PEN

FAM

David Leitch was educated at Merchant Taylors' School and St John's College, Cambridge. His career in journalism began at *The Times* and since then he has worked for the *Guardian*, the *Sunday Times* and the *New Statesman*, covering a wide range of domestic and international news and feature stories. In addition to his bestselling *God Stand Up for Bastards*, he is the author of three investigative books, *Philby: The Spy Who Betrayed a Generation* (written with Bruce Page and Phillip Knightley), *The Discriminating Thief* and *The Cleveland Street Affair* (with Colin Simpson and Lewis Chester).

He lives in London with his second wife, Rosie Boycott, the author and journalist, and their daughter Daisy. He also has a step-daughter, Judy, another daughter, Miranda, and a son, Luke.

FAMILY SECRETS

David Leitch

PENGUIN BOOKS

Penguin Books Ltd, Harmondsworth, Middlesex, England
Viking Penguin Inc., 40 West 23rd Street, New York, New York 10010, U.S.A.
Penguin Books Australia Ltd, Ringwood, Victoria, Australia
Penguin Books Canada Limited, 2801 John Street, Markham, Ontario, Canada L3R 1B4
Penguin Books (N.Z.) Ltd, 182–190 Wairau Road, Auckland 10, New Zealand

First published by William Heinemann Ltd 1984
Published in Penguin Books 1986

Made and printed in Great Britain by
Cox & Wyman, Reading

For Rosie

CONTENTS

TRUDA

1

The story is so strange it makes me shiver to begin. Nowadays I keep thinking of one particular reader out there. It's as if she is waiting on the next sentence, waiting.

She is in her early thirties, the lady in question. There is a strong probability that her eyes are strikingly blue, her colouring blonde, maybe with a trace of auburn.

But this is no more than guess-work, nudged along by encounters in dreams. In reality we have never met. It was only in the course of writing this book that I learned of her existence. Until then she had been the best kept of all the secrets that haunted my fractured and secret-ridden family.

For about thirty years the fact that she existed at all had been obliterated. This cover-up was performed with such skill and resolve that the secret of her origins should have endured safely to the grave. That it didn't was thanks to luck intervening on a level so pure and unexpected it might have been Providence.

Her story and my own overlap in many uncomfortable ways. We were both whisked away from our parents within days of our birth, the intention being to sever us from our roots for evermore. I don't know whether she found this experience as lonely and unnatural as I did. Nor can I tell whether she reacted in the same way, searching for a route back that would connect her adult life to her lost origins. If she did try she failed, that much is beyond doubt.

On the table beside me there is a birth certificate for a baby girl called Linda Elizabeth Chester. She was born on 10 August

1950 in the agreeable Lancashire resort of Southport, and the certificate contains the name of her mother, Mrs Truda Chester, née Madsen. Under the column headed 'Father' there is only a tantalising, empty space.

If Linda Elizabeth has investigated the Register of Births, Marriages and Deaths to trace her genealogy then she may have taken a further step. By going back far enough, to 1937, she could have discovered that Truda Madsen, 'Occupation: Housewife' and John Chester, 'Advertising Agent', were married in London in June of that year.

These names, John and Truda Chester, happen also to be the names of my own natural parents, though I was brought up and named by another couple altogether, Ivy and David Leitch, my adoptive parents.

It would seem to follow that Linda Elizabeth and myself are brother and sister. The story isn't as simple as that though the lady and I certainly have the same blood in our veins.

In the circumstances this birth certificate, which seemed so explosive and pregnant a document when I first looked at it with something close to incredulity, turns out to be an almost useless scrap of bureaucratic paper. It does no more than testify to circumstances in the past, preserving the record of a lie by omission. The moment you try to apply it to the present its coinage disappears like money withdrawn from circulation. It leads to nowhere but a dead end.

As an adopted child, Linda Elizabeth, if she still uses these names which probably she doesn't, has the right to the information on the certificate. The law was enacted in Britain in the 1970s, following similar legislation in America, with the intention of giving adopted children the option to trace their natural parents if they wished to use it. Unfortunately, in this instance it doesn't work. The certificate was not meant to assist future researchers – it was meant to block them and by God it has succeeded.

If Linda Elizabeth has tried to fill in the long emptiness between the present and her roots, she will have found that the birth certificate opens no doors. It is just as useless to me. The law permits her to work backwards from adoption papers to birth certificate, which in this case is the end of the line. There is no legal right for me to progress in the other direction by gaining access to information on file about Linda Elizabeth's adoption. I can't find her name, any more than she can find mine.

So we are both trapped in a bureaucratic stalemate. She has the legal right to acquire facts which tell her nothing without information I possess. They aren't even all correct as far as they go. My information, which is vital for her, offers no legal path along which I can trace anything of her life since she was a week old.

No wonder I have found myself dreaming of a game of Blind Man's Buff in which both the players have their eyes bandaged.

An eminent lawyer whose speciality is in the family courts advised: 'The law as it stands is clear and unlikely to change. The door is closed to you both. There is no way you can trace or find this lady – or vice versa.'

Dead, disappointing words. But there exists another way of prising open the door which has nothing to do with the adoption laws. For all I know, it's been accomplished already by the very act of writing a paragraph containing the names 'Linda Elizabeth Chester'. Out there somewhere she may be saying, 'My God, that's me!'

She will find it all hard to believe I expect. Reading the events I described, she may think it's more like fiction than fact, more like a fairy story beginning 'Once upon a time a young couple in love ran away to London together, hoping they would find pavements lined with gold and see a king's coronation ...' Gradually she will see that the story belongs to her, as much as to the young couple half a century ago, and to myself. Then, if my hunch is right, she will herself take the initiative.

I wonder in what circumstances she will discover this message in a bottle. Above all, how she will respond. My guess is that it will come via a phone call late at night, when impulse rules and the rational mind loses its stark capacity for murdering wild notions before they have time to be born.

Probably I'll have other things in mind, or be expecting a

familiar voice, not one that comes as a surprise from nowhere.

As she will find, reading on, that's certainly how it happened the first time.

2

January 1981

You have to try and visualise a man working on his own at a desk next to a big old-fashioned window without curtains. He can look out over a garden dominated by a jaunty sycamore tree. Beyond, there is a narrow road, then a canal, the Regent's Canal, which runs through the centre of London like a secret path out of the city. The man by the window has often thought how useful it would be as an escape route.

There has been a storm. The rain is still driving down so hard it stirs up those surface patches of water which are illuminated yellow by the street lights. The rest of the water is still, and intensely black like a velvet ribbon.

A barge inches past, engine throb growing louder and merging with the hiss of driving rain, which blurs its outline. The outmoded longboat is no more than a dark shape. It could almost be a surfaced sub or an errant whale. It must be on some commercial, winter errand and is (illegally) unlighted. The observer from the window raises a hand to wave at the undifferentiated shape. His gesture is a legacy from summertime when the canal is thick with pleasure boats taking schoolkids on zoo outings. He invariably waves and there is usually one child, his eyes on the big houses, who nervously signals back. But this is midwinter – no season for waving.

The frustrated waver is living alone in a house far too big for a single person. He has a son of zoo-visiting age, presently domiciled with his mother at the other end of the world. There

is a time gap of eleven hours between London and the Blue
Mountains of New South Wales where the boy is. When they
talk on the phone the father is often finishing breakfast, while
the son is getting ready for bed, or vice versa. The separation
enforced by distance, 12,000 miles or so, is less painful in some
ways than the sense of living according to different clocks,
different seasons. Where the boy is, it is midsummer. In northern Europe winter has fastened like a vice.

The passing boat has halted the man's work rhythm. In the
grip of an impulse to move he has been turning out lights,
putting on a heavy winter coat, preparing to trudge along by
the rain-swept canal to the closest restaurant. This place calls
itself La Venezia, a reference to the area's popular name –
Little Venice. Despite murals featuring gondolas, the owner
and staff are all Romans. They speak the blurred, usually ob-
scene dialect of Trastevere, a kind of Roman cockney. There
is only about ten minutes to go before the kitchen closes for
the night.

His hand is on the door ready to leave the cavernous house
when he realises that the frantic haste has nothing to do with
a need to fill his belly with spaghetti followed by liver grilled
with sage. It isn't even a hunger for exercise after hours at the
desk. He is shocked to acknowledge a sudden lust for his own
youth, or its shadow image. The magnet is the Italian clamour,
the silly macho exchanges about women, how they look, how
they might react in bed, conducted in the hissing dialect he
had once employed himself with a facility now largely a
memory. But Rome, and his very early twenties, have by no
means vanished altogether. He can see himself as he was then,
craning far out of a window on the top of a medieval slum
apartment building, to watch a girl exactly his own age walking very erect but smoothly with an earthenware pot on her
shoulder. Going to the communal well.

The street was called the Vicolo del Cinque, tucked in behind the ornate church of Santa Maria in Trastevere. The girl
(he can even see her shadow on the cobblestones) was a mon-
grel, or bastard, as he thought he was himself; in her case half
Arab, half Hungarian. It had been long after midnight, but still

hot enough for him to be sweating as he leaned out naked, waiting for her to appear from the long journey down the winding stairs, and then to walk with such grace.

Rome, August 1960. He knows the date because they had met just after the Olympic Games.

Strange that he would interrupt his work, in which he had been completely engrossed a minute before, disrupt his peace, go out into the Dickensian London weather he loathed, all for a subterranean whim to re-experience the ersatz flavour of a place and a time lost over two decades before. On San Pellegrino mineral water, too. He doesn't even drink any more. The hedonist Roman habit of convivially putting a match to Sambucca – as much for the pleasure of watching the delicate blue flame, as to burn off some of the excessively raw spirit – is a game he had long stopped playing.

His hand is on the door when the phone rings. Damn. Answer or not? No decisions are more loaded than those involving delaying departures to take unexpected calls. A Roman – an ancient one, not one of the 'Venezia' waiters – would have seen it as an omen, like stumbling on the door lintel, and called off the whole day or, in this case, night. But who knows? Perhaps it will be his small son, on the line from the other end of the world.

The short walk back into the belly of the house to pick up the phone, unless it meanwhile stops, is heavy with premonition. Something unexpected, something very disruptive, is already hovering over the commonplace action of saying 'Hullo?'.

Caller: 'May I please speak to Mr David Leitch?'

'Yes. Speaking.'

It's a strange voice, a woman's. She sounds nervous. The man knows that they have never spoken before, almost for sure. Yet there is the faintest hint of ungraspable, indefinable familiarity about her.

Instead of saying who she is, the caller gasps – the sharp intake of breath sounds like a reaction of astonishment, even fear. Mysteriously, she is completely taken aback. She obviously anticipated an answer like 'He doesn't live here any more.' In these circumstances she is adrift, with no inkling of how to continue.

He says, prompting, 'Who's that calling?' The Italian dinner has almost disappeared. He wishes she'd get to the point.

But even as he speaks, irritated, into the silence, there is a sense of being taken over by ... something that has never previously occurred in forty-three years. The act of answering has launched him into an experience without precedent. Already it has him in its grip. There is a sense of immense external compulsion: and no way out.

Whatever she has to say – and why doesn't he get on with it? – will change him forever. He will never sit at the window again as the same person.

As she begins speaking, the voice increasingly familiar though he has never heard her before, it becomes overwhelmingly clear that this lady in the night is about to undergo an identical experience herself. She is even worse prepared than he is. There are a few moments while he is holding her future in his hands. When he tells her what turn out to be precisely six words, one a minor expletive uttered in a spirit not of blasphemy but awe, then she too finds that her place in the world is unexpectedly altered – and that she has changed at a stroke. She will not be quite the same person at the end of the call as she was dialling the number, leaping in the dark.

A rare speeding car scythes past, destroying the night illusion that this is not somewhere in the heart of a city, but a tranquil backwater, unvisited by virtue of being off the human map. The minor distraction, the noise of engine and tyres, leads to a name being misheard, an instant of misunderstanding and delay resolved when she repeats who she is. After that it all happens so fast as to be virtually instantaneous.

Already there is the strangeness of knowing how easily he might have gone out earlier, decided not to answer, somehow missed the moment altogether. But since the timing was right to the second everyone involved has received a gift of access to themselves. From now on they have identified a dimension which had always been present, yet concealed in the shadows for a lifetime. At a stroke it defines their place on the map.

There is something close to brutality about the absence of warning. It is like learning that you are a target only as the shell explodes – no intimation of gun-fire has offered an instant to dive in a ditch, or even flinch. Yet how else could such an act of illumination come to its appointed hour?

If Linda Elizabeth ever rings in the night then the story that follows will prepare her. At one remove she will have experienced the exchanges between the man by the canal, and the caller, propped tensely on a handy stool, in her kitchen up there in Wales.

It will have to take its proper place in the narrative for the call in the night came only in 1981, a moment when a closed door finally fell agape on its hinges. It was all over in a matter of minutes, and yet it had taken a lifetime.

3

The story begins much further back, at least as early as an unlikely meeting of strangers in November 1937.

The first time I devised a means of communicating with Truda, the mother I only knew for about a fortnight, it was described as follows:

> On Guy Fawkes' Day, 1937, eight days after I was born, my mother Truda published an advertisement in the Personal Column of the London *Daily Express* offering me, in effect, to the highest bidder. She specified a date, one week later, when prospective foster parents could attend a kind of private view of the infant. For this unusual ceremony she had selected the Russell Hotel which dominated the east end of Bloomsbury with its lunatic façade – all in all, a happy choice.

This is how I began a book called *God Stand up for Bastards* which was published in 1973. It went on to say that a meeting had then taken place between my natural parents, 'Paul' and Truda, and a couple who introduced themselves as Mr and Mrs David Leitch. Truda spoke for the parents (there is no memory of a single word from 'Paul') and we can safely assume that again it was the woman, Ivy Leitch, née Ivy Robinson, who did most of the talking on the other side.

As for David Leitch, as will be seen, he became immediately and characteristically busy with a practical consideration to do with my 9-day-old welfare. He left the others to their discussions and quit the hotel in search of baby-clothes. It was a harsh season; my natural parents, unemployed and recent grad-

uates of a shotgun wedding, lacked spare cash for a carry-cot
and warm wrappings.

The meeting soon broke up, 'Paul' and Truda returning by
train to Nottingham much as they had come up to London
early the same morning – only this time they travelled lighter,
without their first-born child.

Without additional formalities, Ivy and David loaded me
aboard their grey Standard 12 tourer and took the familiar
road home to Harrow-on-the-Hill, a leafy London suburb
whose quaint out-of-dateness and unexpected romance moved
the poet John Betjeman to lyrical raptures which most of the
place's city-working inhabitants would be hard pressed to
share. Henceforth I was to live in 'Metroland', the name invented for the between-the-wars commuter belt north-west of
London, served by the Metropolitan line station called Baker
Street, famed for its proximity to Sherlock Holmes's town
address.

The transaction concerning me had been settled on the spot,
de facto as lawyers say, though no lawyers or officials of any
kind had been involved or as yet even consulted. The couples
parted with assurances of keeping in touch. In fact they never
saw each other again. By the time I described these events in
print, aged 35, Truda and 'Paul' might have been figures out
of a nursery rhyme, so shadowy and mythical they seemed.
Since 1937 they had shown no sign of life.

It had not been intended or agreed to work this way.
According to Ivy in later years, Truda suggested that I stay
with the foster parents for a few weeks – 'on approval as it
were', I wrote in the book. 'If they decided to keep the child
the legal details could then be settled.'

Truda, meanwhile, would pay periodic visits from Nottingham, where I always wrongly assumed she and 'Paul' lived.
She never came, as far as I knew, but she did write, quite
lengthily, explaining after her fashion why a visit was always
impossible. When David Leitch died he left me three letters
written by Truda in the weeks after the Russell Hotel exchange.

'I miss the little lamb dreadfully and long to see him in his new bootees, but unfortunately we must go to Leicester by train tomorrow and won't be able to fit in the trip to London as promised . . .'

Quoting her characteristic style from memory, as the originals were lost, I described my first encounter with my mother via the banal words she had written in blue ink – a sense of total recognition, the first experience in my life of visceral family connection and of blood calling blood. I knew precisely her inner discontent, a mixture of pain and guilt and sheer bloody eagerness to be rid of the whole mess, as she forced herself to draft the hallowed, maundering words designed to convey an authentic simulacrum of the Loving Mum.

I could even hear her voice, the *real* voice, struggling to contain an irritation close to nausea behind the (very) conventional phrases she had maybe borrowed from a woman's magazine scanned on the long journey north. 'Why do we have to go through all this performance?' her spirit – and she was long dead for all I knew – seemed to be muttering at me while I read.

Here I detected an authentic link and a shared affinity. But the tug of connection was with my own weaknesses and prevarications, not major vices or glaring, impressive flaws, but small meannesses or acts of carelessness, symbolic perhaps of a greater human carelessness which would forever tie me to my mother's defection. It was the side of me – and her – which instinctively headed for the hills when mundane responsibilities threatened to close in.

After reading these revealing letters it was no surprise that one day they stopped: nor that the sender disappeared for a lifetime. This was why, it was explained, I had never been legally adopted. Ivy and David were left holding the baby. So, without benefit of normal adoption procedures, they simply changed homes, set up afresh in a new neighbourhood called Northwood a few miles further along the Metropolitan line, and resumed life with the baby everyone assumed was the natural child of Ivy's comprehensive loins.

And there might the story have ended in a swift, competent reshuffle of family cards, identities and values undergoing a subtle revision thanks to sleight of hand. I turned out to be a wild card.

While I was writing the first book, I read *The Death of the Family* by David Cooper, an unusually passionate attack on the 'nuclear' family. Cooper was trying eloquently to explode the entity that I was devoting myself to tracking down. Yet he understood a kind of biological imperative afflicting adopted children, the elemental need to make contact with their personal history and origins.

> I still find myself somewhat incredulous when I meet people who were adopted or one of whose parents left the home and has never been seen since, and who so deprive themselves of doubt and curiosity that they make no attempt to find the missing parent or parents – not necessarily to have a relationship with them but simply to witness the fact and quality of their existence.

I had learned about Truda's existence when I was 6. My adoptive mother, Ivy, had sat me on her ample knees one day and said that there was something she wanted to tell me and that I should pay attention. I had done so. The exchanges that followed I have remembered all my life.

There was another mother in my life, or had been, Ivy said. She was called Truda. She hadn't loved me or wanted me. In fact after I was born she had first given me to Ivy for safe-keeping and then disappeared altogether, deserting me for ever.

'I took you because she didn't want to look after you. I love you much more than she did. That means I'm more your mother than she is.'

Decades later the feeling of disbelief was as strong and accessible as it had been at the age of 6. How could anyone be more someone's mother than their real mother? It made no sense. At the same time I felt the world going dizzy and threatening to crack. I was filled with sadness, its edges tinged with panic. And through the pain I could remember another earlier pain, something so terrible that I knew I would die if I ever had to feel it again. Ivy was peering at me closely with her prominent liquid eyes. I said something wretched I've been

ashamed of ever since. 'That's tough on me,' I told her, aping
the vocabulary of the Hollywood movies I'd already seen and
fallen in love with, as wartime kids of my generation fell in
love with everything from the other side of the Atlantic.

It was ignoble, this self-pity. I knew it then as much as I do
now. And so was my other childish reaction – could it be I had
two birthdays, was I really a couple of weeks older than I'd
always imagined?

Ivy explained that there weren't two birthdays and that it
wasn't tough on me at all. I should be happy, not sad. I'd had
the luck to find two parents who loved me more than the real
ones. Who were these real parents? I wondered, and cautiously
asked Ivy whether they would be coming to get me one day.
I could already see that she didn't welcome too many questions
on the subject.

She said irritably that they wouldn't – I could be sure they
had disappeared for ever. I nodded agreement and said nothing, knowing that my earlier question had already been
wrong, and not wanting to make it worse. Ivy suffered from
'nerves' among other things – she lived on a perilous edge of
hysteria, and the tiniest set-back or pretext might send her
screaming over the abyss. In any case I knew inwardly that
whatever she said they would be coming. If they didn't I would
find them for myself, if it took a lifetime.

Ivy warned me that I must keep the story of my origins
secret. Never tell a living soul, never let the slightest hint escape
your lips. I promised. It was no burden. There was no point
in telling anyone else unless they knew this real mother and
father and how to find them. It wasn't likely that anyone
around where we lived did. Ivy had told me she came from far
away, somewhere in the North.

The idea that I would find my real mother and father some
day lodged immovably in my mind from this moment on. It
came up most commonly when people in shops (much of the
war took place for me queuing with Ivy at some empty counter
or another) raised the topic that I must physically resemble
David Leitch, my supposed father. 'Yes,' Ivy would always
reply, 'like peas in a pod.' It wasn't really true, almost nothing

she said to strangers ever was, but the myth was convenient. I certainly didn't look like Ivy. Very often I wondered, or hoped, that David really was what everyone thought. He was a wonderful father and Ivy, in her mad way, tried to be a good mother, succeeding probably better than might have been expected. But I never felt at all like her – indeed her personality was so alien to mine that I often thought I would feel more in tune with a Martian. David I understood, and vice versa. In time, I thought, he himself might aid me to track them down – as far as I was concerned there was nothing he couldn't do if he wanted.

Certainly one day I would find them. The idea was as much a part of my world-view as the conviction that I would become a writer. When I published *God Stand up for Bastards*, it was apparent that the two obsessions had joined forces.

By then three decades or more had passed, all the other avenues I had explored had been exhausted. My own investigations had involved, among other thankless tasks, telephoning everyone listed in the British Isles directories under 'Griffith', a false track as will be seen, like the various others. My hunch was that writing for newspapers would provide the key. With no evidence other than their use of the Personal Column I was convinced that my parents read papers with unusual interest, a sufficiently strong one, I hoped, for them to recognise my adopted name in print somewhere and make contact. It was far from inaccurate as intuitions go, yet the call never came. By producing the noisily named book I was pursuing the same route, only via hard covers: in common with many journalists I had always considered the survival power of written words in book form, as opposed to their instantly disposable counterpart in newsprint, a matter for exaggerated respect. The written word in some form was by then the only weapon I had to hand.

There were only a few pages about Truda in the book, all I knew for sure plus the fruits of thirty years' guess-work.

The preface began: 'This title might seem like a calculated insult to my mother Truda. In a way it is. But I have a sneaking hunch – and hope – that hard words may entice her out of the shadows where she has been lurking, crafty as a trout, for about thirty-four years. She may even bring a father and siblings with her. Mother, where are you?'

The invocation of Truda, a sketchy fantasy about a lady I'd of necessity only known in the womb, made for an unusual and resonant story, full of unanswered questions that may have lodged in the readers' minds. The publication certainly raised a lot of ghosts; people who were elsewhere in the pages, old friends from abroad I hadn't seen for years.

The book's popularity convinced me that Truda, wherever she was, must surely come across it. At first I'd expected to hear from her every time the postman came, every time the phone rang virtually. Yet weeks passed and my optimism left me. The idea that you could find a mother by writing a book had always been a long shot. She had disappeared over thirty-five years before, God knew where. Maybe she didn't read books, even ones that were serialised and discussed in the papers. Maybe she was dead.

Nearly a year after the publication, I was still waiting to discover the outcome of my literary bet with my mother and father. Despite all the dignity and authority of print they had given no hint of life. I had been sure that my method would work – but only, of course, assuming the persons I sought were still around to notice. There had been no trace of either parent for thirty-six years, five of which had consisted of the Second World War.

I had thought to myself in 1973: 'If a year goes by and I still hear nothing then I'll have to accept they're dead.'

4

By the spring of 1974 the statutory year had passed – I had given up hoping and, as far as possible, even stopped thinking about Truda.

There were plenty of immediate problems. In those days I was married to Jill Neville, the novelist and critic, and we were both writing books. It had been a year of constant travel far away from England, the place where I presumed Truda would be, if she was still anywhere.

We had started from Paris, settled for a while in the remote French countryside, shifted to Cassis on the eastern side of the Corniche from Marseilles, taken a boat to North Africa, and eventually another back to southern Spain. At first Jill had savoured the sense of movement with as much gusto as I did and often made jokes about our innumerable, shifting addresses.

In time the jokes stopped. A decade on, it is easy to see that I was killing time waiting, waiting for Truda. Waiting on the move was a device to divert my own attention from an increasingly probable prospect of failure. As far as I was concerned it would amount to an admission that my whole life had failed. Unless I found my true parent or parents I would always be denied access to a part of myself. It was a variation on the theme of Robinson Crusoe marooned on his island, but whereas it was his fate to be marooned and isolated from the rest of humanity, mine was to be cast away, from myself, as my parents had cast me away.

The drive north after we disembarked from the Tangier
ferry at Algeciras was another ideal device for avoiding such
a prospect, in so far as unless you devoted all your attention
to driving there was not much chance of seeing Seville in one
piece, let alone Madrid. The dangerous mountain roads of
Andalucia sometimes faded away into little more than tracks
– a month earlier there had been snow and, after that, flooding.
Only days before the road had been closed and now only a
handful of vehicles were starting to circulate. Any more, across
narrow stone bridges designed for donkey-cart traffic, would
quickly have led to catastrophe. As it was we continued to
Ronda, negotiating one-way passages across sudden abysses
with the roar of water far below, then descended through
spectacular terrain which revealed one trout stream after another, like liquefied crystal in spate.

Only with regret could I continue driving north, leaving
behind the sun and the buoyant, ferocious spring of Andalucia.
At noon, eating floury bread and olives by a stream, the sun
was strong enough to sting your wrist. By night the temperature dropped to only a few degrees above freezing and as we
ate in tiny hotels old women in black appeared with charcoal
heaters to deposit beneath the dining-table. It was a heating
method that probably went back many centuries and was wonderfully effective for as long as you remained in your chair,
eating and then drinking into the night. Once out of range of
your medieval foot-warmer, it could have been midwinter.

As the price of being pregnant Jill was suddenly so physically
susceptible it was as if she had lost all immunity. Any bad
smell provoked instant nausea; the sight of butter on a dish
turned her a ghostly pale. Just as she was exaggeratedly sen-
sitive to tiny things, I was equally insensitive to the fact that
her bewildering symptoms masked a deeper misery.

Only when we arrived in Madrid to spend a few days with
Roy Rutter, an old friend from Paris nowadays resident in
Spain for *Time* magazine, the closeness I thought had existed
on the road vanished. Perhaps it had never existed at all except
in my imagination.

Looking back, it is obvious that our marriage was disinte-

grating, even though Jill was in the early stages of pregnancy.
Yet if a friend, Roy say, had pointed it out, I would have been
taken aback.

Jill had a new novel coming out – when she finally took off
for London ahead of me, one ostensible reason was to prepare
for publication. She was also anxious to consult Neil Perrett
in Paddington, an old friend and the only doctor she trusted.
She was probably desperate for a change, a period when she
wasn't spending all her time locked in with me. I recognised
that the pull of events was nudging me on to London as well.
Like a small boat trapped in a lee wind off the Channel, there
was no alternative landfall but the unreliable coast of England.
The homecoming depressed me more the further north I drove.
I put it down to the fact that some time at the end of the 1960s
I had fallen out of love with England. That my wife had fallen
out of love with me was a notion I lacked the strength to take
on board.

It had been seven years since I had lived in London. Instead
Paris had become my home. I worked there as resident correspondent, first for the *Sunday Times* and then the *New Statesman*. I arrived back in the middle of March and immediately
involved myself in a series of articles. To my surprise, the place
turned out to be poised on the brink of turmoil. The sudden
death of President Pompidou offered a prospect of chaos.
Overnight, by far the most powerful political office in any
advanced democracy was up for grabs.

Hours after Pompidou suddenly collapsed that drizzling
March night, the city was invaded by riot police from the
provinces, 'protectors of order' with the discomforting alien
air of a foreign army. Those I managed to engage in grudging
conversation expressed a troubling nostalgia for the 'effervesc-
ence' of the May 1968 revolution. They were like frustrated
out-of-season hunters, recalling a golden time when students
had been fair game.

In addition to the civil disturbances there were also all manner of political intrigues to write about and when one night
Jill came on the phone line from London the subject she raised
came as from an infinitely remote country.

She had collected some mail addressed to me care of the *New Statesman*.

'There's a letter signed Truda,' she said. 'I think it must be genuine. It makes more sense than any of the others.'

I asked her to read it to me but I was suddenly too excited and eager to take it in properly. 'What's the handwriting like? Can you describe it?'

There was no address, nothing to say where the letter had come from because the postmark was obliterated. All she could tell was that it was somewhere in England. I was desperate to see the envelope and hold it in my hand. There was a good chance I'd recognise Truda's sloping blue handwriting.

I also had confidence in an instinct which would authenticate the physical object itself, as if the fact of it having been touched by my mother would imbue it with what I had learned to call *mana* in the south-west Pacific. I would know at once whether it was real the moment I could feel it in my hand.

It would be like touching my own flesh and blood, an experience that I had spent a lifetime imagining.

After accepting that Truda and 'Paul', as I thought of my father, were most likely long dead, and putting the matter out of my mind, it was now impossible to think of anything else. Even the story I had to write within the next twenty-four hours. There had probably always been a psychological connection between becoming a journalist and the search for Truda. All those stories over the years had only been rehearsals for The Story. And now, here it was.

Hearing the news I had gone into the Armenian cathedral of St John down the road from my apartment, and finding it empty had made an attempt to thank God for a miracle. The Sunday morning mass was always a crowded family affair. In the week the place was like a sanctuary in an area thickly dotted with small workshops where craftsmen made lenses for spectacles or telescopes, polished diamonds and other precious stones, worked gold and silver; the Marais also contained the biggest concentration of rag-trade manufacturers in Paris. Here was a haven in the centre of a bee-hive.

By the next morning my excitement had turned to doubt. This was by no means the first time a letter from a stranger had arrived full of promise. My capacity for hope had been burned.

People in different parts of England, where I suspected the truth resided, but also readers from America and even Australia, had written offering leads. Because the search for a parent or child was such an old story, one of the oldest of all, it moved people to unexpected acts of generosity and an impulse to share their own often unsuccessful experiences.

The comfort of strangers had come in the form of memories of people confessing to them that they had lost a son, or given one away, in circumstances that might have corresponded with my own. The writers had usually been women, their memories most often dating from the Second World War. The correspondents usually wrote to describe someone else, a third party who had told them how she had become pregnant, got rid of the new-born child, and regretted it evermore. They were left condemned to random hopeless searches. They often found themselves roaming the streets, looking into faces of passers-by of the right age for a flicker of illumination or recognition.

I had always begun reading in the grip of soaring excitement. Then, line by line, the high hopes had seeped away. There was always a crucial detail that didn't fit. What the letters had achieved was to give a sense of solidarity and make me aware how common some variation on my predicament seemed to be. Knitting family pieces together after a decisive fracture was a momentous task. One correspondent wrote that she had been trying to find her parents for the whole of her adult life. Now, in her sixties, she accepted there could be no hope of ever tracing them or her siblings. 'Now I know I'll die without ever knowing who I am.'

On the eve of arriving in London to read another letter from a stranger, who perhaps wasn't one, I was sick with apprehension. Jill had insisted that it sounded genuine. Yet so had many others, until you began reading for yourself.

5

22 April, 1974

Dear David,

Until last week I was quite unaware that you had become such a distinguished writer, and charming man.

The talent and charm you inherited from your father, Paul, who died some years ago. Any craftiness or weakness of character must be from me.

It was a bad experience to open your book, most disturbing to my conscience. You must have an answer to the challenge. No David – you are not a bastard.

The pretty blonde has become the old trout. The permissive society had not been invented back in 1937. Then we had mass unemployment. And no social security.

My wish is to remain obscure. But should you like to hear from me further I will write again. The *New Statesman* has a personal column. Give me your answer to 'Crafty Clara', or just D/T.

Do not publicise me further. Promise to keep our secret from the press, especially women reporters or feature writers. You will have gathered by now that I am a coward, lacking in courage. Secretly I am intensely proud of you.

Affectionately, with all good wishes

Truda.

It was a moment of great joy – there could be no doubt that this was genuine. What happened for the rest of the day has vanished from my memory. All that has stayed with me is the happiness, an experience of Grace Abounding, followed by a considerable let-down.

When I came to examine Truda's letter in anything approaching a cool state of mind I realised that the tone, which involved a careful weighing of words and had probably cost her a lot of thought, was one I had heard before. The handwriting was familiar too, I had seen it before, fifteen years before to be exact, and over the years it hadn't much changed.

While she had made the first step, my mother was still keeping her head down. Her communication might have fallen out of the clear sunny sky. She had not compromised her personal anonymity by a millimetre, except in so far as she had let it be known she was alive.

The letter was written exactly as I have transcribed it. No address, no identifying name beyond 'Truda'. And fortune had favoured the timid; even the postal frank was nearly obliterated, though under scrutiny the area name seemed to begin with an 'N'. This I (wrongly) guessed indicated the Midlands city of Nottingham, my birthplace according to the certificate I had located in the course of previous researches, which gave my name as Paul Griffith.

Wherever it originated, the letter had arrived at the venerable offices of the *New Statesman*. These were at the bottom of a Dickensian passage leading to Lincoln's Inn Fields, London's equally Dickensian legal district set round a park where pin-striped lawyers watched office girls play netball, and students from the London School of Economics walked purposefully towards the future. Like their counterparts at the Sorbonne, they were showing early signs of being a conservative, career-orientated generation.

Here I sat one sunny morning, composing my Personal Column response to this almost anonymous letter. It involved as much care and concentration as anything that I'd ever produced on the editorial pages.

'CRAFTY CLARA: Wonderful news. Complete Discretion Assured. Please write or phone ...' and I added the details of the temporary address where Jill and I had borrowed a *pied à-terre*.

It was to appear on 3 May, a fortnight after Truda had broken her cover. I don't think time ever moved so slowly.

The 3 May arrived, and my by now expert eye examined the relevant section to make sure my 'Crafty Clara' ad had seen the light. Sure enough, there she was. The *Statesman* printers were a fine body of men, whose capacity to get even the most inaccessible foreign names precisely right had long excited my admiration. To them 'Crafty Clara' was child's play. No errors in the address or phone number: I settled down to wait, seldom straying far from the phone, and greeting the postman on the doorstep each morning.

London was recovering from a bad winter – the first of the energy crisis and the grimmest for a quarter of a century. The city had been blacked out, the government had fallen after the miners' strike, people bought car-stickers reading 'Will the last businessman leaving London please put out the light.' The 'please' was very British; so was the wry pleasure in collective adversity. I remembered this wartime humour, without nostalgia for lost childhood. After Paris, which had retained its stylishness and efficiency, London appeared to be in terminal decline. Only foreigners, and those like myself who had been away, appeared to notice. The natives carried on regardless.

Every morning I exchanged pleasantries with the postman, who was under the impression that I was awaiting a long overdue cheque. Having told me it hadn't arrived, he would thread his way whistling through the long uncollected garbage, as blithely as if the putrefying sacks were spring crocuses.

The inner city, especially now there was an extended garbage strike, was experiencing ostentatious decay, but my mum's trusty Personal Column was enjoying a manic renaissance. New-born babies were no longer on offer but plenty of other more rarefied commodities, including self-realisation and even happiness, were being sought and offered in the little boxes.

My ad was the only one containing a phone number – from Thursday afternoon onwards I waited by the phone.

Perhaps she was out there on the grimy streets, fighting her way into a call-box with the *New Statesman* in one hand, her coin ready in the other.

There was no need to wait very long.

'It's about, er, Clara, Crafty Clara,' said the first voice, a male one.

'Yes?' I said encouragingly, waiting.

It had never crossed my mind, but now I wondered if Truda could have asked a friend to make contact on her behalf. Maybe this was her husband, or boyfriend if she had one. And then suddenly I found my hand shaking. For all I knew it might be Paul, my own father.

There was only the sound of a throat being cleared at the other end of the line. The caller was obviously in a public box.

'You want to speak to . . .?' I coaxed.

'Clara, of course,' he said irritably. 'Isn't she there?'

'No. Are you sure . . .?' But already at the other end the phone had been banged down.

Almost instantly it was ringing again.

'You're *sure* Clara isn't in?'

'She isn't. I'm afraid there's been a mistake.'

'That's the right number for the ad, isn't it?'

'Yes, but . . .'

'Is she going to be there later?'

'No, but . . .'

Once again a throat was cleared, the phone went dead. I was, however, to hear the same voice again, much later that night. This time there was a background of juke-box music and alcoholic singing at his end. He sounded a different man, brisk, confident, and with an authority that had been absent before.

'She's not there, I suppose, Clara?' he began.

'No.'

'I thought not. Listen, if there's a password or something I don't know, that's OK, no sweat. But just tell me one thing – I've been wondering about it all evening. What is it exactly that Crafty Clara *does*?'

Now I knew why the other advertisers, whether seeking a lodger, an encounter group, 'a kind man', a linguist, a fellow

cat-lover or someone to share a cottage in some remote and
economical part of Europe, all restricted themselves to a box
number.

Between phone calls, because they rang and rang again, I
studied the Personal Column for the first time and realised
what was happening.

Those hoping to find sex talked of companionship, com-
patibility, culture, humour – anything except sex itself. These
wants were laid out in an insiders' code, easily comprehensible
to those with access to the right mental cypher book. Mine
defied instant cryptology. Presumably its appeal was pursuing
the spoor of some novel sexual action they could not allow
themselves to miss. A debased Freudian intuition had convinced them that something substantial, like 'Clara' herself,
lurked behind the words. They wanted in, whatever it was
... they wanted in desperately.

The calls were unstoppable – and I had to answer them all,
just in case. Jill got drawn in too. Under normal circumstances
she was seldom downcast very long. At first when she lifted
the phone without thinking and a voice said, 'I'm all yours,
Crafty Clara, your place or mine?' I heard her laughter from
the next room. But after a few days she was no longer prepared
to go near the phone, let alone speak to it.

In a catch phrase of the time, everyone was suffering from
'pressures'. Those bearing down on Jill increased when the
news arrived that her own mother had now been diagnosed as
gravely, possibly terminally ill at the other end of the world.
It was one pressure too many. Her book had just been published and within a few days the travel arrangements were
made for her flight to Australia, her mind already 12,000 miles
away. Jill and I had been getting on badly in London but now
she was gone I felt lonely and dispirited. I had lost the knack
of single life.

There were no longer so many responses to the Clara ad.
But those who phoned were even more insistent, desperate
even. It was as if they feared they had left it too late by failing
to react, like the majority, within the first three days of the
paper appearing. They adamantly refused to accept there could

be a mistake. She must be there. She must have what they wanted. It might have been a matter of life and death.

One morning very early I decided on impulse to go back to France. Truda would answer, if she did, in her own good time. I would never have been able to resist dialling the phone number. She was different, I realised, infinitely more cautious and less given to unconsidered action for its own sake. If such things are inherited, then this impatience, certainly absent from the personalities of my foster parents, must have been derived from my father Paul.

It was a relief to leave the strangers' voices behind. But they had taught me that I was by no means the only one trying to break a mould of isolation. All over the disintegrating city people were trying to make connections and find, if not kin, at least a kindred spirit. The thick, pleading note in so many voices went far beyond a lustful quest for a sexual variant that would give them satisfaction. They felt incomplete, cut off. For an instant they allowed themselves to be overwhelmed by the unrealistic notion that Clara would somehow make them whole.

We had a lot in common, these strangers and myself.

6

A few days later the London friend I had asked to check the mail for likely-looking letters left a message to say he thought it had arrived. I wanted to call and ask him to read it to me straight away but resisted the temptation. Irrationally, I felt that some confidentiality would be broken, the fragile link jeopardised.

Rather than risk the letter disappearing between London and Paris, I crossed the Channel yet again. The familiar greenish envelope, the familiar handwriting – there was no doubt who it was from. This time there was even a readable postmark: Birkenhead, the docks and ship-building area of Liverpool south of the Mersey I knew from my days as a young reporter on a paper in Manchester.

10 May, 1974

Dear David,

Thank you for your message. I feel happier having your promise, in return you have my word not to embarrass you in any way. Definitely I shall not be landing on 'your doorstep', although I do have an address to write to. The phone number too is appreciated. So tantalising, perhaps I may avail myself of it later, but for the present just accept my thanks.

It is not easy writing to you. Since I had your message I have written two letters, slept on them, re-read them, eventually torn them up, and this one I must send or you will be thinking I have forgotten all about you.

I am fully conscious that you would spot insincerity, just as

easily as you will know that I did not earn my living by the pen!
However, one does one's best hoping for a kindly understanding
and the turning of a blind eye.

I expect you would like a complete documentary of all the events
and facts neatly typed and set out. Please forgive me for not
doing this. It will be best for you to have regular letters from me.
Gradually you will get to know me and something of the family
background.

It would be easy to make excuses for myself but this I will not
do. 'Paul' is not here to give you his story, and I must not take
advantage of him. I would like to think he would consider me if
it were otherwise.

He was a sports lover, cricket and tennis mainly. As a schoolboy
he was over-enthusiastic and suffered heart strain. As a result he
spent a long time in hospital and so was to a great extent self-
educated.

We did not meet until we were twenty and twenty-two so I am
[not] clear of the precise details of his early years. I do remember
he was very good at table tennis and snooker.

Here I must put you right about 'Paul'. I promised you only the
truth and so I intend to refer to him as John for that was his
name. As I will not be keeping copies of my letters to you it is
important that I do my best to be truthful for my memory is not
as good as it was!

Should I repeat myself in subsequent letters, I beg of you to bear
with me, for at sixty-two years of age I am not as 'slick' as I was!
I do not regard myself as a poor old pensioner, although I retired
from regular work on my sixtieth birthday. I managed all right,
supplementing my pension by a little homework which pays for
cigarettes, the odd bottle of Martini and occasional night out. I
also go dancing at a local Widow and Widowers' Club – mostly
'Old Tyme'. Not as strenuous as Rock 'n' Roll, but a lot more
graceful, don't you agree?

John was not interested in dancing – I think he had two left
feet. I tried to teach him but soon gave up the effort.

Well, David, this must be all for now, I hope you have found it
interesting.

There is one point that did not come through very clearly to me
in your book. Did you feel love from and for your parents? To me
you sounded rather cynical when you referred to them. Surely it
was undeserved? Any bitterness against me I am prepared to

accept, even antagonism built up over the years would be natural
with the little knowledge you had.

I promise to write again. Meantime stay out of danger zones.
Take care of yourself.

Affectionately,

Truda.

My first concern had been to look for an address, even a
poste restante one, but there was nothing. She had been
tempted by the phone number, but not tempted enough. My
mother was still keeping her head down.

As for my father – John it seemed, not Paul, if Truda was
to be believed – his head was permanently down. If she was to
be believed.

It was clear that she had studied *God Stand up for Bastards*
very closely – in all probability the relevant pages were open
beside her as she wrote. Hence the reference to my 'spotting
any insincerity'. Hence, above all, the astonishingly self-
revealing sentence about not keeping copies of what she wrote.

It read like the confession of a professional liar aware that
with the passing of the years she was losing some of her expertise. She would do her 'best to be truthful', not because
truth was on her mind, but for fear of being found out in lies
she might forget without a record to remind herself what she
had invented last time round. I too consulted the book that
had tempted her to make contact and found this paragraph:

> Whatever Truda's other defects she wrote a pretty slick and
> convincing letter when necessary ... to me they spoke loud and
> clear. A good deal of my education had been concerned with
> examining what people had written and extracting the ultimate
> nuance. Truda's few hundred words evoked a sense of total com-
> prehension and sympathy I had never previously experienced ...
> Before [reading the three letters from Truda which David Leitch
> had left me] I had never known with absolute certainty precisely
> how someone else was feeling at a given moment.

There followed the passage about missing 'the little lamb'
dreadfully and regretting whatever factor it was that prevented
her from making a previously arranged visit. Behind the token

gesture towards maternity and its gushing vocabulary I recognised 'an undertone of bothered petulance – why do we have
to go through all this performance, I can hear her mutter
irritably.'

This section of the book had been based on my memories
of letters I'd seen fifteen years earlier. Now I was sure I'd got
it amazingly right – and that Truda recognised the fact herself.
Unfortunately, the brutal approach I'd used, like the 'bastard'
challenge, had now become a liability. By sprinkling ground-
bait indiscriminately on the water, I had managed to encourage
the fish to rise. But Truda didn't intend to allow herself to be
hooked very easily all the same.

The more I studied her letter, the more I felt another kind
of sympathy with her, much as I'd described in the book. She
didn't want to be blamed, she didn't want to hear that what
she had done for the best, according to her lights, had worked
out anything less than ideally. Blame was the last thing on my
mind. The fact that she had revealed herself, or come close to
it, paid off any old debts instantly as far as I was concerned.
I felt very loving and protective. Frustratingly though, she had
provided no way for me to let her know – except via a few
words in a small ad column.

As for John, as I had to get used to calling my father, or at
least thinking of him, I could only hope that she was lying,
and that one day I would hear the story from his own lips. I
was sure from her words that he was dead to her. But I could
not get rid of a flicker of hope that all the same he might be
still around somewhere, possibly very much alive to someone
else. The main concern though was not to lose contact with
Truda.

Thanks to my connection with the paper, I was able to get
my response printed in the issue of 17 May. This time no
chances were taken with references to 'Crafty Clara', whose
name I hoped never to hear again. No phone number was
provided either. Belatedly, I had learnt the name of the game.
The message read 'D/T. Delighted by your letter. Please write
again giving box number. DL.'

My theory was that though she was probably still too

cautious to reveal her home address, a box number might work
as an acceptable half-way house. If I could write to her, I
calculated, then with the right kind of reassurance I could
probably persuade her to tell me how I could meet her face to
face.

This time the reply came with encouraging speed:

Sunday 19 May

Dear David,

Thank you for your message, it was kind of you to express your
delight at my letter. I had not thought that you would wish to
write to me, frankly the idea of being on the receiving end of what
you might say directly and personally disturbs me. Perhaps I
should have let the whole business remain as it was.

Selfishly (I realise now) I imagined that a letter from me now
and again would suffice, but obviously complications were inevitable. We have lived very differently, David.

I live in a pleasant enough flat in the house of an old lady. It is
not self-contained and over the years it has worked well. Sadly she
is now 85, depends on me for company, and practically lives in
my pocket. I feel a certain responsibility, although she is no relation.

Now I believe it is time her family took over, possibly soon as
I shall get a flat of my own and for once have my own front door
and letter-box.

On Tuesday 21st I have to go to hospital for a minor eye
operation, following this I am to go away till after Whit – possibly
looking like Moshe Dayan for a day or so.

I am hopeful that perhaps we will find ways of solving the
communication problem. Oh why did you put me in your book?
The moving finger indeed wrote in capital letters.

Normally I'm a cool type, not easily upset or given to panic,
having been through Hell and High Water, not forgetting the Blitz!
But right now I'm full of butterflies and very definitely uneasy.

This is a poor letter, not very informative of what would interest
you.

My grandfather was a Danish Master Mariner. He died many
years before I was born. My father survived the First World War
but died as a result of his service in 1920, when he was just 39
years of age. The Danish blood stirs in my veins for I love all

Danes and my happiest holidays have been spent in that lovely
country. Perhaps you have been there in your globe-trotting. If so,
I'm sure you must have felt happy there.

My maternal grandfather was a goldsmith (craftsman). He made
beautiful watch cases.

My trade has been jewellery – specialising in pearls (and known
as the 'Pearly Queen'). I worked in Hatton Garden at one time as
a grader and stringer. Now I must be the oldest in the business for
I still work privately for a few clients. Did I tell you that John was
a copy writer at Harrods where I also worked at one time?

I was looking for a photo of John to send you but sorry to say
I don't seem to have kept one.

Expect a letter from me in about two weeks. So for now best
wishes, have a happy week.

Affectionately,

Truda.

It was a tantalising communication – Truda was hovering
on the brink, but still reluctant to dip her toe in the water. For
the first time I began to discern an impression of what her life
was like in the present. It was clear that there would be no
more progress until the end of the month so I set off to do
some work in Paris and Brittany.

Years later, when a London publisher was making a collection of my journalism, I read a selection of articles I produced
that summer, including two written over the following three
weeks. I found them unusually interesting to read because as
far as I was concerned it was the first time I had come across
them. I neither remembered reading them before nor writing
them. They could have been the product of a ghost. I was
impressed that he had been so industrious and convincing.

In an attempt to get a compass bearing on the lost weeks I
worked through a collection of notebooks and found a brief
entry underneath a précis of a political speech. It read: 'June 3/
4 Temperature 82 degrees. Horrors at 11 Rue de Poitou.'

The address was my old bachelor flat where I had been
staying off and on. The note was enough to bring back an
experience I had managed to wipe out altogether.

I remember passing an evening alone, sitting by an open

window and watching the blue drain out of the sky, gradually merging with the grey of the slates on the roof-tops opposite. I had been studying Truda's letters, the last one particularly. It had struck me that there was a frightened and even death-like quality about it.

I became convinced that Truda had laboured to produce these stilted phrases, like dead flowers in a funeral parlour, in the grip of some terminal impulse to neatness. There was a testamentary ring about it, an echo of the fright she felt as she wrote, which made me frightened in turn. This was Truda 'getting her affairs in order'.

John really was dead, I was now convinced of that much. She had written, I could see, to pay off a personal debt, and having done that she felt as if the slate had been wiped clean as she could make it. John was a long way from her mind, triggered only by remote, unimportant memories of the past ... 'I don't seem to have kept a photograph.'

The memories had stayed with her, but she would have been happier without them. They were an intrusion, a reminder of what she had done wrong, and what had gone wrong. She had only referred to my father as an afterthought – she knew me well enough, via her intuition, to see that I was anxious for news about him. But there wasn't news, only a flicker of history. By the time she reached him the letter was on the home straight. She was anxious to be finished with the burden of writing it. She was beyond lying, or bothering to work out some cosmetic tale. He was long gone for her, so long gone that it had been an effort to discover whether or not she had retained any souvenirs, and apparently there were none.

He had gone to the grave without making contact and for all I knew this was the last contact I was going to have with her. If the operation went wrong, then she had done her best, or at any rate done something. Even if everything had gone well a few days before, she might now decide to convalesce undisturbed, and leave me to assume that she had died, or whatever I wanted.

I had never experienced such anxiety and isolation: it was like being marooned on an ice floe, despite the intense Paris summer heat. There had been a letter from Australia saying Jill had arrived but I had received no news of either her mother or herself since. I remembered the time when the child we had hoped for miscarried in that same Paris apartment. I was filled with premonitions of another disaster and my mental state was so shaky that sometimes I heard the voice of the lost child trying to call me but using words I could not understand.

There was nothing I could have done to help this baby who had never been born, never had the chance to become even a little boy. Now I was equally helpless to bring aid and comfort to Truda or Jill. She was pregnant with another child, who might suffer the same fate, and 12,000 miles away. Dial as I did, late into the nights, it was impossible to get through. Australia was in the grip of a long communications strike. For all I knew there might have been another miscarriage, or termination as the doctors tersely called it, without anyone having succeeded in telling me a word.

It was perfectly possible that these letters, added to the memory of those she had written to my adoptive parents, were the closest contact I would make with Truda. The original correspondence had ended without warning, and even, as I remembered, with a promise to write again soon. The only thing that had followed was a silence that had hung over my entire life.

This time, thank God, it only took three and a half weeks before I received the following:

9 June

27 Alvanley Place,
Grange Road West,
Birkenhead,
Merseyside.

Dear David,
    You have been much in my mind these last few days, especially regarding your wishing to write to me.
    Not knowing your temperament you could be furious with me, possibly feeling terribly frustrated and impatient.

So David say it as you will.

I feel that you must have been sincere when you promised discretion. Forgive me for doubting your word.

Whilst not completely illiterate I find the *New Statesman* most informative but to one whose reading is restricted to the *Daily Mail* with Vincent Mulchrone my favourite writer, the *NS* is in some ways over my head.

The *Mail* crossword is more simple. Perhaps I have a lazy brain!

You must appreciate the classical education and the contrast the lack of it brings. I'm glad you live in Paris where there must be much beauty and gracious living. I await your letter with some trepidation.

Still my best wishes to you.

Truda Bucknall.

I remember nothing of my reply, except that I was jubilant and wrote from France by return of post.

She responded as follows:

21 June

27 Alvanley Place

Dear David,

Thank you for your lovely letter. Your Joy, High Spirits, together with the whiff of that Paris bar, made my day.

I am certain now that I did right to send my letter, although at the time I was unsure.

My eye 'op' was a great success, the injections were unpleasant, a 'darkie' nurse held my hand throughout and the doctor (dark brown eyes and a voice to match) was so gentle.

My sight is good, improved I think now that the swelling has gone down. I have a lot of work in, so a stay-at-home weekend for me.

Have just been to the library, Jill's latest book was on the shelf so I have that as relaxation. I have already read *The Girl Who Played Gooseberry* and *The Love Germ*. The latter was unusual, rather!

You will miss her while she is away. My congratulations to you both on the news of the baby. I trust all goes well, also hope you have good news of her mother.

Coincidence that Birkenhead is the location of Jill's printers. The shop which I managed until my retirement was just a car park away from the printers – many of the staff were my customers. Small world!

Welcome back to London. Holiday or permanent stay? John and I lived first in Barnes and later – guess where – Happy Hampstead. The Olde Bull and Bush, Jack Straw's Castle. Memories.

Well, David, that's all for now. Have a happy week. Thanks so much for cheering me up as you did with your letter.

Love from Truda.

Eureka! Now I could risk no more delay. Truda had been so elusive since November 1937 that it was always possible she would pack her bags and head off again, destination unknown.

I sent a telegram warning her to expect my arrival. I calculated that it would reach her only a few hours before I did myself. This would give my long vanished mother time to prepare for the meeting. But not time enough to leave town in the grip of second thoughts.

Truda's capacity for disappearance was highly developed. Once, it seemed to me, was quite enough.

7

So early one Sunday morning in high June I found myself walking down Primrose Hill in north London bound for Euston station. There I would take a train bound for Liverpool in the north-west. A banal enough itinerary. Yet for someone who had spent most of his adult life crossing the world on the way to somewhere or another, a journey like no other. The journey.

Never had the edge of anticipation been so sharp, so unbearably consuming. Never had I looked at my watch so often, even as a child waiting for a trip to the seaside. Never had the minutes stood so resolutely still.

Being Sunday, and so early, it was as if England had died in its sleep. No taxis. No people. There was something terminal about the train too. It was completely empty, stretched out alongside platform four as if it had succumbed after its last trip. It was remarkably dirty, filled with the breath and the cigarette smoke of the previous overnight passengers. Trying to open a window I smeared one cuff of my immaculate, mother-visiting white shirt. It was as if I'd rubbed it with a piece of coal.

Already it was uncomfortably hot, though the patch of sky visible through long neglected windows gave no hint of a fine day. The sun had to be there somewhere but it was totally obscured behind even cloud cover, the colour of a very old battleship. There was a hint of moisture as if the sky was sweating.

Gradually the train began to fill with shabby, unshaven, sleepy people. They wore that English look of resignation, a hangover from the war probably. No discomfort, or delay, no waiting in line for a bus that never comes, can faze us, the look says. We were born without expectations, and we'll die the same way. The more enterprising began to unpack sandwiches of industrial bread.

Some of this I put down in a notebook. The way I felt it was impossible to allow my mind to settle on whatever lay in store at the other end of the line. Accordingly, I tried to divert myself with a mental Kim's Game, that childhood contest where you have a set time to memorise the contents of a tray before a cloth covers them over.

No war-zone take-off in a blacked-out military plane had induced such turmoil in the stomach. I found my eyes were closed as if I was enduring a very long fall.

It was only when the old train gave a wheeze and shuddered forward that I realised how frightened I was – as frightened that the journey wouldn't begin as I was about facing its end.

This won't do at all, I thought, as we edged out of Euston into the secret past. Get a grip, read your book, anything. I fished out Graham Greene's *The Honorary Consul*. I'd already worked through it once to write a review and had promised myself a more leisurely study when there was time. Since the train was one of the slowest in service there was plenty of that ahead. After a few pages things seemed to improve. I looked up, sniffing an unexpected animation in the air. Something was going on.

The something turned out to be a bar on the train, not a miracle apparently, but an obscure administrative legacy of the soccer season. We were on an 'excursion special'. The merry sound of beer cans being snapped open was enough to provoke unsuspected stirrings. Apparently moribund passengers were at once on their feet, moving quite briskly too. Thank God there were not many of us. We invested that little counter like a tide.

My taste for English domestic beer had evaporated in years of expatriation. Now I could scarcely get the stuff down unless frozen so near solid that it paralysed the throat, tasting only of cold. This batch was tepid with a distinctive flavour of

forgotten copper coins: still it came in the nature of a bonus.
It let me buy a delay before I needed to approach the whisky
in my bag: as close as I had come to making preparations for
the trip.

Scotch, according to my personal scale, was a drink for
acute occasions, offering the primitive catharsis of sex and
violence, and demanding in return a fairly steep entrance fee
– most importantly, a certain donation of self. You might
pretend, like Charley Fortnum, Greene's Consul, that by treat-
ing the stuff with extreme judiciousness, topping it up with
just the right amount of water and sipping away through
pursed lips like an alcoholic dowager, you could achieve a kind
of benevolent equilibrium. But realistically this was hardly the
case. If the truth were told – and sooner or later it always was
– Scotch was no ally in the pursuit of any kind of mean. It
excluded finesse, delay or compromise. It also drowned the
noise of alarm signals.

We kept slowing down almost to a halt. By now we were in
the industrial heartland of England. The tracks periodically
passed within a few yards of long rows of nineteenth-century
factory dwellings. So close that the train seemed on the verge
of demolishing the identical backyards; and even the identical
kitchens. There were plenty of people about now, men going
to clubs, kids playing next to hen-coops, and all of them as
perfectly indifferent to our physical presence, almost within
touching distance, as the hens were. Impressive Anglo-Saxon
phlegm. Visually it was looking up – Day of Rest or not the
factories kept smoking, and now the sun was like a Cyclops' eye
through the pollution, lurid, wounded and deep, furnace red.

I had actually managed to shift my mind away from
Liverpool and the end of the journey when the barman caught
me unawares. His appearance was such that I had assumed he
was incapable of speech, or close to it. His face was a literal
example of professional deformation, the skin blossoming with
burst capillaries and covered with carbuncular swellings so he
resembled those cartoons of freaks that used to appear in
druggy comic books. At first I didn't catch what he said.

'A very nice drop of beer,' he repeated, the words coming

out with relish and disproportionate conviction. He leaned
across the bar, and the close range effect was startling, like
talking to some winter vegetable, a turnip perhaps, that had
been disinterred, mounted on a stick and draped in a dirty
white jacket to scare the birds.

My intention was to make some beer-fancying and appropriate reply but it never happened. Instead before I knew it I
had looked at my watch, made some normally long-winded
calculation without thought, and remarked without particular
expression:

'In three hours, give or take ten minutes, I am going to come
face to face with my mother, someone I have never seen. Or
at least not for thirty-six years and a few months. The last
time we met I was getting on for 2 weeks old.'

'Oh aye,' he said, in a voice as unruffled and tranquil as my
own. 'That's a funny thing.'

Time to return to my seat in search of the right level, like
Charley Fortnum. It was one of those exchanges which destroy
their own potential for ramification, like a very large bomb.

The zombie barman and his warm beer raised my spirits –
it was even possible to let my mind dwell on Truda, and my
urge to find her again. It was 'again'. For something had been
retained from those nine or so days before the baby had been
whisked away and turned into a new human entity called
David Leitch. There was no memory of those days of course,
nothing that could literally be called 'memory', yet some kind
of imprint had stayed with me. It was something that belonged
to me. A ghost-like thing, which all my life I'd been casting
round to exorcise.

I can only describe it as an impression, devoid of human
content and yet as complete in itself and as unlike anything
else, as a taste, a scent or a colour. Truda was somehow in it
at one remove, and presiding over it, perhaps like music issuing
from behind drawn curtains.

The worst moment of all was standing in front of number 27
Alvanley Place. All I had to do now was ring the bell. Something that had always been impossibly elusive was for the first

time within my grasp. A tiny physical act would make it happen.

I stepped forward a pace, squared myself up, took a deep breath and pushed. There were a few seconds of complete silence, then footsteps. Someone was coming downstairs and towards the door.

And there on the step, well turned-out as for some formal occasion, was Truda. Our eyes met: recognition was total, instantaneous. Her expression revealed a moment of fear so acute it was like a pain. I don't know whether I looked the same, but very likely I did. We embraced and I was aware of glimpsing her blue eyes, a variant of my own, flashing around somewhere over my shoulder.

'My God,' I thought. 'She's looking to see if I've turned up with a camera team.'

I wanted to laugh but too much was going on for the thought to take shape. Instead I was full of the sense of her smallness and of wanting to protect her. We were sharing a mutual impulse to dissolve the pain of the moment by reaching towards physical contact. Holding her I knew here was something we shared, a physicality that lived close to hunger, an expression of need more than warmth.

It didn't last long, this doorstep embrace. She had disentangled herself and was saying 'Come through here' in a low, even conspiratorial voice, while I was still taking in how remarkably tiny my mother was. It had been hard to put my arms round her without simultaneously yanking her up off the ground, an action that she was far too dignified to have undergone without feeling ruffled.

Before leading me inside she took another quick peek around. Again I had the thought about TV. But perhaps she was simply checking in a spirit of propriety. Alvanley Terrace was a decorous little row, one whisker up from the slums. The tiny material gap was therefore all the more significant to the inhabitants. They were not given to embracing outside the front door at noon on Sundays, that much I could see.

'So I'm still a secret,' I remember thinking. Another impression that came and went, only to reappear afterwards.

I followed her brisk, self-important steps along a narrow
hallway, up some stairs, and into a small and immaculate
kitchen. I might have floated up those stairs, or stepped
through them – it was as if my body had been displaced by
the density of emotion. I stood grinning at her, feeling weight-
less and dizzy.

She dabbed at her extremely well-arranged grey-blonde coif-
fure, a gesture at once coquettish and serious.

'You must always make sure you give me time to get my
hair done in future,' she said in an admonishing tone.

I started to tell her it looked fine, which was true. But she
stopped me, a finger over her lips.

'Keep your voice down.' She pointed at the ceiling. 'If the
old lady hears she'll come down. Any excuse is good enough
for her. If she comes, we'll never get rid of her. She just won't
leave me in peace, that's the trouble.'

She sighed with irritation and started making tea. I stood
grinning like an idiot. The incongruity was too much for me.
You invest a lifetime in dreams of such a meeting and when it
happens the talk is of hairdressers and old ladies upstairs.

Again time had to pass before these first exchanges came
back out of memory. They were not as trivial as I thought at
the time. The way she looked was desperately important to
Truda. So was the need for peace – she had spent a lot of her
life trying to protect her personal space against intrusions and
disruptions. I was the last of these and potentially the most
intrusive of all.

Meanwhile the small lady was efficiently making tea. To my
relief she made no more than a token demur when I produced
the whisky. The glasses organised, she shifted me into an ad-
joining room, her sitting-room, as authoritatively as if I'd been
a pawn on a board. Truda might be small, but this did not
hold her back when it came to getting things done exactly the
way she wanted them. You could almost feel her will vibrate
– it was quite palpable in the cramped room.

She indicated a place on the sofa and started fluffing up the
cushions preliminary to sitting. I watched her with growing
affection and amusement – she was so busy, so determined.

The cushion shifting, however, generated an unforeseen consequence. A copy of my book spilled out from under one of them. It sat there shamelessly, like a cat with dirty paws.

There was a silence while we both looked solemnly at *God Stand up for Bastards*, its unregenerate yellow cover, a photo of myself, bearded and aggressive, peering at us both from under a cowboy hat. I think she would have put it back under a cushion if I hadn't asked her where it came from.

'I ordered it from the library. They're very good there – they get me everything I ask for.' She had read about the book somewhere and, as I had hoped, the strident title had lodged in her mind. Later she had seen part of a TV programme when someone had been discussing the book and I had been interviewed.

'Did you recognise me?'

She gave me a look, half coy, half appraising. 'I thought perhaps it could be ... I wondered,' she said. 'I asked them in the library. They knew about it but said it wasn't in stock so far. I reserved it – the manager's always keeping books for me, he's very kind. Then when I went in one day to get my usual books he came up and said it was in. I took it – but I didn't look at it properly until I was outside. On the steps.'

She held the book in her thin, well-kept hands, looking from it to me and back again. 'I looked at the cover and then opened it to read a few words before I went to catch the bus. Then I saw this picture.'

The inside cover had shown a baby photo which I had dug up for a magazine serialisation. To me it looked like any old baby, except there was a recognisable blue gaze, precisely the gaze Truda was focusing on and through me at that moment. Her eyes were partly concealed behind large glasses but as she looked from the book picture to me and back I caught the reflected flicker of blue through her lenses, a flash of colour like catching a dragon-fly on a river bank in the corner of your vision while watching for fish.

'And you recognised me?' I prompted, wondering if a memory of a new-born child's appearance could have survived so many years.

'I fainted, fainted on the steps,' she said, quite dryly.

In an overflow of protective emotion I took her small hand, our eyes meeting before she again seemed to lengthen her focus through me and beyond. The trouble was we were so much alike.

I was sure that she had the same thought at the same moment. There were so many samenesses between us, too many. As I watched her holding the book in a gingerly way – was it going to explode and shatter her careful world? – I saw she had my shape and probably the same tendency to be too plump and round and stubby. She, poor child of the First World War and the depression years, was built to a smaller scale – she might have originated in my body rather than the reverse.

Those eyes were the same blue, they had the same glint others sometimes found charming, the same coldness in repose, the same tendency to move through and beyond the object ostensibly in focus towards a wider, secretly egotistical abstraction. They sat in faces the same shape, with the same beakiness, the same slightly unfinished look. The shared soaring forehead and high cheek-bnes were something I'd noticed elsewhere before – on Moscow airport years ago, meeting a group of Russian dignitaries at the start of a portentous official visit that soon lurched into farce.

'Were you all right?' I asked, or rather prompted. She had lost the thread of the story about the library. Without my question I think she would have left it there contentedly. She took no pleasure in telling stories or guiding them through to the end.

'When you fainted. Did you fall down the steps?'

'Yes. I grazed my knee. There's nothing wrong with it now.'

She didn't care for the memory. As if to exorcise it, she walked a few steps round the room, head held as high as possible, a model of small persons' deportment. Her prettiness and vitality would have enabled her to pass for several years younger than her age. The thought came into my mind that the manager of the library, who went to so much trouble on her behalf, flirted with her. She would not have made any effort herself, I guessed, but accepted any services as her due.

She had the complacent quality of someone who had been
spoiled or even worshipped at some stage in her life. Judging
by what I could make of her current circumstances it had
probably been a long time in the past.

Truda and I soon became highly compatible, we settled
down on her sofa, smoking each other's cigarettes and working
through my Scotch – drink suited her well, making her relaxed
without being silly, and giving her the confidence to suspend
at least some part of the deep-seated caution which she had
cultivated like a privet hedge round the borders of her life. I
was full of gratitude. The more I saw of her the clearer it
became that writing to me had been an act against her nature.
She was a very timid person. Anything unknown or improvised
worried her. Risks she abhorred.

As the afternoon drained away she gossiped on about the
old lady who owned the house and her job as manageress of
a jeweller's shop nearby in Birkenhead. I enjoyed it all very
much. We were as companionable as a pair of collusive old
whores.

The subject I most wanted to hear about was my father, my
dead father, if what she had written was true. All the same it
was impossible for me to accept until I had heard it from her
own lips. There was certainly no trace of him or any man
around the place. Yet I retained a tiny nugget of hope.

There was something deceptive about Truda, something
hard to pin down. I was very conscious of it at this first
meeting, though later I lost or suspended my scepticism about
her. I forgot my initial reluctance to believe what she told me,
all of it to do with John, assuming that was his name. While
she talked I found myself praying that she had lied for some
reason of her own. I was frightened to ask her and hear the
ultimate bad news. She herself was no keener to experience
pain. Her chosen habitat was the shallows. She had lived there
a long time. I began to see that she intended to get around to
passing on serious information only at her own pace. It was
pleasanter to talk about other matters. There was, she hinted
with a mixture of coyness and complacency, no shortage of
suitors, 'even at my age'.

One she had met in her shop. He had come in one day with
a button missing from his shirt and asked if she knew where
he could have it sewn on. This enterprising approach was fatal
in Truda's rigorous book. He had wooed her with expensive
dinners, a vision of his own comfortable circumstances which
included 'a large bungalow', and finally a proposal of marriage. These efforts had been insufficient to erase the bad
impression he had made with the shirt.

'He's got children,' she said with distaste. 'They are grown
up but all the same – I told him what he really wants is a
housekeeper.'

There was something comic about her emphasis which made
me laugh. She hushed me up urgently, indicating the ceiling
and the potentially troublesome landlady. She herself didn't
share the laughter, or even condescend to a smile. Truda didn't
think there could be anything funny about herself, that was
certain. She was too determined to stand on a level of dignity
for that. It was a shame ... With her lofty expression in contrast to her small stature she had the potential to be a gifted
deadpan humorist.

She was talking about the old lady, how she had known her
for years, how generous she had been and now, in retirement
and near senility, what a damn nuisance she was. At the slightest excuse she would intrude if Truda had visitors, particularly
if they were male. Increasingly she was coming to rely on my
unreliable mother, calling in the debts of the past. Truda was
desperate to get out. She made no attempt to conceal her
irritation when people made too many demands on her. Widowers who wanted her to play mother to their children, de-
pendent old ladies – no one was going to catch her like that.
She didn't try to pretend to a generosity of spirit that was
absent. I had got her uncannily right in the book, lying now
on the sofa between us. She had employed baby-talk (very
unconvincingly) in her letters to my adoptive parents while
making excuses for not coming to see me. It was the voice of
an adolescent being asked to tidy her room when she was eager
to go out dancing. Even at 62 there was something less than
grown-up about this small, assured figure.

On impulse I asked if she would think of marrying again.

'At my age ...?' She looked thoughtful as if the idea were not so impossible all the same. 'If the right person came along, not the one I was telling you about of course.'

The time had come to get it over. I poured us both a pre-paratory drink.

'You're called Bucknall – no wonder it wasn't any good trying to find you. The only names I had were Madsen and Griffith.'

She nodded, her expression impassive. I expected she might exhibit some curiosity. When I was 20 I had worked for a newspaper in London as night reporter. Since the paper was *The Times*, in those days not a great pursuer of very late stories, I had filled many hours scouring the phone books for the British Isles, dialling first all the Madsens, Truda's maiden name, and then all the Griffiths, the name under 'Father' on my birth certificate.

These researches had yielded no one. As I told my tale of frustrated filial devotion Truda listened without detectable in-terest. She made no comment when I finished. If she was pleased that I had been so anxious to find her, or my father, she gave no sign. I had the feeling of interviewing a subject who was anxious to give nothing away.

'You were married to someone called Bucknall?'

This seemed to be the right stop to press – with warmth and evident pleasure Truda talked of her life with a man called James Bucknall some twenty-five years earlier. I listened atten-tively – there was a lot about Bucknall, whose name she had taken, though she had never married him. I wondered if she was going to say why at some point, but she did not. They had been very happy – her eyes grew misty behind the glasses as she described their life together. It didn't seem to have lasted very long. He had always been ill, ill from the start. In due course he had died. She spoke as if she had always known this outcome was inevitable.

Truda had nursed her sick lover, the owner of a business which she had tried to save from collapse, to a point where she had become ill herself. 'And there was his daughter too –

Lois.' She paused a long time and then allowed herself a single sigh – it might have represented disillusion with the child's subsequent life or a deeper regret for the whole human condition.

'He'd been married before – I mean the girl, Lois, she wasn't your daughter?'

'Oh no. She was Jim's daughter. I already had Margaret.'

Truda got up briskly, changing the mood, and handed me a framed photograph of a girl aged about 7 in school uniform. She wore a navy-blue blazer, by coincidence similar to one I had worn for school at the same age. Not that I needed it to make the connection. I felt plenty of resemblances with Truda, uncomfortable ones mainly, but they were nothing compared to the familiar image of what beyond all possible doubt was a picture of my sister.

Somewhere I had school photos of myself at the same age – we could have passed as identical twins.

My God, a sister. Why hadn't she volunteered the information in her letters, or told me before?

I looked at her enquiringly. She looked back at me, as unruffled and unresponsive as a tortoise.

'This one, Margaret, is your daughter? That is, yours and John's?'

She nodded.

'Younger than me?'

'Yes.'

'When was she born?'

'It was during the war – in 1942.'

I felt very excited – I remember the impulse to phone her at once but Truda didn't have a phone.

'How is she? What does she do?'

'She's married.'

'Happy? Does she have kids?'

It was wearisome nudging her along to give me the essential information. It was like drawing teeth. I managed painfully to establish that Margaret had a small daughter, that she had been very clever as a schoolgirl, that she might have gone on to a university if she had wanted to – but she hadn't.

Truda's almost still-born narrative capacity began to move now. She described how Margaret might have married the son of someone rich and influential, a person Truda had clearly regarded as highly suitable. In the end she hadn't.

I wanted to go ahead now, get on with it, get it over. I asked whether 'John', I wasn't even certain that John was the right name, had given an opinion on Margaret's suitors.

Truda looked quite surprised, as if I should have known the answer already. 'Oh no. He wasn't here then. It was after.'

After what? I could imagine all too well. Even with virtually nothing to go on about my father. Ever since I was a small child there had been clues about Truda, including her name, the fact she was blonde, her prettiness. About him there had been nothing. He had always resided in an unknown territory without signposts or maps. He might have been a shadow.

I said to her: 'He is dead, isn't he? Not just gone away or disappeared?'

'Oh yes,' she said very briskly.

He was no longer even a shadow. The sense of loss was agonising, even though it was for someone I had never known, and had failed to find. It was too late now, all too late. Nevermore. It was like a door closing.

Truda leant over the sofa and produced an elaborate box of chocolates. I wondered for a moment if she was going to offer a bon-bon as you give a child a sweet to divert his attention from pain. This proved to be very far from the case and yet another misreading of Truda. I don't think it occurred to her that I might have any strong feelings about my father one way or the other. She riffled efficiently through a collection of papers in the candy box, shut it up again, and produced a second repository of old souvenirs. Judging by the experimental way she examined it, this one had remained shut for a long time.

'These things were to do with him – I've been trying to find them,' she said absently. The moment had been prepared then, after all. She had been putting it off, just as I had.

I wanted to ask about his life, but first she had to find what he had left behind. What he had left behind was no more than

could be contained in a smallish box, originally intended to
contain an inexpensive set of chess-pieces, some of which had
disappeared while others, chipped and imperfect, had remained
to accompany my inheritance from my father, which accordingly was not so ample that it needed much space. It consisted
of a death certificate, a silver-plated cigarette case and a photograph of him with a party of other people on board a boat
of the kind you hire once a year for an afternoon outing on
the river.

He was in the very front of this group, his hair dishevelled
in a manner I recognised, his grin broader than those worn by
his fellow boaters, most of whom were timid smilers. He was
evidently prepared to try anything with a certain gusto, even
when it came to an expression for a boating group photo. The
same could be said of his approach to the question of identity.
No wonder I had failed to track him down.

'John Chester, also known as John Griffith-Chester, also
known as John Chester-Griffith', the death certificate read. I
held it for a while. The date was my last year in Cambridge.
I was fifteen years too late.

'How did he die?' I asked, having a reasonably vivid picture
of precisely how.

Truda said that she hadn't seen him for nearly ten years
before his decease (aged 48). Accordingly she had heard the
account second-hand.

Nevertheless it had the ring of conscientious and accurate
reporting.

'One day he was in his office as usual – he was working in
a club in Leicester, it was called the Constitutional Club and
he was the Social Secretary. He suddenly put his hand to his
chest and asked the girl there if he could have a glass of water.
She went to get it and by the time she came back he'd passed
away.' Truda tried this phrase on like a fur coat belonging to
a richer friend. She was forced to admit that it wasn't her style.
'Dead,' she clarified.

We paused for mourning, me holding my cigarette case inheritance, Truda pondering over the event without pain. 'I
think it must have been the only time in his life he ever asked

for a glass of water,' she continued without ironic intent, or any that could be detected.

Looking at her sideways in the course of the ensuing silence I saw she had taken on a curious roundness, her baby chin supported on her palms, her blue eyes – my blue eyes – aimed in the direction of her impeccable net curtains, but focused on nothing much outside herself. Her emotions had long been isolated from herself, their core frozen in layers of some exquisite crystal through which no light or sound could pass. All the things to do with John, the pain, had been stashed away somewhere irretrievable. She was listening, I thought, not suffering, making sure that John was far away, beyond all echoes, somewhere so distant that she could not hear him.

She had wrapped him up and put him away in some obscure place where he had lost the power to hurt. It was the same kind of thing that she had done to me. Only in my case the process had begun as soon as I was born. I felt very close to my dead father.

The pity for him which overcame me suddenly was the same emotion, damp, acute, foolish, that he had felt for himself. Of this I was convinced. It was as if his feelings were a tune I had started to hum.

I suddenly wished she had died first instead because she was no use to me. She had whittled away her emotions like a stick. There was almost nothing left. Certainly there was nothing left for me. She was not in the giving business.

'You left him because, I suppose, you had to?'

'Oh, I couldn't go on,' said Truda virtuously, as if she were the guardian of the exigencies of life, the voice of getting by. Yet she was uneasy now. She had the air of someone about to suggest making a cup of tea. I got in first, tilting the Scotch bottle, and asked the obvious question.

'John was a bit of a drinker, I suppose?'

'A bit.' She threw her head back and made a kind of gargling noise from deep in her throat, a sound of posthumous indignation.

'Whisky and so on?'

'Oh no, beer, always beer. He liked to be with a crowd in

the pub, buying drinks, always buying. "Miss, how about some service for my friends?" That was John. He always liked to put on a big show. As long as there was anything left in his pocket. *Friends*.'

It was unexpected to find oneself blushing, embarrassed at the fecklessness of a father I had only known in boyhood dreams of paternal heroism. I had told people he had been killed in the war. Once in Spain, when drunk, I had assured a rat-faced waiter that he had died gloriously in Huesca – on the right side of course. This was a fantasy that he had fought with the International Brigade. In reality he had fought with no one – unless you counted Truda. She explained that he had managed to get himself discharged from the army in 1941 as unfit. As a boy he had strained his heart after a bout of rheumatic fever. The heart – and flat feet – had been enough to keep him well away from the firing line. Truda said he always refused to wear army boots, it had been a matter of pride with him. And he had always kept his medical discharge certificate about him to show to stranger soldiers in pubs who asked: 'Why aren't you doing your bit?'

'He had a bit of money when he died. They told me he'd been saving. Yes, saving.' She repeated the word as if I had expressed incredulity.

'For his old age?'

'No, he was hoping to buy a caravan. He'd always wanted to live in a caravan.'

A man of modest ambition, it seems, and those thwarted. If things had panned out, I might have set off to visit him in some trailer-home colony in the Midlands.

My regret for this unmade journey must have shown. Truda suddenly started talking very fast, perhaps to dispel illusions. It may have been that the alcohol had finally loosened her leaden tongue: more likely it was anger. Even after so long my father's memory had retained a capacity for enraging her.

As she talked I understood what she had meant in her letter about him not being able to speak for himself. Very likely she had originally penned some late-night indictment which had never been sent. The fact that it hadn't implied no deference

to my feelings. She had probably decided in the light of day
that too much bitterness looked bad – better to present herself
as magnanimous, despite his bad behaviour – but she hadn't
been able to suppress a broad hint of disreputable truths, gen-
erously censored.

She was no longer in a censoring mood.

'He could be a right, er, bastard,' she hazarded, swallowing
the unfortunate word with some delicacy, as if it were a repudiated digestive noise. And then, gathering pace:

'He didn't want you, you know, or your sister.' *Sister.* 'He
used to say to her, I'm just off to get some cigarettes, I won't
be a minute, love, you just wait here like a good girl, and once
he was in the pub he wouldn't be back till all hours, and there
she was with no one to look after her. Only a little girl, that's
all she was then.'

Now the flood gates were open Truda wasn't going to stop.
From my father's shortcomings towards my sister she switched
to what he had tried to do to me, or my embryo. His solution
to her unwanted pregnancy had been to arrange an abortion,
a modest economical affair, I deduced, since a kitchen table
figured. It was only thanks to Truda that I had survived to
hear the tale. Not that she pretended it was my future life that
was on her mind. My prudent, self-protective mother had deduced that the practitioner was likely to botch the job and do
her damage. Accordingly, she had hopped off the table, even
though the cash had already changed hands.

'We never got it back, either,' she concluded bleakly.

For the second time that day I saw terror in Truda's eyes,
a glimpse of an old panic that went way back to 1937. It was
gone in a moment because she busied herself closing the boxes,
sealing them with tape. Her nimble jeweller's fingers hurried
through the job – she had the air of someone leaving the scene
of a crime. I wondered about the fear. Was it the memory that
had frightened her? A set of lurid images – the abortionist, the
kitchen table – which had long been consigned to a secret
closet in her mind, and had now surfaced unexpectedly, abetted by the Scotch and my presence?

It must have been partly that, but there was something

more. Her own candour had perhaps taken her aback. Certainly she looked furtive now, like someone caught out in a lie. But it obviously wasn't a lie. It was something very real to her, so much so it had made her turn white.

My small mother, who had decided self-protectively not to have me knifed in the womb, had been caught out in a truth. I think it made her feel as vulnerable as she had been at the time. She had recovered already.

'You've got the cigarette case safe now?' Her voice was solicitous and maternal. I found myself glancing round for it, unaware momentarily that I was still holding it tight, tighter than I had held Truda's hand.

'It's here.' I showed her. 'Thank you for giving it to me. I'm glad to have it.'

The thanks surprised her. Clearly she didn't think of the case as a gift. It was more something she was glad to get off her hands, a piece of incriminating evidence.

Truda was a person of neat habits. The next step was to return the boxes containing her meagre souvenirs of my father to their home in a cupboard. I caught a glimpse of more ornate boxes, a stack of the things. Then she closed the door decisively, though without any hint of a slam that might have alerted the old lady. I was intrigued by this brief vision. So, like me, she kept things, or tried. I preserved notebooks; words. She preferred objects. There would be boxes dedicated to James Bucknall, the man she loved, and to her daughter Margaret, my sister. The thought came: perhaps she will start one for me?

Then I was shaken to realise something that should have been obvious from her whole account of seeing the TV show, ordering the book, glancing at the cover, and yet still remaining uncertain about whether or not I was her son until the moment of sighting the baby picture. It was clear beyond doubt that she had kept no record of my adoption in 1937, nothing of the correspondence with David Leitch, my adoptive father. I had lost her side of the correspondence through youthful fecklessness. She had in all likelihood destroyed the letters David had sent her. She didn't want anyone else to find out. More important, she didn't want her own memory jogged.

It was an episode to forget and she had deliberately forgotten it – just as she had 'forgotten' the abortion, or prevented it from surfacing, until a few minutes before.

God Almighty, of course: she had forgotten my name. I had spent all those years trying to find her. She had spent the same period wiping out everything about me, right down to the names of the people who had adopted me. She had allowed the whole thing to vanish. 'David Leitch' meant nothing to her at all. In 1937 she had met the man who had given me his own name. She had also written him at least three letters. It was a very uncommon name outside certain parts of Scotland – there were less than twenty examples in the London phone book, none in the Liverpool directory at all.

And yet all those years I had been trying to find her she had succeeded in losing me to the point where she had consigned the name to oblivion. She had baulked at killing me physically, but only because she feared to harm herself. There had been no such mental sanction to stop her killing me in another way. In the mind she had been rid of me for evermore.

Only a visual image of the baby had lain dormant to be reawakened, powerful enough to make a respectable lady faint outside a library, for all the world like a secretly pregnant adolescent.

'I never thought you would have forgotten my name,' I was about to say. But she was ahead of me. Some delicate antennae detected anger or rebuke in the air.

She was on her way through the door to the kitchen as I began to speak, saying something about making tea, that fine English stand-by in moments of emotional stress, over her departing shoulder. Truda reckoned enough had been revealed – far too much probably. The Scotch had been a great help. It had taken nearly half a bottle to oil her hesitant recall mechanism. It had helped her to get it out.

Now it was tea-time, an end to the season of revelation. In her absence, I put on a record, trying to change the mood. She had a good collection of dreamy, romantic music. There was

an overture by Tchaikovsky sitting on the turntable. When she
returned, her floral tea-set decorously laid out on a tray, the
volume alarmed her. She rushed over to turn it off. Then she
hovered listening, her face a study of anxiety. I must have been
pretty drunk, as I remember wondering if she feared the arrival
of John's bibulous ghost, clattering in from the pub to give his
version of the past. Truda was concentrating every nerve on
listening.

She turned to me and whispered: 'If she comes down you
can say you're a friend of my brother's son.'

I was entirely taken aback. It sounded so complicated and
it was such an unexpected way to learn that I had an uncle. I
started to laugh, but she hushed me urgently.

'Wouldn't it be easier to say I'm your son?'

'Later perhaps,' Truda said soothingly.

They were the same words she used when I suggested making contact with my sister Margaret. My impatient impulse
was to press on, make the connections, ventilate the house of
secrets. But Truda had taken a risk and put herself in my
hands. I was in her debt and crippled with magnanimity. There
was a spark of anger in me at still being repudiated after so
many years but I couldn't express it in these strange circumstances. I was also as prone as Truda to accept an easy way
and avoid too much pain. It was pleasanter to charm and be
charmed. Somehow over the tea-cups two quick light people
make a quick light accommodation. The greatest kindness I
could do for her was to emphasise that I wasn't going to
demand anything.

Soon after arriving I had told her the time of the return train
to London. Now we agreed to go out and reserve a taxi to get
me back across the river Mersey. Truda's narrow economics
didn't run to a phone of her own. Instead we called from a
pub a hundred yards down the gritty main road. It was a big,
sweaty, noisy bar and it reminded me of the times I'd spent
covering dock strikes in Liverpool and Birkenhead as a young
reporter. I felt at home immediately, much more so than fas-
tidious Truda, who sat, prim and wretched, anxious to get
back to her own oasis.

The final hour was the most relaxed – Truda's fears that a
prodigal son might settle in for the duration had been allayed.
She was happy to reminisce now, though the memories were
of a distant uncontroversial past long before John and I had
come on the scene. I learnt that her father was Danish, one of
eight children brought up in a Liverpool orphanage for the
families of sailors lost at sea.

So my great-grandfather had been a maritime Dane, who
died suddenly and young. His son, my surviving grandfather,
had been wounded in the First World War to die at home in
1921, when Truda, her two sisters and baby brother were still
small. He had been a religious man. His brother, Erasmus, had
devoted his entire life to Liverpool's Anglican church. 'Ras'
had been too poor to become a priest: instead he had earned
a living photographing church affairs and churches – his illus-
trations had appeared in churchly and missionary magazines.
Surprisingly, Truda's mother was Jewish. The family had come
to Liverpool from Odessa. They had established themselves as
jewellers and watch-makers well back in the nineteenth century. They had been dug in around the Mersey for a long time,
well before the Statue of Liberty appeared in New York.

Without the famous landmark to warn them, they had
accepted that Liverpool was Manhattan, and had disembarked
under the impression that they had arrived on American soil.
Thereafter they had survived, if not thrived.

In Truda the two apparently incompatible strands of ances-
try, the Danish sailors and Russian Jews, had come together
with Liverpool as the melting-pot. As a girl she had been
apprenticed to a jeweller. At 19 she had set up her own tiny
shop in Penny Lane of Beatles' fame. In her twenties she had
worked in London in the Harrods jewellery department. She
was proud of her skill with precious objects. She loved pretty
things like a child or a magpie. But she also knew their worth.
She was proud of having acquired bargains because she knew
what things were and others didn't. She had wanted to work
as a jeweller on one of the great Cunard liners on the New
York run. But something had gone wrong. Her face clouded
at this point in the story and she trailed off into silence.

The anecdote struck me with some force: as a small boy during the Second World War I had devoted two summers to building a boat out of old planks and rusty nails. I too had been planning to sail to New York. It was apparently a family ambition, doomed through the generations to be disappointed. I had also built two boats. In my imagination I had captained the craft, while my younger sister, Margaret so it proved, acted as rear-gunner.

Truda, despite her timidity, had a core of toughness. Her collection of tiny, pretty objects was like a small person's armoury. They put a screen of prettiness between herself and the harshnesses of the world. I had to admire her determination, the odd air of self-satisfaction which must have taken a lot of work to achieve. Here was someone who had lived as her own person, and managed to get by pretty well.

She was a survivor. When the car came to take me away I could sense a lightening of her spirits. She felt she had got away cheap: no tears, no fuss, no recriminations, no responsibilities. We had spent all day allowing our underlying needs and obsessions to achieve some kind of balance, an exhausting process. We were like dogs who had exhausted themselves with barking at the unknown.

Her unspoken bark had been: what is this decision to let the past catch up with me going to cost? Mine had been of triumph. I had won a bet against crazy odds. Standing on her step I was overwhelmed to think how much of my life had been devoted to making this meeting possible. It wasn't just that I had been forced to write a book to tempt her out of this obscure terrace. I had even been forced to create a life which contained the right ingredients to manufacture such mother-bait.

We parted with kisses and assurances: but not too many. Truda was now cocky enough to allow herself some judicious maternal bullying to do with missing the train (goodbye, you'll be late if you don't hurry, goodbye). Somewhere under the Mersey Tunnel, my eyes resting on the driver's cropped nape, her elated relief that it was all over settled on my own shoulder like a domesticated bird. Back in Alvanley Terrace she had made herself a milky drink and put her feet up. Thank God I got through that, I could hear her sighing.

I remember opening and closing my father's cigarette case, and noticing the decisive metallic snap that he too must have noticed long before. He had wanted to have me killed while I was still in the womb. Truda's version made it sound as if he had been only one degree more friendly towards my sister. A right bastard, no doubt. Yet already I felt myself missing him, felt my spirits sinking as I took in the knowledge that he was definitively beyond any recall.

At least he might not have forgotten his son's name. He might have felt some flicker of emotional sympathy. No matter what a disaster he was, poor old John, he couldn't have been more out of tune with me than Truda was. He would have been able to guess something of how I felt – he might even have had a sense of humour.

Yet her insensitivity, or indifference to feelings not her own, carried an advantage, I thought. In the future it would enable her to talk freely about the past. Listening to her was like reading an autopsy. It provided cold, unembellished, reportorial facts. A kind of coroner's truth. No fun in it, none at all, but given time it would enable me to learn what I needed to know.

How wrong I was again.

LUKE

8

It was five in the morning when the Liverpool night-train drew into Euston and along with the other rumpled, sleepless passengers I walked out into the cold pre-dawn. It was not very welcoming either for me or the southbound optimists with jeans and cheap suitcases coming to try their luck in the capital. Compared to what we grew to expect a decade later, London unemployment in 1974 was as low as in Utopia. Yet a southbound exodus by young people who couldn't find work in the traditional industrial centres of the Midlands and the North was already underway. It was hard not to think of Truda and John in their twenties, facing economic conditions that were only too similar, disembarking adventurously in London off a cut-price night-train in search of – what exactly? I hadn't learned enough about either of them to know. It was only certain that whatever they were seeking had proved elusive, or an illusion. Within two or three years they were riding the same 'excursion' train back where they started, only licking their wounds.

When I got back to the borrowed apartment in Primrose Hill, I went straight to bed but I couldn't sleep. In the end I got up and started a letter to Australia.

'So it all went off amazingly well,' I found myself typing, and then stopped, wondering what I meant. How could I be describing meeting my mother in terms appropriate to a party that had turned out fine, despite doubts about whether the guests would mix? And why if it had gone so well, which in a sense it had, was I so overcome with distress and disappointment?

My real father turns out to have used *four* names... His first name was 'John', not 'Paul' as I thought. He was brought up to be called John Griffith. Later he became 'John Chester'. On his death certificate it adds: 'Also known as "John Griffith-Chester" and "John Chester-Griffith" '!

Truda calls herself 'Bucknall' – the name of a man she lived with in the early 1950s, but never married. She had left my father and dropped his name (or names!) well before that. Her first – and only – marriage was over by the time she was 35, Bucknall died young, even her father, my maternal grandfather, was dead at 38, the aftermath of being in the army in the Great War ... None of the males in her life seems to have lasted.

As the sole exception to this rule, my turning up from oblivion has made her jumpy – she had certainly blown me away in her mind. All those years thinking a 'David Leitch' byline might one day produce a letter or call out of the blue, what a fool I was. If it hadn't been for TV, and the baby picture on the dust-jacket, she would never have made the connection at all ... She had forgotten the bloody name years ago ...

The letter tails off and I remember going back to bed, though not for long. I awoke with the bedside phone ringing, picked it up thinking it might be Truda, and found it was only the start of another story in France.

No memories of the journey are accessible any more, but from my notebook I know that I flew to Le Touquet and went on by rail to Paris, a route I often used because the train journey offered four hours' uninterrupted work time. Notebooks like this, as well as press cuttings and an appointments diary, are my hoarded equivalent of Truda's boxes. Without them I would never have been able to recall the extent to which I was disturbed and saddened by finding her, at the same time as being buoyed up by the miraculous chance of it having happened at all.

One note, interspersed with details and phone numbers required for a long-forgotten story, begins: 'Is there something wrong with her, or with me, or with both of us? It is unbearable to see so much in her that I recognise in myself. She can seem so cold, shallow, evasive, indifferent – as if nothing of significance exists on the other side of her own skin. Have I inherited this chill, and will I bequeath it to the future?'

Some process akin to crack-up must have been going on – I kept it at bay through work and a matter-of-fact brightness, another quality I could now recognise in my mother. Afterwards I obliterated the experience, much as she had tried to obliterate me. Until I found a heavily annotated copy of a book by Georges Simenon, not a *Maigret* but a piece of autobiography published in English as *Letters To My Mother*, I would have bet confidently that I had never seen or even heard of it. I had copied the beginning: 'It is nearly three and a half years since you died ... perhaps only now am I beginning to understand you.' Perhaps this was meant to encourage myself – understanding Truda would take time, it would be as hard for me as Simenon had found it. And having written it down, I was free to forget it, or very nearly.

It was sheer good luck that there were plenty of diverting and comparatively undemanding stories coming out of France in the course of that long, claustrophobic summer. Some of them are quite funny in their way, though reading them now all I see is a desperate brightness, like a grin on the face of someone who suspects he may be dying.

9

Truda could easily have gone through a similar shock reaction but at the time we next spoke she had more than recovered. It was like talking to a different person altogether – someone younger and freer. If I hadn't known from the operator that the call was coming from Liverpool it would have been hard to recognise her voice at all.

She must have picked up this uncertainty because the first thing she asked was whether I was hearing her properly.

Yes, fine, I replied, already convinced of her ecstatically high spirits, and feeling momentarily guilty that my own mood had been so different. At least, I thought, I've made my mother happy. She was experiencing the joy of reunion I had always imagined I would feel myself though for a reason I didn't understand, my father's death probably, it hadn't worked out like that.

'I feel as if a miracle's happened,' she was saying.

'It is a miracle, or close to it,' I replied.

'You don't know what it is yet,' she cut in.

'What?'

'It *is* a miracle,' she decided, 'a miracle from God.'

Before the last word there was an infinitesimal hesitation – either it didn't come naturally to her, or my cautious mother was concerned that by saying 'God' she was taking a risk. It might attract His supernatural attention and undermine everything. I told her how marvellous she sounded. In Liverpool she had been full of hesitations, weighing every word like gold-dust. Now she spoke in a rush, and in a tone of pure triumph.

'I've come to the *top*. At last. They sent a letter yesterday. I had hopes, of course, but I never really believed ... it's been so many years.'

'Top?'

'Of the list. The housing list. I phoned straight away and spoke to the lady. A very nice lady – so helpful. I've got to make up my mind very soon, she said, but there's no trouble about that. I've decided already, of course ...'

Only then, belatedly, I realised that she was not pursuing the theme of reunion between long lost mother and equally long lost son. Far from it. The euphoria, the exultant voice of someone who had hit the jackpot after a lifetime's frustration, was entirely unconnected with the fairy-tale happenstance that had taken me to Merseyside, and brought about this precursor of so many long-distance phone calls in the years that followed. She was not offering her almost tearful gratitude to Providence, and the mysterious coincidences of family fate. Pragmatic Truda was rejoicing over this – long delayed – benefaction flowing from the Merseyside municipal housing department.

It was stupid, ignoble even, to feel so hurt, but I did. She had been blessed with something infinitely more desirable, and essential, than the rediscovery of her first-born child. A place of her own. Her own turf where no one, not me, not even John's ghost, could intrude on her privacy and self-sufficiency.

As yet she had not clapped eyes on her new home. But it sounded as if the official dealing with Truda's application would be hard pressed to delay her inspection visit beyond the end of the day. She had already managed to see the specification, which included central heating, an exotic luxury in Merseyside, and power points so distributed that no awkward bending was ever necessary. 'They're designed for the ...' she paused, baulking at the word 'elderly' in all likelihood. 'For what they call senior citizens. I get my,' another pause, this time to avoid the qualification 'old age', 'pension next year, you know.

'There's a bathroom, with shower, and quite a nice-sized kitchen. There's a view from the kitchen, the lady from the council said. It's meant for a single person. All my own. No sharing. I'll never have to share again.'

I suggested making another visit to Liverpool: Truda vetoed it at once. She said it was better to wait until she had moved. It made sense and I accepted her wishes. Later I realised that her motives were largely to do with keeping the landlady and myself apart. I was struck by her affectionate tone – two unpredictable events had changed her life at the age of 62. She connected the one with the other. She thought I had brought her luck. When we talked on the phone as we did often during the summer, I was reminded of a gambler on a lucky streak. I had felt that way myself a few times. It was a rarer experience for Truda probably. I was pleased for her but there was never any danger of thinking that her joy was to do with me, except indirectly. She said as much herself.

On 12 August, selecting paper exuberantly embossed with bluebells, she wrote:

Dear David,
    The Postman calls at 7.30 a.m. Your note was the first delivery on my first morning here (apart from Bills etc.). I look upon this as a happy omen, thanks for your good timing. I love to hear from you.
    My new home is lovely. I'm still in a dream, can't believe my good luck. Already I feel so much better and enjoy the peace at night, sleeping undisturbed right through. Margaret and Bob have worked so hard to get me settled in. Yesterday they came to tea.
    How is your work going? Tell me what you are doing. You are more like John than I thought at first. Don't ask me to define this! Love to you both.
    Truda.

The 'both' was a reference to Jill – she had just flown in from Australia as if returning from a temporary, though extremely distant, summer migration. She was set on having the baby in the same London hospital where Judy, her daughter by her first marriage, had been born in the 1960s. Her own mother's health had apparently taken a turn for the better. She no longer felt obliged to stay in Australia. The omens for London were good, she thought.

10

Until Jill's return I don't suppose I had spoken of her pregnancy to more than a couple of friends, and then only briefly. I was frightened that talking about it, thinking about it even, could endanger it.

Now she was back, full of confidence about Charing Cross Hospital, she made her first direct contact with Truda, who was 'christening' her newly-installed phone. She was inordinately proud of having a phone of her own, and of the improvement in her status. After they had spoken I asked: 'What did she say about the baby?'

'Not much. She says the new flat makes her feel like a princess. She's going to come and see me in hospital.'

Jill visited Charing Cross for examinations the next day. When her daughter Judy was born over a decade earlier the hospital still stood in the very heart of London, abutting on Trafalgar Square. Now the old Victorian hospital had been demolished and replaced by a lavish medical palace whose looming towers were located 'out west', as taxi drivers said, in Hammersmith. True to some English conservative reflex, it was still named 'Charing Cross'.

Ante-natal out-patients visited a spanking new clinic, presided over by an aptly named baby-doctor, Hugh Jolly. He had arrived, via his baby books, at an eminence equivalent perhaps to that Benjamin Spock had enjoyed in America. The doctors conducted examinations, produced an X-ray photo of the stocky embryo *in situ*, and in the course of the morning it emerged that we were expecting a boy. He was even allocated a card with his Expected Time of Arrival, 27 October, inscribed on it. The fact that this was my birthday seemed a happy omen. It was like his final set of flight documents. Already, *in utero*, he had flown round the world and back.

Truda's lucky streak was spreading out to all of us like ripples from a gold coin dropped in a pool. From now on I knew the cards were going to fall our way, I could feel them growing warm. Luke was on the home stretch. Jill had chosen his name as far back as January, when 1974 was first showing its claws. The cards then had been cold indeed. And Luke had not even been conceived. Terrified by the possibility of having to undergo serious surgery, Jill had solemnly sworn that if it all turned out well she would have a child, and name it in honour of the ward where she had waited for the verdict. It had sounded a melodramatic act, but somehow it had worked out. No operation had been necessary, she discovered the ward was called 'St Luke's', and now in a few weeks her part of the bargain would be complete.

I phoned Truda and assured her she could expect a grandson. Her response was wonderfully authentic, at once commonplace and double-edged. 'Girls are much less trouble to bring up,' she assured me.

Because the new 'Charing Cross' was still not completely finished, their maternity patients occupied an annexe a mile away. The first time I visited Dr Jolly's spectacularly joyless annexe, I turned away from the entrance. The place was more like a forgotten nunnery than a maternity hospital, or perhaps an unusually extravagant fundamentalist church, built on a grandish scale 150 years before, and then transformed into some collegiate function, maybe a seminary for missionaries. Inside the marble vestibule, the heavy neo-classical pretensions of the marble curving stairway led upwards to circular galleries, filling me with foreboding. More than anything it made me think of a fancy morgue.

The section devoted to birth began on the third floor. The two beneath were disaster zones, densely populated by terminal patients and traumatised relatives. In the elevator you could see good Samaritan visitors, carrying boxes decked up with indomitable ribbons and wearing more sanguine neckties than were probably habitual, practising a brave face for the encounter ahead. The new hospital, I suspected, had found it convenient to shuffle off their hopeless cases to the Gothic annexe.

I hoped Jill didn't notice; very likely she didn't. The baby world, starting on the third floor, was completely different, and almost as empty as a pub with no beer. There was still lots of growth potential in death, despite the adverse economic factors in the air. It was only entering the maternity section that the catch-phrase 'zero growth' came instantly to mind. Jill was installed there herself within forty-eight hours of the examination. Her blood pressure was high, there were doubts about the position the baby had adopted. Dr Jolly said: 'It's best to keep an eye on you.'

I became a connoisseur of the daily underground journey to Hammersmith, sucking in long-forgotten odours of the London tube. These were the smells of armpits sweating under heavy clothes, of sopping raincoats, of bottled Guinness, of dogged, uncomplaining failure. It had crept up on me too. The last time I had become attuned to a regular in-city train journey had been in Paris, travelling from Denfert-Rochereau several days a week to the palace in the Avenue Kléber for the Vietnam Peace Talks. The Paris métro had been a haven of order and cleanliness, the train popping overground for three stops and crossing the Seine on a fine suspension bridge. I had travelled first class and contentedly enough. Someone had even been paying me for my industry. Now, as I sat bound for Hammersmith, the Paris memories came back often, mixed with Vietnamese ones – above all, the Saigon orphans' hospital, where the babies had learned to rock themselves perpetually, partly because no other rockers were available, partly as a kind of auto-hypnotic distraction from constant emotional pain.

Distraction, though of a different kind, was at a premium in Jill's ward too. She was one of six expectant mothers in an area designed for forty beds. It was so spectacularly under-occupied that you felt any day now the entire operation would be wound up and arriving visitors would find nothing left

except the last removal men. It was a fine room, built with
Victorian conscientiousness and the occasional imperialistic
plaque or curlicue, epitaphs to a cockier age. Now it was like
a church; once the heart of some flourishing and uplifting cult,
now in the last days of decline.

Four of this six-strong congregation were putting most of
their resources into waiting, like stranded passengers in an
unusually well fitted out airport lounge. They just lay there
and let it happen as if under heavy sedation. Perhaps they
were. Even Jill was comparatively docile. All over the hospital,
conspicuously amateur posters advertised a review, called 'Hey
Presto!', which the staff would be performing in a lecture
theatre a few weeks later. One night I was visiting at the same
time as a young doctor trying to sell tickets for the show. The
expectant patients were so unresponsive that I took pity and
purchased a batch. 'They don't like the waiting,' he said.

'I know how they feel,' I replied, stashing away my open
sesames for 'Hey Presto!' night. Except, of course, I didn't
really. It was an experience from which males were largely
excluded, physically in that their presence during the birth was
allowed only as a grudging concession, psychologically and
physiologically as this is the point where the sexes are most
remote from each other. The women seemed elsewhere.

With their god-like trick up the puffy sleeves of their bri-
nylon nighties there was no pressure to parade minor accom-
plishments. The patients lounged in a trance – the ward was
one of the most boring places I had ever known.

Two of the expectant mothers did their best to make up for
the excessive placidity of the other four. Their methods were
very different, but they shared a taste for physical activity. The
'Egyptian', a lady who had arrived with a maid known as the
'Slave', specialised in fits of Egyptian hysterics followed by
mimed – and in one case genuine – departure. The first issue
was her right to keep the 'Slave', who squatted on a mat beside
her bed. In the end the authorities gave in – the place was so
empty that another human being, particularly one happy
squatting on the floor round the clock, made no difference.
The second, graver dispute took place one day before I ar-

rived. The 'Egyptian' had walked out in a rage and the authorities had insisted on extracting a waiver first. She hadn't
wanted to sign. According to Miss Collins, the second maverick, the 'Egyptian' had been insulted by this bureaucratic re-
quirement. She suspected it was a way of humiliating her by
demonstrating in view of the other mothers that writing as
well as reading were beyond her.

Miss Collins had got it wrong, as she got everything wrong,
including her bet that letting herself be fucked in a Ford Cor-
tina after a pony club dance would not, inevitably, lead to the
pregnancy she so abhorred. The 'Egyptian', who returned the
next day accompanied this time by her husband and his chauf-
feur as well as the 'Slave', was far from illiterate. A lot of her
time was probably spent signing credit card slips.

Miss Collins, in contrast, was by temperament a pacer. Her
normal mood was one of blazing indignation at the way life
had treated her. Almost before I had met her, she was telling
me, as she had told the uncomprehending Egyptian, about the
Night of her Betrayal. She was a beefy, countrified girl, but
rusticity and naturalness had not merged in her – she was fake
right through. Her anger was also inordinate. When she
buttonholed me, she gave off so strong an impression of
reined-in violence that I sometimes found myself trying to remember whether you stood in front or behind horses of uncertain disposition, in case they suddenly lashed out.

At first I had thought Miss Collins was calling herself 'Ms
Collins'. Many feminists I knew were deliberately getting pregnant, having babies, and setting themselves up as 'single-parent
families', partly because the nuclear family was so unpopular,
partly because marriage was as socially unacceptable in some
circles as Miss Collins's unmarried pregnancy was in her own.
After a Sunday encounter it became clear that her parents were
the arbitrators she accepted on social and ethical matters. Like
a ventriloquist's doll, an exceptionally bulky one, she was re-
citing someone else's words.

They were a frozen stoical couple with a quality of hidden
anger she shared. Mr Collins was a retired real-estate man
dressed in tweeds with a matching cap. It was hard to know

whether they hated the seducer or the baby more. 'It's going to be adopted, Antonia's signed the papers. They wanted her to wait until after it's born in case she changes her mind but Antonia's not trying to have any of that, are you?'

Miss Collins said she wasn't. I was fascinated to learn her first name.

The Collins clan had chosen Hammersmith because it was far enough from home for the birth to be kept secret. I wondered whether they had been attracted by its Victorian décor as a complement to their daughter's Victorian predicament. She was a heroine out of Thomas Hardy, out of Victorian melodrama, and I thought of her often in capital letters: she had been Wronged, Seduced and Betrayed. I never discovered the name of the seducer, he was 'him' to her, too degraded to be given a human appendage. Just as the impending baby was always 'it'. 'He' had tricked her, maliciously, promising marriage, even giving her a ring. When she had said this I looked for it on her hand and she followed my glance. 'I sent it back,' she said. 'It wasn't much, a lot of little diamonds.'

'I don't think they were real,' said Mrs Collins. 'You know they can make them cheap, in Russia or somewhere. They look real but when you come to sell them they might as well be dirt.' It was a striking contribution, the only one she made.

'I made her send it back,' Mr Collins said proudly.

When they talked about the adoption there were more mental capital letters. 'We all think,' Mr Collins said, 'It's By Far The Best Solution.'

Surprisingly, he asked what I thought.

'It's certainly a final one. Mothers do change their minds, of course.'

'*She* won't,' Mr Collins said, putting on his driving gloves preparatory to exiting. 'After all, it's not her baby, it's his.'

'That's right, dear,' said his wife.

After they left I heard Miss Collins telling the saga of the ring to the 'Egyptian', whose husband was paying a brief call, as if to a bank manager.

Miss Collins, who couldn't wait to discharge her baby like a housemaid working out her notice, glowed with health. It was as if her permanent anger, her sense of personal outrage, nurtured her like the sun. She was obviously going to drop the child as easily as if it had been a foal of doubtful pedigree.

Jill, a more complex and emotional creature, was having a much rougher ride, despite the early hospitalisation. The indications were that the baby was positioned to enter the world backwards, or feet first. For over a month before she started labour, efforts had been made to shift him or persuade him to shift himself into the more conventional head-on approach, left occipito anterior as I learned it was called in the profession. Finally it had been decided that the foetal position was not going to change. Preparations were made for a 'breech birth'.

In these circumstances, the size of the head became critical, I was told by a reassuring obstetrician called Mahmoud. Since the baby needed to be born quickly, probably assisted by forceps, it was a bad idea to let the head grow too large. Accordingly, they decided to induce labour nearly ten days before the projected date of birth.

There had been a recent controversy about induction machines. Jill, fortunately, had confidence in the hospital and Dr Mahmoud – since there were so few expectant mothers in the place, it was obvious that she could rely on expert attention. She was benefiting from the falling birth-rate, whose steady decline had been felt in all the European countries and the USA – in France they had arrived at 'minus growth', the sinister demographic point where there are more deaths than births. Jean Dutourd's novel, 2024, had just been published. It was set fifty years hence in a Paris populated almost entirely by senile survivors of the mid-twentieth-century 'baby boom', where anyone under 50 was a rarity, and the appearance of a child on the streets caused a sensation.

In Jill's ward it was easy to think that Dutourd's science fiction might be prophetic. Here, perhaps, was the last generation, waiting to be born in a lonely and unwelcoming desert. But Luke's birth, thank God, was not like that at all.

There had been a phone call early in the morning. I arrived at the hospital in a violent storm to find Jill already in the

labour theatre. She looked enormous and preoccupied – she
was reserving her powers of concentration. There was already
a lot of pain and she received an injection in the spine with
long-suffering resignation. Her first labour had been easier, she
told me, lying back with her eyes closed, surrounded by hard-
ware of various kinds. It was easy to see why the induction
machine had led to so much angry debate. As feminists pointed
out, this was a man-made and male-designed system, and
looked it. Jill could not see its facia but I sat staring at it for
hours, my eyes glued to the green monitor indicating the foetal
heartbeat.

Early in the labour it turned to red. In a panic I dashed off
to find the nursing sister in charge of the afternoon shift. She
diagnosed 'machine malfunction' blithely, and said: 'The
bloody thing does it all the time.' She didn't seem to like the
machine any more than I did. It looked an amalgam of a
computer, a deep-freeze and an institutional safe.

Jill now wore a look I recognised from battle-zone stretcher
cases who were gravely wounded, or suspected they were. She
was abstracted and turned inwards, martialling her powers.
Despite the injection there was still a lot of pain. The nursing
staff came and went erratically, I hunched by the table, holding
Jill's hand and staring grimly at the white enamel of the machine, its lights flickering, its programmed drip inexorably im-
posing its robotic will on any human contrariness. I felt useless
holding Jill's hand. In due course I was directed to a waiting-
room, where I found the husband of the Egyptian 'Slave-
owner', as the nurses called her. She was to have a Caesarean
some time that afternoon. The husband was reading the
Financial Times, gold bracelets on his wrists jangling as he
turned the pages.

When the birth finally began it happened much faster than
I had expected. Dr Mahmoud, who had lectured to me about
breech births, exuded the same cheeriness from behind a green
mask. 'Push – very good,' he was saying. Then, more fiercely,
'Don't push. You must be very careful now ... Don't push
... Don't ...'

His voice was now commanding, imperative. For the first

time he transferred his attention from the mother's dilating
cervix to look her straight in the eye and make sure the
message had been understood. This was the moment of danger
he had mentioned so lightly a few weeks before, casual in blue
blazer and a tie with squash rackets on it. Now he spoke like
an officer in uniform, an image that went deep with Jill.

It seemed a very long time before he spoke again. I sweated,
prayed, felt useless behind my mask, though Jill later remembered holding my hand and squeezing it hard to transfer some
of the hurt. It was the nearest I came to a useful act – I became
aware that the theatre was almost packed with people who,
like myself, had no discernible role except to observe behind
masks, and maybe pray.

Just as the waiting became unbearable, Mahmoud said:
'Well done. Good. Very good.'

More happened in the next twenty seconds than seemed
possible to keep up with. Suddenly there was a new voice,
besides Dr Mahmoud's, a very distinctive one.

Jill had exercised the control required. It had been like feeling your finger on the trigger and knowing you mustn't pull it,
she said later. Her father was a senior army officer: 'It was my
military upbringing. When the doctor gave the order, and
looked at me directly, instead of my body, I knew I needed to
obey.' If she hadn't she felt the child might have been de-
formed, might have died even. It was certainly the moment of
maximum risk.

This was why she had insisted on Charing Cross and fled
Neuilly in Paris. She didn't want there to be any possibility of
a misunderstanding of language, an order confused in a flurry
of voluble French. Once, sailing on a yacht in the Mediterranean with an all French crew, she had thrown the unattached
anchor overboard to the depths of Capri harbour. She had
thought the Parisian skipper had said: 'Throw that rope over
the side.' He had really said the equivalent of 'Don't let that
go, for the love of Jesus and Mary.'

This time Jill had got it right.

A bright pink rump, glowing almost, appeared. And a
moment later, it could have been a moment before, there was

a voice, a kind of waking up voice as if from a very small animal. It was somewhere between a whimper and a mew.

Instantly, more rump, much more. Then a pellet of shit, round as a pebble and pea-green, was propelled into the world. Before I'd taken that in, an arc of urine, for a beginner a Giotto-like perfection of peeing, followed Luke's pellet as if to water it.

There was an instant before everyone burst out laughing. Luke filled it with his new voice, more tiger than kitten. It was something between a roar and a scream, an infant cry which Frédéric Leboyer among other researchers claims is the world's one truly universal language.

Then everyone was laughing, including myself and, very likely, Mahmoud too behind his mask. There was something witty about Luke's arrival. What a way to enter the world – to a chorus of young people laughing.

After the birth the audience dispersed with astonishing speed. They were nursing and medical students who had seen breech births on instructional films and were seizing a rare chance in this 'zero-growth' period to observe the real thing. The mood of comedy persisted until they had all left, jostling each other for coats in the ante-room and talking about 'the show' that night. It was a ribald, even sexy atmosphere.

The crowded room became empty, Dr Mahmoud and his team disappeared to take care of the Egyptian lady's 'Caesar' and a benign English charwoman out of the past appeared to pour tea out of a daintily festive pot. She clucked over Jill, who sank into sleep before she had time to drink anything and gave Luke a cooing, which he accepted with composure.

As recommended by my obstetrician friend in France I had turned down the lights as soon as possible. No one minded and the baby, calm now with the air of someone who had been obliged to do a lot in a hurry and was now taking it easy, examined everything with eyes bluer than his blanket. I had settled down to rock him in a cosy spot behind the table but quickly stopped because soothing him was unnecessary. He was already perfectly soothed.

Like everything that had happened that day the exchange

between us was not at all what I had expected. The events had
surprised me but not, apparently, the baby. His blue gaze roved
round as if compiling an inventory, taking things in calmly one
at a time, only moving on to the next when he had satisfied
himself everything was in place and in the right order.

My impression was that he found nothing new. Instead, the
different elements were all familiar – the matter in hand seemed
to be recognition, satisfying himself that nothing necessary had
been lost or overlooked. I had seen him going through the
same process with Jill, from a vantage point on her stomach,
that he now embarked on with me. It didn't engage him long.
When I smiled and stuck out my tongue he seemed to hesitate,
considering a mimic response, and then decided against. His
only concern was verifying my presence – what antics I got up
to were by the way.

I had expected to feel possessive but was taken aback to see
that his was the proprietorial air. I had the impression that he
recognised me: we had met, as by long-standing appointment,
at the right place and at the predetermined time. He seemed
graciously pleased that everything had gone off smoothly and
in due course, entirely his own man, he took advantage of my
arms as if they were his reserved seat and settled into sleep.

His mother was deeply asleep too. The tea-lady had left to
pursue her humane vocation somewhere else; the shadowy
room might have been a cave. I closed my eyes, feeling planted
deep down in the earth like a tree.

Much later, on the way out, I met the maternity ward doctor
with whom I'd had dealings over the Amateur Night tickets a
few weeks before. He was hurrying.

'Aren't you coming?' he asked anxiously.

'I've just had a son,' I said.

'That's good,' he said. 'But I guess he's a bit young for the
show. Come along.'

He took my arm and led me in an unfamiliar direction in
that only too familiar hospital. I remarked it was the wrong
way for the exit. 'Are you all right, my dear chap? Not in
shock or anything?'

'Where are we going?'

'To the hall for "Hey Presto!", you haven't lost your tickets? I can probably get you in. It's not entirely amateur, you know. We're having that magician who's always on TV – he's going to saw a nurse in two.'

I disengaged myself, I hope without giving offence, and set off into the urban desert of Hammersmith, my step so springy it was like experiencing weightlessness. I'd experienced enough magic that day to last me till the grave.

11

My eyesight was better than my mother's. Waiting at the barrier I spotted her coming along the platform off the Liverpool train long before she knew I was there.

Truda looked dapper, unencumbered, as self-sufficient as thistledown in her matching beige outfit with a little hat, gloves and a cameo brooch at the throat. She was also a model of deportment. There were people all around her, an eager, distinctly shabby crowd thronging off the excursion special, but at fifty yards it was evident that Truda was apart from them all. She was not the kind of person to fall into conversation with strangers to beguile a long journey. Not for her the exchange of snapshots, gregariousness for its own sake. Truda did not give parts of herself away without consideration for the sheer joy of the thing. I am a cat who walks alone, her platform demeanour proclaimed. Do not think that this is an accommodation I have been obliged to reach with necessity. This is the way I have chosen.

I was delighted to see her, delighted with my own delight. There was something very endearing about her personal complacency, the silky sense of having selected her clothes with care, arranged her newly-set hair to perfection. She carried an umbrella so frivolously tiny, so carefully matched to the rest of her outfit, that it might have been some purely decorative outfit item like a fan. Clearly no anarchic rain would dare fall on her.

I kissed her on the cheek with care not to disturb her skilfully applied make-up. We set off across the forecourt as if we had really known each other for a lifetime, instead of this being only technically the case.

We drove in the rain to Hammersmith in west London, Truda throwing little glances periodically out of the window like a feeding bird making sure nothing hostile is creeping up. My own mood was still dominated by paternal euphoria, blinding me to the self-evident. My mother in no way regarded visiting her grandson, now aged three days, as a treat.

Her reaction when I'd phoned on the night of his birth might have given me a clue to her growing unease, clear now as we stopped outside the hospital. If I was euphoric three days later, that night on the phone I'd been babbling. Truda had been pleased, gratified even, but markedly cooler.

'What a shame the little bugger's grandad isn't still around to take a peek at him,' I had said fatuously down the Liverpool line.

Mersey people take as much pride in their supposed warm-heartedness and family feeling as in the Beatles, but on this occasion Truda was in no mood for any sentimental evocation of an extended family reunion. '*Him*,' she responded acidly. 'You'd never have found him – he'd have been lost for a month wetting the baby's head. I'm surprised *you're* in tonight.'

As if to emphasise her own superiority, she reconfirmed the details of her arrival in London. Like all her arrangements, it had been made weeks before. We had assumed at the time that it would fall shortly before the 27 October birth – Luke's approach to schedules was more cavalier than that of his methodical grandma. He had jumped the gun (with a little encouragement) by nine days.

As we crossed the marble vestibule I felt her shiver. It still didn't cross my mind that her plan to visit Jill before the birth was deliberate. It would have been easier for her to meet Jill without the baby. The emotional load would have been lighter.

'I hate hospitals – I'm allergic to them,' she said, waiting for the antique lift. I hated them too, loathed them. Yet I assumed Truda's natural discomfort, like my own, would evaporate in excitement at seeing the baby. I prayed we wouldn't have to go up three creaking levels with some parchment-faced cancer

patient. It would have a bad effect on my mother, I thought.
For my own part I always felt an affinity with the dying;
sharing their company was no ordeal. It probably wasn't for
Truda either. It was the new-born, not the nearly dead, who
opened her dark places.

The lift was crowded with various visitors. What was left
of Truda's composure was melting like wax.

Jill was now established with her baby in a new ward on a
yet higher floor. Along with a few others, still no more than
seven or eight, she had passed through the valley of birth from
Ante-Natal to the glories of Post-Natal. It was a very different
emotional setting, though still incongruously over-sized, as if
a cottage industry had been set up in premises designed to
handle a mass-production line.

During the waiting period, the mothers (except for Miss
Collins and the 'Egyptian') had been noticeably placid. Now
the post-natal ward pulsated with maternal passions, raw as
blood, orchestrated – and augmented – by the babies' own
aviary chorus. As far as I could see every single mother had
fought a pitched battle with at least one particular nurse, often
with several. Jill had told me of the small-hours quarrels,
usually to do with feeding, which broke out in the yellow
corridor connecting the mothers' ward and the babies' nursery.
Jill already recognised Luke's huskily pitched SOS – an Irish
nurse had tried to tell her the cries came from another child.
Jill had come close to hitting her.

The spirit of Mars had entered into the mothers. They didn't
like the hayseed Irish nurses; they didn't like the reggae-
crooning Caribbean ones. They positively hated a militaristic
English matron, who criticised their breast-feeding techniques,
or lack of them. I hoped that we might avoid this woman,
whom so far I knew only by repute.

As we walked along the corridor, the combat ground for
battles that marinated during the long non-visiting hours,
Truda's eyes were everywhere. 'There's a lot of darkies,' she
commented when a pair of Jamaican nurses walked by. Then
she spotted what she sought – a door marked 'Visiting Ladies'.

'I'll just powder my nose,' she announced, and vanished

almost at a trot. I suspect she wasn't using the expression to
be genteel – she wanted somewhere to touch up her face.

I had wanted to avoid the matron. Instead there was a
different barrier to penetrate. Miss Collins was standing, arms
threateningly akimbo but immobile as a statue, in the centre
of the ward entrance. Her hair was wild – the new mothers all
complained of lack of access to hairdressers – and even in her
pink, floor-length nightgown, fastened primly at the throat
with a complicated ribbon, she looked barbaric. She examined
every visitor like those 'physiognomists' employed by French
casinos for their capacity to recall the faces of clients guilty of
dubious cheques. But they perform their fiscal vocation with
arithmetical detachment. Miss Collins's expression could have
raised a heat blister at twenty feet. She could have been a
valkyrie marking down those who were to be slain.

She ignored my brisk 'Good afternoon'; Truda eyed her
doubtfully. Jill was waiting in bed, a welcoming, equable figure
by comparison. She and Truda shook hands, oddly formal. To
accomplish this act, Jill had to reach across a white-shawled
Luke who was dozing, using Jill's left breast as a combination
mattress/pillow. The baby doctor Leboyer had assured me that
this position, the usual one of 'Madonna and Child', was
adopted to ensure maximum physical proximity to the
mother's heartbeat. He thought it soothed and reassured the
infant. It certainly seemed to have such an effect on Jill. Her
manner was pleasant and, as far as we were concerned, uninvolved. She dealt with Truda and myself on an automatic pilot.

The 'Egyptian's' husband interrupted us to show me his
baby – he was carrying him as deftly as a briefcase. We exchanged macho compliments with unforced bonhomie. His son
wore an expression of profound abstraction with no hint of
evading any painful reality or memories. The Caesarean had
left his mother depleted to a point where she was almost physically absent. It didn't seem to have bothered her husband
much. He and I had exchanged maybe twenty words during a
month of short meetings. Suddenly we were blood brothers.
With a gesture of infinite charm and a jangle from his bracelet,
he passed me his child to hold. His cranium, much darker than

Luke's, seemed covered with a thicker fuzz of hair. The fon-
tanelle, still imperfectly grafted to my eyes, looked as if it
would crack under the pressure of a falling leaf.

Such a well-meant eastern compliment had to be recipro-
cated. Jill saw it too, and interrupting some exchange with
Truda about how Luke got his name, invited the Egyptian to
inspect our local product. She exhibited no anxiety as he
scooped Luke up and gave him a professional going-over. It
struck me that his habitual haste may have been that derived
from a need to commute between wives as well as business
deals.

Then it was Truda's turn. She delicately avoided a plastic-
lined bin, conveniently to hand for what she probably intuited
were soiled nappies, and lifted Luke as if he were a china
teapot she had a premonition of dropping.

Luke was not looking his best. His skin looked somehow
rubbed, his neck was no more than a row of fatty folds so his
plum-sized chin appeared to rest for support on his chest. His
lids were heavy – they gave him a debauched look and, I noted
without enthusiasm, suggested a physical resemblance to his
rapscallion Uncle Richard. His gaze remained steady, though
distinctly less curious than it had been immediately after his
birth. One chubby paw flopped out, disarranging Truda's
prominent glasses. She instantly returned him to Jill, concentrating her attention on smoothing down her ruffled blouse
and checking it surreptitiously for damp.

The whole exchange couldn't have lasted more than ninety
seconds. It was enough to establish that Truda was as fluent
with babies as an Eskimo-speaker taking his first steps in Man-
darin Chinese. Regaining some of her poise, Truda bent over
and tried cooing and clucking. Probably a canary or a catfish
would have been as responsive as her grandson. He was ready
to doze again but accepted her advances with uninvolved good
nature. At this moment, with no prior warning, or none I had
seen, Truda started to sob.

She looked infinitely more vulnerable than the baby. I can't
remember how long it went on, but it was awful. Jill said
something comforting but unavailing. I patted her uselessly

on the shoulder, as illiterate with mothers as she was with babies. It was clear she wanted to leave: somehow we did. On the way, Truda's sobs subsiding now, she stopped off again at 'Visiting Ladies'.

While I waited Miss Collins moved in, carrying her baby this time. She couldn't have been more confident with him – it was as if the bundle was an unsuitable gift she was on her way to exchange for an item that fitted better. She handled him briskly, toughly even, and periodically inflicted little blows on his back: 'Helps it burp,' she explained.

She also explained her anger. The formalities of adoption were more bureaucratic – and much slower – than she had expected. She was going to phone her father's lawyer about it. The matron had been very rude and said she might have to keep 'it' as long as six weeks.

I had hoped that Miss Collins might move on before Truda returned, but she didn't. The novel pleasure I took in introducing Truda to people as 'my mother' warred with embarrassment. I made awkward introductions, blurring over the 'Miss', and after a few seconds, tiny and once again immaculate Truda, face to face with the sturdy new mum, shapeless in her dressing-gown, we moved off.

Truda hadn't bothered to pretend she wanted to admire the baby. Nor had Miss Collins gone through any routine about displaying her son. But Truda was sharp – she had caught the word 'adoption'.

'She's letting the baby go, isn't she?'

'Yes,' I said. 'She's waiting for the formalities to be worked out. She's getting fed up.'

It was a subject which Truda might find painful. Yet she returned to it. As we walked down the portentous staircase, out of the underpopulated floor dealing with maternity into the crowded sections dealing with the chronically sick, she asked, surprisingly, if I knew Miss Collins's 'background'.

I said what I knew. Truda listened attentively. 'I thought she came from a nice family,' she remarked finally. 'I could tell from her voice.'

By 'nice', my conservative-minded mother meant 'middle-

class', which the Collinses undoubtedly were. That was the
source of their problem, or one of them. They were unable to
make judgments about their daughter's baby in terms which
were not social – that was why she was holed up in London,
far away from friends and neighbours who might have discovered the secret. The parents had made sure that their
daughter shared their views, out-of-date and unhelpful as they
were.

'She's making a great mistake,' Truda said unexpectedly.
There was something in her voice that entirely engaged my
attention – she spoke with a long pent-up emphasis, a kind of
shrillness, that was many miles away from her habitual mod-
ulated tone. 'A great mistake,' she repeated in the same voice.
She sighed. '*And* she'll live to regret it.'

We had reached the hospital exit. Ahead were some steps,
the pavement, a swirl of evening traffic flowing in to the centre
of town. Truda was hanging back, keen to delay stepping out
beyond the shelter of the portico, where the insidious drizzle
could get at all her neatness.

I took her arm, then transferred my hand so I was holding
her suede-gloved paw, and stopped walking altogether, anxious
for her to continue. Miss Collins had touched my mother.
Perhaps this was the moment I had been waiting for. I was
sure that she was going to say what I wanted to hear, even
though until that moment I hadn't known precisely what it was.

She looked up at me and I smiled encouragingly, squeezing
her glove. Her expression overflowed with conviction. I felt a
moment of joy – a deep relief – in advance of her next words.
I also felt grateful to Miss Collins. It was hard to imagine her
as benign. But by waddling along the corridor at that precise
moment she had somehow sparked off the reaction in Truda
I so badly needed. An acknowledgment it amounted to.

Now she would be able to say how easy it was, through
youth and emotional disturbance and outside pressures, to
make an error you would regret until the grave. She was going
to say that mothers should not give away their children. That
Miss Collins would curse the day she had let her first-born son
go, just as she had herself.

'I nearly told her,' Truda continued. 'I would have done only I was upset after seeing the baby. It looks so much like you.'

Waiting for her to continue, I was surprised that she still thought of Luke as 'it'. She had stopped again.

'What were you going to tell her? Perhaps you should have carried on. Miss Collins needs advice.'

Truda agreed warmly.

'Yes. It's a great mistake walking around hanging on to the baby like that. She should get the nurses to look after it, that's what they're there for. The more she coddles it, the worse it will be when they come to adopt it.'

My astonishment was lost in Truda's vehemence – she didn't notice that I was rocked back on my heels as if punched.

'I made sure that never happened with you. I hardly touched you once. You ought to tell that girl when you go again.'

Truda spoke proudly as if parading a virtue, some quality of mothering in which the inexperienced Miss Collins had proved deficient. Never touch the baby, then it will be easier to dump, less troublesome to forget, as she had forgotten me.

I remember the welcome sight of an empty cab heading east and withdrawing my hand from Truda's to flag it down.

12

The day was redeemed through sheer luck. I was so relieved to get Truda out of the hospital and into the cab that I told the driver simply to take us to the West End. As we pulled away she let out a sigh. It could have been relief, yet such was the intensity behind this muted expulsion of breath, I felt it might easily have come out as a scream. I'll never understand her, I thought. I'm too dumb, and it's too late. We'll always be intimate strangers, out of step, out of synch. So we sat, side by side, flesh and blood, absent.

Then came the mood change, instantaneously and with no warning. We had reached Knightsbridge, scarcely moving now. The traffic was probably stationary all the way to Hyde Park Corner.

'Oh look,' Truda said. 'Look at it!' Using my shoulder for leverage and with unusual disregard for dignified comportment she was sprawling across my side of the cab to get her nose as close as possible to the steamed-up window.

'Isn't it beautiful?'

Through the drizzle across the road was Harrods, focus of her delight. The luxury store was decorated for Christmas, prematurely it seemed to me, indeed it was lit up like a Christmas tree. We exchanged seats to give her a better view. She wiped the window clear with her glove, and when it smeared over within seconds, polished it yet again.

We moved past infinitesimally slowly, but it was still too fast for her. She might have been trying to imprint on her mind an image of the Taj Mahal by moonlight.

'Do you know, I think it's even brighter than it used to be. Aren't there more lights?'

My mother's eye for glitter, I suspected, hadn't let her down. The display seemed more lavish – and garish – than in the past.

Perhaps it was a reaction against the oil-crisis winter of the previous year, the three-day week, the blitz-like black-out. More likely, the excessive neon reflected the way that the store's personality had changed in rhythm with the shift in world economics. In the past the house speciality was opulent good taste. Nowadays, judging from what I heard, they just concentrated on the opulence.

'I'd love to go and see it again. Oh, let's go tomorrow. Do you shop there?'

'Hardly ever.'

Truda made a little disappointed noise. The traffic started to pick up and she turned to watch the pleasure domes of her personal Xanadu, decorated now with reindeer, recede through the rear window.

I hadn't wished to spoil her pleasure by implying indifference to the cosmopolitan fairyland where the kid from the remote provinces had lived out her dreams of participating in the ultimate in metropolitan chic. For her the journey from Liverpool to Knightsbridge must have been like traversing the globe. She had worked there long ago, of course. Before I was born. Worse, until she became pregnant with me, thus disqualifying herself as a suitable young lady to pander to the aristocracy from behind her beloved jewellery counter. Once she could no longer conceal the bulge I made in her immaculate uniform, they had expelled her from dream-land forever. If it had been hard taking the high road from north to south, then she must have gone every step along the low road back to Liverpool with a taste of ashes in her throat.

On impulse I knocked on the partition and asked the driver to take us to the Ritz. Truda, at once delighted and businesslike, turned the light on and employed her handbag mirror.

The downstairs bar was almost empty and we settled in a corner banquette. I suggested Buck's Fizz, and again I was able to indulge the novel pleasure of ordering for 'my mother'.

There was something about Truda's unseamed neatness
which always provoked an urge in me to embark on something
spontaneous – her hospital breakdown had been profoundly
untypical and I never saw her react in a remotely similar manner again. I would try to inject a sharper vitality via the improvised, the unexpected, treats. What was unavailable inside,
I attempted to replace with drinks that sparkled.

Daintily sipping her fizz from a crystal goblet, Truda was
by now sparkling herself. Harrods was still on her mind. She
was telling a story which, with repetition over the years, I
came to see summarised everything she had longed for as a
girl.

'The department managers were very strict – everything had
to be just so. Immaculate. We were inspected every morning
from top to toe. They examined everything. Your stocking
seams had to be exactly straight, your fingernails manicured.
The girls used to do them for each other – but no coloured
nail varnish mind.'

In tribute to the standards prevailing in the Harrods jewellery section about thirty-seven years before, I observed that my
mother's nails, though perfectly shaped, were glossed with
colourless varnish.

'That was our regular morning inspection. You can imagine
what it was like when royalty were expected – and that happened quite often. Sometimes they would come at a special
time and the whole store or the floor that they were on was
closed to the general public altogether.'

'Which ones came?'

'Oh, they all did. We had the Queen Mother when she
wasn't much more than a girl, she was still Duchess of York.
She'd come with her little daughters, the present Queen and
Princess Margaret. They called her Margaret Rose then. And
the Prince of Wales before he was Duke of Windsor, poor
man. He was so handsome, smaller than you'd think though.
And Mrs Simpson, of course – we all knew about her long
before the papers did. She was *thin*.'

Truda, as might be expected, was no fan of Wallis Simpson.
She had served the future Duchess of Windsor often without

getting over-excited about the experience. But Truda's apotheosis, a story I came to know down to the subtlest inflexion in her voice, concerned the royal mother of both the Duke of Windsor and George VI. 'The old Queen Mary', as Truda called her.

Queen Mary had not only bought some old silver. She had asked Truda's advice about a hallmark first – and Truda had got it right. Afterwards the manageress had complimented her. Truda looked modest. 'I've always had a feeling for silver,' she said, as if it were a quality people inherited at birth.

I nearly made the error of asking whether Queen Mary, having 'bought' the silver Truda recommended, had actually paid for it. Certainly in her old age, I knew, the formidable old lady had a reputation for kleptomania, or 'forgetfulness', about such matters. She had always been a great visitor of London department stores. Apparently they made a point (probably even at Harrods) of detailing a discreet employee to check the items she slipped into her bag so they could bill Kensington Palace for them later.

But this was much later on, in her declining years – and also in Truda's. The occasion my mother liked to recall with such savour had taken place during the legendary Good Old Days with no shadows to sully their cloudlessness. For Truda this experience stayed with her like a jewelled crest on the wall. It was my mother's personal royal warrant.

We went on to eat in a restaurant on the edge of Hyde Park. Through the big glass windows there were fine, melancholy vistas of the park in the rain. Truda adored it. She also spotted that some other diners were talking Russian. I told her that it was popular with personnel from the nearby Soviet Embassy. When I had been doing research for a book on Kim Philby, 'counsellors' from their diplomatic mission had sometimes tried to pump me here over vodka-drenched lunches.

Truda hated and suspected Russians, probably one of her few morsels of inheritance from the Odessa ghetto generations back, but Philby fascinated her. We talked for hours about this black prince of double-agents, who had served Soviet intelligence for twenty years without either Washington or London entertaining suspicions that he was anything but the truest-blue patriot.

Her endless interest in the man surprised me as much as I had been surprised by her reactions in the hospital. It was a long time before I discovered the two apparently disparate strains shared a common ground. Truda herself was a natural double-agent, an implacable guardian of secrets, a masterly purveyor of 'disinformation' exquisitely calculated to mislead and deceive.

Half way through the meal I phoned the hospital to fix what time we should visit the next day. It was bad news. Luke's slightly worn look, the roughish texture of his skin, had been the first symptoms of jaundice. It was probably better if we didn't go. Truda affected disappointment, but without too much conviction. A little later she enquired delicately whether we might fill the gap by an expedition to, inevitably, Harrods.

We went the next day. For me all department stores were a claustrophobic nightmare: a reminder of the last days of the Second World War when Ivy, my adoptive mother, had gone on a shopping orgy, dragging me behind her, to take advantage of a fashion for 'Victory Sales'. But Truda sniffed in the very air with relish. It was not simply that she responded to luxury and style. I think she could smell something that had been even rarer in her life: total material security. Here was a world where fathers did not suddenly die, leaving their offspring in poverty, and where husbands (or so she believed) never disappeared in a haze of drink and debt.

She insisted on buying Luke an expensive chimp, despite my protests. 'I'd never spend that much on a toy.'

'That's your Jewish blood talking,' she replied, accepting her green- and gold-wrapped parcel with a regal air that would have done credit to the old Queen Mary herself.

At the station there came a lesson in the inconsistency of mothers, or of my mother. When I suggested upgrading her ticket to first class because of the crowds, she rejected the notion indignantly: 'I've had quite enough treats already, thank you.'

It was the nearest she came, or so I thought, to referring to my father. The rebuke in her voice was not exclusively directed at me. She was really addressing a ghost, whose taste for limitless treats had led only to tears.

I felt sadness and a mistiness around the eyes as she disappeared down the platform. Each parting probably triggered memories of the original one. Then I must have been kicking and screaming, though by no means torn from her arms if I had read Truda's variant of the Miss Collins approach correctly. In 1937, when she had carried out her illegal and almost piratical do-it-yourself adoption, Truda had ensured that someone else, anyone else, was holding the baby.

During her visit I had lost my innocence about mothers. I had thought they loved you, as I loved Luke, without really having any choice in the matter. It was somehow enjoined by the music of the blood. I hadn't grasped it could be something that needed learning, or teaching, or the seasonality of growth, to develop. It made me ashamed to think that it had taken thirty-seven years to see something so obvious.

The idea of Truda and I leaving each other in peace for a while was attractive.

13

Judging by the card that arrived a couple of days later, Truda must also have felt the strain. It was embossed with the identical motif of bluebells she had chosen to announce her change of residence in the summer. I recognised her celebration stationery. Her note concluded: 'By the time we see each other again I suppose it will be 1975. It's sure to be more restful than 1974, don't you think?'

We were already preparing to return to France. I was going to write a series about President Giscard and his first six months 'at the helm', the nautical slogan he had used to win the June election by a whisker. Since then I had devoted infinitely more time to Truda's progress than Giscard's. It was time to catch up on work.

Once the Paris articles were done, there was a trip to Washington in the offing. Journalist colleagues in the US were excited about the applications of the Freedom of Information Act, which were opening up in the wake of Watergate. Rumours from the other side of the Atlantic hinted that a new 'Open Government' policy meant that all manner of previously sacrosanct documents, among them NSA, CIA and FBI files, could now be inspected. The *Sunday Times* of London wanted to find out whether we could prise open new material on the British spy ring, a subject I'd been writing about for a decade.

Yet, against the odds and contrary to our expectations, only a fortnight later Truda and I were face to face again, getting through a surprisingly swift lunch in the plush dining-room of the Adelphi Hotel in Liverpool.

The Adelphi was the Ritz of Liverpool, though older and, if anything, more cosmopolitan. For well over a century it had catered for Liverpool's cotton aristocracy as well as served as a home-from-home for passengers using the weekly Liverpool–New York transatlantic service provided by mighty liners like the *Aquitania*, the *Queen Mary* and the two *Queen Elizabeth*s. The Liverpool-USA link went a lot further back than the steam and iron liners – there had been a monthly paddle-boat service to Philadelphia as far back as the 1830s, and there were fine oil paintings of New York-bound vessels under sail all round the restaurant.

Truda loved the big passenger boats. She had been aboard one of the *Queen*s on an 'Open Day', though an ambition to sail on her had never been fulfilled. Still she spoke with the authority of a veteran. 'You can't imagine how beautiful the accommodation was,' she told me. 'Perfect in every detail. It was like being in Harrods – only afloat.'

There was a boat-like aspect to the Adelphi too – an under-booked ocean liner, perhaps, with as many waiters as passengers, though without the motion of the waves. Apart from a convivial group of Roman Catholic priests from the United States, we were the only clients. These godly men, topping off their black-cherry cheesecake with rounds of Irish coffee, very much the local speciality, belonged to a church architectural committee and were visiting Liverpool's new Catholic cathedral.

'I wonder if they know everyone calls it "Paddy's wigwam",' Truda commented slyly. 'It's a horrible eyesore. They put it up in a hurry to make the Church of England look old-fashioned.'

On her native turf Truda was tarter, more authoritative. She had read about the American priests in her local bible, the *Liverpool Post*, and took satisfaction in passing on the infor-mation to me. I know what goes on here, she was indicating. You can't tell me anything about Liverpool.

There was also a legacy of prickliness. She had taken offence over something I had said on the phone when setting up the meeting. An unexpected day's work had come up in Man-

chester. This meant that I could drive over to spend half a day
with her in Liverpool on my way back to London. It was short
notice, according to her hairdressing scale. There was a silence.
I imagined her calculating whether she could fix an appointment in time. But her eagerness for me to see her flat was
paramount.

'But how are you going to find the new place?' she asked
finally. 'You do realise it's in Birkenhead – on the wrong side
of the Mersey?'

'Easy. We meet in the centre of Liverpool, at the Adelphi,
say. Then after lunch you can guide me through the city if you
know the route by car.'

'By car!' Truda was outraged. 'Of course I know the way.
I'll have you know I've walked every inch by foot – many a
time.'

Now she was eager to get going before the abbreviated
winter afternoon disappeared. No Irish coffee or liqueurs for
her. 'We can have coffee in comfort at my place,' she remarked
grandly. On the way out she produced a rare spontaneous
reference to my deceased father. 'That was one of your dad's
favourite spots,' Truda said, indicating the plush entrance to
the hotel's 'Sefton' bar, much patronised by race-horse owners
before and after the classic Grand National at Aintree. 'When
he was in funds, of course.'

Because I had parked facing the wrong way for Birkenhead
and the Mersey, we had to join the traffic system flowing east,
the enforced diversion leading us past terraces of decaying
Georgian mansions and a sighting of the pyramid-shaped Catholic cathedral. It did indeed resemble a wigwam, though on a
gigantic scale. Truda hated it. But, despite her dislike, she took
an acid relish in pointing out that the Catholics' site, on a hill,
had been chosen so that worshippers crossing the forecourt
could look across and down and see Liverpool's second new
cathedral, the Church of England variety. Truda liked it much
better, an enormous neo-Gothic edifice of sandstone already
turned murky in the prevailing grime. The Anglican cathedral
was manifestly unfinished. Truda none the less looked at it
with the eyes of love.

'I used to live near there. It was wonderful, we used to watch the processions.'

I couldn't help wondering if my father had been a procession watcher too. 'Was that when you were with John?'

'Oh no, it was long after he ... after that was over. I was sharing a flat with a lovely lady who played the violin. It was before I went to Denmark for the first time to see the relations.'

She had mentioned these Copenhagen Madsens several times, particularly her cousin who was famous, or at any rate distinguished, as the founder of a children's orphanage. I knew that Frederick, Truda's father, had been brought up in an orphanage for seamen's children in Liverpool and asked whether there was any connection.

The idea had never crossed her mind. 'No, it's just coincidence. Like meeting you.'

'That's Dale Street,' said Truda. 'I served my apprenticeship there.' She was pointing to a large jeweller's shop. I only glimpsed it on this occasion. Later it was pointed out to me many times, accompanied by stories about the long hours and iron discipline – 'We never got off before eight o'clock on a Saturday night,' she invariably said.

By chance I too had served an apprenticeship in Liverpool, or part of one. I started to tell her about my time as a (very young) labour reporter which had often brought me to the Cammel Laird shipyards in Birkenhead to cover one of their innumerable strikes. She gave me one of her 'you would' looks, as if to say: trust you to be drawn to this sleazy terrain. When I said how much I had enjoyed working on a variety of industrial disputes up and down the Mersey the look came back again, only more explicit.

'I thought you'd always worked abroad?'

'For years now, yes. But I started in the provinces. I was only 21 or so when I came to Liverpool for those strikes. To me it was like abroad – I'd never seen anything like it.'

And nor I had. Manchester, where I was based, had seemed exotic enough then. It was entirely different from the southern pastures of middle-class England where I had spent all my

time apart from a spell of vagabondage as an evacuee during
the war.

There had been a running story on the Liverpool docks. It
involved rivalry between two dockers' and stevedores' unions,
the 'Reds' and the 'Blues', who were fighting for supremacy,
and fighting dirty. To add to the waterfront mix, as if it were
needed, came a break-away group from the National Union of
Seamen, calling themselves the Seamen's Reform League, who
favoured what was called 'direct action', an odd forerunner of
1970s terrorist politics. As far as I know it was confined entirely to Liverpool. It was the only city in Britain capable of
anticipating world-wide tides, instead of limping in their wake,
just as it was the only one with the *chutzpah* to build a brace
of cathedrals.

The result was a Liverpool season which much resembled
On the Waterfront. This was no coincidental resemblance. All
the Seamen's Reform members, blue-jeaned, black-leather-
jacketed, and with brilliantined hair-styles which suggested a
cultural mating of Marlon Brando and Elvis Presley, belonged
to a category known locally as 'Cunard yanks'. It was by no
means a term of approval.

These disreputable seafarers, often stewards or deck-hands,
brought their own brand of mid-Atlantic 'hip', as you said
then, to a Liverpool ethnic mix that was already rich as a
stoker's armpit. They smoked 'weed', they sniffed 'scag', they
drank duty-free rye or bourbon or both, they worshipped
Brando and Charlie Parker, Buddy Holly and Chuck Berry.
They knew Times Square better than Piccadilly Circus. They
introduced me to America by proxy. They also knew many
places I later visited and fell for: Marseilles and Naples; Athens
and Istanbul; the parching, insane ports of the Gulf where you
drank home-brew called 'rat'; the jazz clubs around Bondi
Junction in Australia where 'scag' was by now 'smack'; the
dangerous, alcoholic and disaster-prone township of Darwin,
on Australia's northern coastline, where there were only two
seasons, the 'wet' and the 'dry', and the inhabitants often went
'troppo', or comprehensively crazy, for six months in every
year.

'Do they still use the expression "Cunard Yanks"?'·I asked her.

Truda let out a little snort of indignation, like a spluttering kettle. ' "Cunard nancies", people said. You know what that means?' By now we were getting very close to the Mersey and she had opened the window. She was sniffing the damp gritty breezes coming off the north Atlantic by way of the estuary.

'That's the Pier Head where the ferries to Birkenhead leave from,' she said.

'Do you want to stop for a minute?'

'I suppose there's time.'

She was keen to unveil her new home. But the Pier Head, centre of all Liverpool's maritime activity from the tiny ferries to the big liners, drew her like a magnet. It always did. Over the years we seldom managed to get past without a visit. She liked to strut around, invariably in the cold and rain, like the lord of the manor. Now she allowed me to park as if she was indulging a whim of mine, instead of vice versa.

When we got down to the Pier Head I could see why she was so attracted. It was officially called St George's landing-stage, a name which very misleadingly suggested something lightweight and even provisional, and not this masterpiece of mid-Victorian engineering floating securely after nearly 150 years on a series of gigantic galvanised iron pontoons. By now Truda was surprising me with a running commentary. Here was her special local expertise, the equivalent of her professional know-how when it came to antique jewellery. The universal hinge had been invented for the Pier Head, she told me, so that it could rise and fall in rhythm with the tides. From high to low tide the difference was thirty feet. 'If you fall over, whoosh, you're gone forever,' she said. 'You get sucked under – deep.'

Even the great Victorian engineers had failed to tame the savage tides of the Mersey estuary completely. Beneath your feet but very deep, communicable like a seismic tremor, was the movement that reminded you everything was floating. Deep down there somewhere was the power of the Atlantic, tugging delicately at your feet like the Devil's magnet.

On one side were boats of all varieties, on the other a set of
buildings so stern and portentous that they resembled the
gaudy British palaces constructed throughout the world under
the Empire, a Roman impulse to astonish, which had the in-
cidental virtue of filling the natives with respect, very likely
with awe. Here was status on the grandest scale. This is no
less than the greatest port of the industrial revolution, the
façade proclaimed.

'Grandad said standing here was a poor man's boat ride,'
Truda said, echoing my thoughts. 'Not that he was poor. You
never saw him without his gold Hunter watch and chain. It
was wonderful, a real antique, made by Jewish craftsmen in
Russia. And he'd have twenty sovereigns in his purse too.
Nowadays he'd have been mugged.'

'This is my great-grandfather? And he used to stand here?'

'Yes, Will Eagels. But he didn't stand. He used to come
every day to the coffee houses they had. He liked to write, and
read the papers and shipping registers. He knew every ship in
and out. He was famous here, they used to tell the time by
him. He was retired, over thirty years, so he came here for the
papers, those kind with wooden handles he said they had in
Vienna. He was economical, a real Jew. He said he could have
his shoes shined twice a day with the money he saved not
buying *The Times*. Sometimes he bought me cream cakes.'

'Did your brother and sisters get cakes too?'

'No. Fred was only a baby. The other girls wouldn't listen
to all his stories. I liked them. He showed me the manacles
from when they chained the slaves for auction. In his father's
time there was still a slave trade, he said.'

'His father's? That must have been, my God, during the
Napoleonic Wars.'

Truda looked vague. 'It was a long time ago, before the
Statue of Liberty. Otherwise they'd have gone to America.
They got put off here thinking it was New York. If there'd
been the statue, they'd have known the Captain was cheating
them. There used to be a joke – only dumb Jews ended here,
the smart ones refused to leave the ship at the first port and
got full value for their passage money.'

There were some small shops close to the Quay. On this intriguing note she dived into one, and I went on ahead to the very edge of the water.

Ever since the Beatles, the 'Mersey Beat' or 'Mersey Sound' had been an international cliché. Trying to retain the outline of a vanishing ferry as it disappeared into the mist, I detected a specific Mersey smell. This was what had drawn Truda through the car window.

It was really a mixture of smells – big city and sea coming together. It was also the smell of adventure – and risk, of hazardous journeys ending God knows where, but somewhere strange and unknown, that was for sure. For not only had innumerable passengers, including, it seemed, my remote fore-bears, arrived in Liverpool from strange places: many more had sailed away. Millions of emigrants had merely passed through en route to the New World. A few hundred thousand others had set off for Australia and New Zealand, literally the other end of the earth. At least the Irish, who had always formed a sizeable chunk of empty-handed, empty-bellied voyagers, would find a shore with a language more or less in common.

But what about the Jews, the Letts and Lithuanians, the variegated Slavs and Balts and citizens of countries with names long obliterated by history? Many of them couldn't even say the name of their destination. They must have been terrified. And also filled with wondrous anticipation of strangeness. They knew that what they found was sure to astonish them, as much as Marco Polo had been astonished.

It was good to be home again and so much in my skin. So good ... and then I realised. Again? Because I'd never been there before. Never – even through the 'Cunard Yank' period. I had often noticed the Pier Head on my way to and from the city centre. But there had never been time for sightseeing, or crossing the estuary by ferry. Yet for a few seconds it had felt entirely like home, more even than the Luxembourg Gardens in Paris, a place I had adopted and come to love with the excessive passion of an expatriate enchanted by someone else's country. I would have liked to visit the Pier Head every day of my life, as my great-grandfather had apparently done.

Only with great reluctance did I turn my back against the grit-filled incoming wind, and walk towards the city side where Truda was waiting. Coming off the estuary with the North Atlantic pursuing it like a mugger with a knife, I felt the wind propelling me. It should have numbed me to the marrow. Instead I was elated. Someone else, this coffee house habitué ancestor probably, had been through identical experiences here before, many times. It was like receiving a handshake across the generations.

There was a flower-stand by the exit and on impulse I stopped to buy Truda an azalea. I also picked up all the local papers from a vendor outside and carried the lot towards the car.

Truda, waiting for me to catch up, looked suddenly pale and somehow startled. I said: 'Are you all right?'

She moved her lips, but whatever she said was lost among the rasping, endlessly circling gulls. In any case she turned away quickly and made for the car.

Once inside she looked better – I assumed it must have been the cold. 'Here.' I showed her the azalea, a beautiful one with soft pink flowers flecked with white along the edges. It should have been decorating a geisha's apartment in Tokyo, not Truda's in dockside Birkenhead.

She took hold of the gift without comment, parting the plastic wrapping so that she could submit it to scrutiny. She might have been verifying its hallmark. It was suddenly easy to visualise her behind a jeweller's counter, shrewdly assessing a piece of silver someone was selling second-hand. She gave no hint of a response: was she going to make an offer, or not? As often happened, her feelings were in some other country as far as I was concerned. They were unavailable, and unfathomable as a cat's.

I drew her attention to the sharp spring green of the buds, nudging for some response.

'It's a terrible extravagance for this time of year,' was all she said. I was beginning to learn that the mother-son relationship was rich with such disappointments, tiny emotional set-backs and reactions, or lack of them.

I had been eager to tell her about the strange way I had felt on the Pier Head, and ask more about my great-grandfather. But she was directing me towards the tunnel entrance, 'Right here, at the lights', and the moment was lost. We plunged down into the winding, yellow-lit tunnel, Truda warning me that there was a toll-gate at the Birkenhead exit. While I fumbled for coins she said that as a child she had crossed both directions under 'Queensway', its original name, on the only free day in its history.

'Opening day, you could walk, or go by bike, for nothing. It's very long, three miles, so by the time I cycled back I was tired out and had to push. Everybody was excited though. In those days it was a wonder of the world, the longest under-water tunnel ever built.'

It had been the final element needed to make both shores of the Mersey combine to provide the biggest and best-serviced port complex in Europe, a process that had begun with the Manchester-Liverpool ship canal link, continued with the railways, and turned Liverpool into a model of advanced industrialisation. When I had worked there as a young man the port was split by industrial conflict: there were signs of decline. There were even more now. We drove along deserted streets and past the ship-building yards where so many strikes had been fought out. The biggest was Cammell Laird which for a hundred years had competed with John Brown, their Glasgow counterparts, for supremacy in a world league of two when it came to building great ships. Now the cranes were stationary. There was no hint at all of work.

The Birkenhead boat-builders had led the world in mercantile industrialised achievement, now they looked as if they were serving for a different kind of advance model – one of post-industrial decease. Not a derrick moved, the intricate patterns of cranes and lifts and scaffolding surrounding the vast dry docks looked as if they had been frozen and inanimate for so long their purpose had become decorative. There was no work bustle. No hint of life in any form.

'Is there a strike – I haven't read about one?'

Truda replied reluctantly, in the tone of one whose knowledge of dockland affairs was, deliberately, only superficial. 'I think they've all been on short-time since last year.'

Very probably they had. 1973 had been the year of oil crisis, power cuts, a mass strike of miners and a three-day working week. Truda had followed instructions about saving energy to the point of cleaning her teeth in the dark. She was a most responsible citizen. Unlike the dockers, in her view. 'All they do is hang around waiting for the pubs to open. Work or not, there's always money for beer.'

The Pier Head, devoted to passengers and overlooked by the great mercantile buildings of Empire, was the acceptable face of the Mersey as far as my mother was concerned. Dockland, whose proximity to her own residence irked her, was like a splinter under a nail.

Laird Street, Truda's new address, turned out to be very long. The proportion of pubs to premises engaged in other forms of commerce became clear as light after light came on and little knots of well-muffled men in caps started to build up under the shadows. They had a well-drilled look like players taking up their positions in some complicated field sport. Clearly, they each had their own spot.

'I know it's a bit near the docks,' Truda said apologetically. 'But it's lovely when you get there.' A man crossed the road ahead without looking. His rolling gait might (just) have suggested a long life at sea. Truda, looking fastidiously displeased, pointed through the windscreen. 'You see. He can't stand up and the pubs are only just opening. They're all the same.'

It must have been the cry of Liverpool women from generation to generation. Now, the gross reminder of the feckless, anarchic Merseyside male community, overflowing with Guinness-sodden dockers' macho, filled her with bitterness and spoilt her pleasure in showing off the fabled world of 114 Laird Street.

'It's in here. Be careful when you park. There's always a lot of broken glass at throwing-out time.'

I chose my spot with care. She was right. All round fragments of broken bottles shone like frost in the yellow lights. We picked our way towards her apartment block, a square four-storey building, as though we were on thin ice. Under our feet, glass particles crackled with a hard, percussive snap. I took her arm and felt she was grateful for the support. We had arrived at her place, a long-imagined dream of home-coming finally real.

'Here we are,' she said triumphantly before the little front door on the second floor, '114B!'

We entered a small warm flat, Truda ushering me forward. Simultaneously the thoughts came to me that here was her first emotional address, the home of her heart, and also that it was the place where she was going to die.

Opening the door she tinkled the musical bell almost girlishly. She was showing off its three tinny notes. This made me think for a moment that there must be someone inside, but once I felt the atmosphere, the blanket of all-soothing warmth, with no hint of a draught or an open window, of any human or animal content at all, I knew this was space that Truda shared with no one. Not even a cat or a canary.

Her first impulse was to conduct me on a tour of inspection. It even took precedence over putting the kettle on. Truda's nest was crammed with wonders: the jackdaw items she had snapped up in her beak over more than forty years covered every surface. Finding a suitable spot for the pot plant involved major reorganisation.

Truda had created a little temple to comfort, an oasis virtually. Inside there was perfect peace. But every so often you could hear an angry shout or the sound of something breaking from Laird Street. There might be storms out there on the heath. But Truda, at last, was hunkered down by her own fireplace, under her own roof.

I admired her objects. Some I had seen before at Alvanley Place. Could it have been only five months before, when she was surviving on such a meagre domestic diet, whispering as in church for fear of calling down the wrath of her senile landlady only one floor up? In any case, it had been a long enough gestation period for her possessions to have bred. She favoured little objects in porcelain, odd cups and saucers, tiny

statuettes, the occasional snuff-box, all manner of delicate minutiae. Once in a shop in London we saw an eighteenth-century
set of monkey musicians, all playing their instruments conducted by a simian Toscanini. It was Aspreys, it was an incredibly rare mint set, and it would have been too painful to ask
the price. But I could still remember the expression on Truda's
face.

We always did things together. In a way we had to. We
were not companionable sharers of long spells of propinquity
while nothing much went on. We were the kind of people who
might have played chess or cards together. But it never came
to that. Truda's mother Gertrude, after whom she was named,
had been apparently a bridge fanatic. Truda bore the scars of
years of making up a fourth. It was one of her most developed
personality traits that she never, or so I then believed, allowed
herself to suffer in the same way twice. Mention cards to her
and she snorted like a miniature dragon.

As promised, I had brought her the photographs of Luke's
christening. For the occasion he had been dressed in an antique
lace shirt, an excess he had accepted very equably. My friend
Bryan Wharton, whose photos of babies had generally been
shot in war zones, had seized the moment to take probably the
most sentimental picture of his life. It portrayed Luke, serenely
asleep above his lace collar, with a rainbow striking poetically
across the breast.

Truda was enchanted. She clucked over it with an unforced
delight she could never have summoned up to deal with Luke
in person. She still showed a tendency to call him 'it' periodically. In Truda's psychology babies had to be like Shirley Temple, cute, with a pink ribbon in their locks. The nuts-and-bolts
of maternity, the odour of fecundity which she had breathed
so distressingly in the post-natal ward, were another matter
altogether.

I asked her whether she had found any more souvenirs of
my father: so far she had dredged up only one cigarette case,
one commercial snapshot of him sailing down the river Dee
looking expansively tipsy, and one death certificate.

Truda disappeared into her bedroom. There was the rasping

of keys in locks, a door creaked. She returned bearing an Edwardian chocolate box, bestrewn with scarlet ribbon, but sealed with utilitarian contemporary Sellotape. There was also a more demure, dark-green oblong box, originally designed to contain preserved ginger. They were both filled with photographs, letters, cards and even more small china items or collections of necklaces and brooches, all of which Truda had made herself.

It was as if she had saved everything with the slightest personal connotation. I expected to see seashells; perhaps they were too heavy, or she kept them more substantially housed, in a shoe-box possibly. But here was the archeology of Truda's emotional and romantic life since girlhood, only a fraction of it on the new carpet between us, but endless more layers, some of which I had glimpsed in the old house, stacked prudently away next door, very likely in her vast wardrobe. It was her narcissistic history and she dealt with it as cautiously as a CIA official letting classified documents out of his grasp. She never passed over any photograph or letter without a canny skim through first. Her mental blue pencil never stopped operating.

When it came to my father, I think she must have long since employed the ultimate censorship: either he had left so little to mark forty-eight rumbustious years that he had cultivated a monkish austerity, not his style at all from all evidence, or someone had consigned all traces but three to the shredder. Truda was handing me a most exciting picture – one of her Pier Head grandfather out for a walk in his ninetieth year, yet somehow she caught my thought. It may have been sparked because, to make more space, I had moved the big pile of newspapers I had picked up earlier.

While I pored over a studio portrait of a splendidly fierce old man, a most formidable customer, Truda was mentally skipping two generations ahead. 'You gave me quite a turn down by the ferry,' she said. 'Buying the flowers, and all those papers. All of them.' She nodded disapprovingly towards the *Liverpool Post*, the northern edition of the *Daily Telegraph*, and all the rest, disfiguring the spanking-new surface of her fitted oatmeal carpet. 'It was your dad again. That's just what

he used to say – "Give me all the papers you've got love" – I
saw his ghost. Laughing too, like you were.'

'But I don't look like him, surely. Judging by the boat picture you gave me, you know, that life-and-soul-of-the-party
one, he must have been four stone heavier than me for a start.'

'It was the papers – and then the flowers. I couldn't get him
by without stopping. Even when there wasn't money for rent,
cigarettes. He lived on papers. You know they brought him up
in a newsagent's and he said he started the habit when he was
7, doing the round at six o'clock. Read, read, read – and never
forget a word. I think he knew more about more things than
anybody in the world. It was a shame they didn't have those
"Mastermind" quiz shows then. But what good was it? There
was always an audience in the pub. Sometimes when I wanted
to find him I could follow him from bench to bench across
Sefton Park like a paper trail. He could talk himself into jobs,
and I'll say one thing: he always got good service in bars.
Especially the Theatre Royal. We must have gone there a dozen
times and I don't think he was ever out of the bar in time to
see the last act.'

It sounded a harmless enough biography, if somewhat ineffectual. Truda, sifting through the boxes as she spoke, described it in the tones of a judge donning the black cap. To
her, it was a litany of evil. That it had popped up, recalcitrant,
like a jack-in-the-box on the Pier, had disturbed her profoundly. She had thought him safe in the past, under twelve
feet of sod, in a Leicester cemetery.

The coincidence of our taste for flowers and newsprint had
involved her personally in something she had shucked off over
fifteen years earlier. As before, the way she talked about my
father was very shocking to me. This had nothing to do with
the content, which had been sparse in any case. It was her tone
of voice. She spoke of him with less enthusiasm than she would
have given the TV listing or some anecdote about a third party
in which she herself played no part. Almost whatever she said
about him, she said in the same flat way. When she described
him leaving Margaret for hours on the pavement outside a pub
she spoke as if the vignette was without moral weight. She

might have been saying that Dad had woken up, cleaned his teeth, and put on a shirt. Anything, everything, to do with him had long lost all relationship to the way she was now.

You can't interview your mother. It would have been easier dealing with some veteran spy at last unveiled, a professional aware that virtually any word he uttered was probably against his best interests. Maybe Truda believed the same. Trying to get a fix on 'Jack', as I thought of him, was like extracting an eye tooth. All my professional skills had gone for nothing. Far from employing them to set Truda chirruping, my progress had been so feeble that I was still unsure of my father's family or christian names. There was more to it than mere curiosity. I had come about my own names in an arbitrary and, strictly speaking, illegal fashion. The man who had adopted me, again without any legal formalities, had simply passed his own names on for me to use, plus an additional 'Paul', supposedly as a memento of my natural father. There was something broadly humorous about this, I was beginning to see. David Leitch had conscientiously tried to retain the link with my real father, but his 'Paul', and mine, had somehow missed the target. There was a strong suggestion around that I had been named after a myth.

'Why did he have so many names?' I asked.

For a long time she went on sorting through her souvenirs without replying. In the end she said, 'He changed them to suit himself', and in the same instant disappeared towards the kitchen, leaving me to examine my great-grandad's photo.

It was in a folder, dated November 1938, and addressed to Truda's mother, as well as to Truda herself. It had been prepared well in advance because the inscription read: 'With best love and Hopeful Wishes for Welfare and Compliments of the Season'.

Below, there was some verse, penned in black ink, in a lucid but idiosyncratic hand. It was the calligraphy of someone who cared about the act of writing, and had put in some work at it.

> In my 92nd year, out for a ramble,
> Time flies, Life's lease now a gamble.
> Instead of a card, I think a good plan
> To send you a postcard, for critical scan.

His verse had plenty of vitality for 91, but compared with
his portrait, studio-posed against a background of soaring
Alps, it was almost tepid. Here was an old boy so delighted
with himself and the world that his ego might have hopped
kangaroo-like out of the venerable mounting on cream-inlaid
paper. He wore a narrow bowler hat, its sheen under the
hard lights as brilliant as the diamond pin in the tie he
wore with a stiff collar, or the parade-ground glitter on the
toes of his fine black shoes. He was equipped with gloves
and an umbrella: a tightly rolled model with a prominent
ferrule, possibly of gold. The way he held it suggested neither
an instrument for leaning on nor a protection against the
Mersey climate. Its function was decorative. He bore it like
a swagger-stick.

His eyes dominated his expression. They were dark, knowing, quick to anger, probably, but above all pregnant with
triumph. It was 1938; probably names like Auschwitz and
Theresienstadt had not yet filtered through to the Mersey. But
he, and certainly his father, had experienced a kind of dry-run
for the Final Solution a century before Hitler. Survival, with
the Cossacks as racial enemy in those remote times, had been
bred in the bone.

No wonder he hated the Russians, and no wonder Truda
had inherited an identical blood aversion. There was a story
about a Cossack skewering a baby from horseback in some
tiny village, the name long since forgotten. The fact that the
rider had been laughing had however lodged in the family
memory. Truda's grandad, a marathon, city rambler, was far
too swift on his pins, even at 91, for anyone to skewer him.
Instead he was the one laughing, towards posterity.

I found myself grinning back with cordial familiarity. I noticed again that November 1938 was the date embossed by the
photographers he had patronised: Jerrold's of Oxford Road. I
had been adopted in 1937, on 5 November, Guy Fawkes' Day,
when bonfires blaze and fire-crackers explode to honour a
failed yet noble endeavour to dynamite every politician in the
country. Thus, it was virtually the first anniversary of my
adoption. Could the awkward reference to 'welfare', and the

fact that the dedication included Truda as well as her mother, mean that the old survivor was somehow involved with the circumstances of my birth and adoption?

Not a chance, I knew instantly. This jaunty fellow was in the business of seeing the tribe grow, not disposing of un-wanted members who had chosen an inconvenient moment to check in. Even less did he look like one of nature's abortion lobbyists. Truda would never have dared breathe a word to him. I could see it in her eyes as she came back into the room.

We were both tired enough to want an early night. After a dispute about who was going to sleep in her room, and who on the sofa, I gave in and accepted her double bed to please her. Before we settled down for the night she took me into the kitchen to show me a view from the window – the summit of a steep hill a couple of miles away crowned by a building with a green light. Truda said it was an observatory called Bidston, built in the classical style she admired. She had tried, but failed, to find more souvenirs of Will Eagels, and had packed her boxes away. Now she came up with one from her memory bank instead. From the Bidston vantage-point, he had observed Halley's Comet in 1910, the year before her birth. He had joked that it was always possible that he might see it again on its second twentieth-century visit (he would have to live to 141), but in case he didn't, she should look out for it on his behalf. 'You'll still be young,' he had said.

By 'young', I later worked out, he meant 78.

Will Eagels had been her mother's father, and though there were no more photos of him, or any of her mother, she showed me another nice studio portrait of Frederick Madsen, her own father and my grandfather. She propped it up on the bedside table but I was too tired to examine it closely. All I knew was that after starting life in the Seamen's Orphanage, and surviv-ing that, he had been through the Great War, surviving that too only to die very suddenly four years after the armistice. He had left four children, the youngest, named after him and the only boy, only a few months old. They had been prosperous and overnight they became very poor.

There were two other photographs on her table. One of a

Liverpool church, St Margaret's, taken by Frederick's less
successful brother Erasmus, 'Uncle Ras'. His lack of success
might well have been in the material sense only – since he
spent his life photographing churches and their interiors, it
sounded as if he was the most spiritual of my immediate fore-
bears. He had also helped provide the money for his younger
brother, another William, to train for the priesthood. In due
course he had become an Anglican Church cleric somewhere
in the West Country.

The final photograph was an old-fashioned 'snap' taken
probably with a box Brownie. It notably lacked Erasmus Madsen's professional touch. This was Truda's shop, which she
had taken on at 19, the moment her jewellery trade apprenticeship was over. The premises were tiny. 'No bigger than a
box-room with a window,' she said. It had been a lane
crowded with market stalls and similar mini-shops, an obscure
street yet known to everyone in Liverpool and, by coincidence,
to tens of millions over the globe who would never go near
the city in their lives. For Truda's shop had been located in
Penny Lane.

It was an easy room to sleep in and I drifted away almost
at once, cosseted between an electric blanket and an expensive
swansdown duvet. I remembered what Ivy, my adoptive
mother, had called me – 'a blue baby', because I had been blue
with cold when she and my adoptive father, David Leitch, had
first seen me on that November afternoon in London. I had
always thought that my hatred of being cold could be traced
back to the first ten days of my life. Now, on the edge of sleep,
it struck me that its genesis was a generation more remote.
Truda too found it desperately hard to survive without a
warmth that was only incidentally connected with the weather
in the streets. She had always needed to find an oasis where
clement temperatures and security combined.

Her father, despite his complacent and reassuring expression, had proved ultimately unreliable – he had died on them,
which meant the end of their pony-and-trap, the destruction of
Truda's doll's-house world. She had been only 10. All her life
she had been trying to get back round the family hearth and

only now, after half a century, had she succeeded. No wonder she had been happier about finding a place of her own than about rediscovering me. All her men, I thought, drifting off, had left her in the end. First, her father. Then Jack, my father. And finally James Bucknall, the man whose name she had taken, and who had died on her as well, leaving nothing but trouble behind. I was very pleased that she had come in after a lifetime out in the cold.

I left early and hurriedly the next morning. I had to be in London by lunch-time. Truda herself was doing one of her periodic 'day jobs to help out' in the jeweller's where she had long worked as manageress. She had to be off by eight.

Over coffee in the kitchen Truda looked worried. She had examined her slender morning post. When she said, 'I've something to tell you' I had a strong premonition that it was bad news.

'What's that?'

'Margaret's having a baby. Another one.'

There was not time to pursue the matter: Truda betrayed no grandmotherly enthusiasm. Her tone was more appropriate to news of a decease than impending birth.

'I thought they'd said she wouldn't have another,' she added finally. She sounded positively aggrieved.

'Margaret and her husband, you mean?'

'No, the doctors. Her health isn't as good as all that.'

This was a new factor. I had imagined my sister as robust. She was five years younger than me, and from all accounts, Margaret liked 'a quiet life'. I imagined her bedded down in long-matured domesticity in the Welsh countryside.

Now we said goodbye in haste and I was leaving the city limits before it occurred to me that babies in Truda's biography invariably implied trouble. No wonder the Liverpool euphemism for unmarried pregnancies was 'in trouble', that's what it usually meant. Perhaps it wasn't so different if, like my sister, you were respectably wed, yet living on a tight budget.

Radio Mersey was having a Beatles Request Hour: perhaps it was a daily fixture. I listened to some fragments of interviews, including John Lennon's famous remark, made during one of the disputes about his right to reside in the USA: 'Ever since I first heard Elvis Presley, I've been half American.' It was a remark straight from the Liverpool soul, that longing to make it to the USA which accounted for my mother's wistful look when I told her about the plan to go to Washington. She would have preferred it, of course, had I been planning on cruising to Manhattan by Cunard (first class naturally) rather than a run-of-the-mill economy return via Pan Am.

I can't remember whether Radio Mersey played 'Get Back', the song Lennon had written just before the group split up, and he was feeling rootless and confused about the crazy world they had inhabited in the few years since they had left Liverpool which, in itself, had been crazy enough. But I recall thinking how strange it was, working through the traffic on the edge of Birkenhead, how I myself had 'got back' to the city of my forebears long before Truda, long before there had been a clue that this hard northern city contained my own roots. I could see why Truda found it irritating, rather than agreeable or just plain weird, to discover that I had put in so much time there, and with such gusto.

Except occasionally when drunk, or 'tipsy' as she preferred, it was plain that she hadn't spent much time considering her son's fate between November 1937 and the spring of 1974. But whenever the memories had forced their way through her self-created amnesia, it must have been nice to think of me grazing contentedly in the lush pastures of the 'golden triangle' comprised by Oxford, Cambridge and London, far from the industrial filth and sweat she so fastidiously loathed. She had abandoned me, not on a mountain top, but in a softer world where life, at any rate in her imagination, was not so unremittingly, unforgivingly hard. Thanks to coincidence and character, or rather bad character, in any event that same irredeemable element in my rapscallion father that had defeated her, I had managed to spoil these dreams of instant gentrification. Like a bad penny I had come rolling home.

That was why she had given me the 'you would' look when I'd told her what a good time I'd had on the waterfront. It wasn't a new expression, that 'you would' blend of exasperation and, what was it, yes, recognition. For a moment she had 'seen' me, and seen my father again. She hadn't liked it. Anymore than I had liked the discovery that my own well-nurtured fantasies of her, just as self-deceiving, and in their way even more sentimental, couldn't be reconciled with the reality either.

14

For Christmas we returned to Jill's big apartment in Paris and almost the first object I encountered, lugging Luke in his carry-cot through the battered oak front door, turned out to be a reminder of a friend irrevocably lost. On top of the mail in the hall there was an elegant and heavily embossed envelope from a diplomatic mission. There was no time for careful examination but I put it aside thinking that it contained a yet more grandiose card summoning me (as I wrongly assumed) to a Christmas celebration.

We only stayed indoors long enough to set down our luggage before rushing downstairs into the Rue de l'Abbaye de l'Epée and along to our local Vietnamese restaurant in the Rue St Jacques. Hunger and the desire to take up the old threads of Paris street life had driven us out so urgently. As far as I was concerned there was another factor. The apartment, which had been empty throughout November, felt strange and dead. Through prolonged emptiness it had lost its reassuring quality of everyday human presence. Already, by returning, we were setting this right, spreading our possessions around, turning on lights and the antique central heating. But there was something else, a new element altogether, which made me uneasy. I found I was constantly listening for something without knowing what it was.

There was some residue there beyond the familiar sounds of old wood floors shifting under the weight of people or winter weather – the apartment was on three storeys. It had oak flooring and steps of elm which contained deep furrows like geological signals of 300 years' wear. Sometimes at night the creakings were so loud that you had the sense of being in an old galleon.

Much later when everyone was asleep I began sorting through the accumulated mail. Looking at the seductive party envelope, I discovered that the intended guest was not me at all, but 'Monsieur Hope, Francis'. There were several other items for him too, messages that had spent time gathering dust and would now never reach their destination.

Francis had been posted to Paris as correspondent for the London *Observer* about two years earlier, a welcome addition to the Parisian tribe of foreign correspondents, cleverer than the rest of us, more stylish and also, it transpired, more vulnerable.

I had known him only casually before his Paris arrival – he had never been a part of the chain of friendships underpinned by professional relations and often dating back to university in the 1950s or early 1960s which was sometimes called the 'Cambridge/Fleet Street mafia'. Unlike many of the people I was most closely involved with, Francis had in fact studièd at Oxford, where he had been the star of his generation.

Yet getting to know him in Paris had been more like finding yourself close to a relative from a different branch of a large family than a run-of-the-mill social or professional friendship. His elder brother, Donald, had been a university contemporary of mine, and a constant visitor to the disorganised and easygoing house in Cambridge where I had lived during my final year. But by an odd coincidence the closest connection was via his comparatively new stepmother, Helen Hope, a powerful, endlessly entertaining woman who had long been important in my life as a mixture of confidante, ally and Bohemian reveller. I had first met Helen a decade earlier because of my friendship with her twin daughters, Laura and Jenny, children of her first marriage. Their mother turned out to have an unusual talent for bridging generations and cultures. At her house in Little Venice, an area of London she introduced me to, she gave famously rowdy parties where apparently incompatible figures discovered unexpected affinities, right-wing Washington

officials and left-wing African exiles spilling out into the dawn
like old, impassioned partisans of the same cause. At her cottage by a lake in Oxfordshire, there were more parties, and an
annual cricket match, and if anyone exemplified the optimistic
hedonism which flowered for a while in the London of
the 1960s it was Helen Hope. As she grew older, she had
turned into something approaching a tribal mother, wry and
generous with her experience, harder and wiser than most of
the internationally distinguished figures who would turn up to
drink her gin and ask her advice whenever they passed through
London.

The fact that a by-product of her last marriage was acquiring Francis as a stepson amused her as much as it did him. 'I
hope you are showing my glamorous new son the ropes in
Paris,' she would remark huskily. 'Not that he needs showing
much.' And nor he did.

If Francis had been the star of his university generation,
Nicholas Tomalin, with whom he had much in common, including dark good looks, a sardonic wit, and the confidence of
independent means, had been the equivalent figure in mine.
Nick and I had shared offices, stories, experiences of various
kinds, and when I had written God Stand up for Bastards he
was one of the friends who had read the manuscript and made
suggestions. Thanks to savage bad luck, Nick had also been
the first of my close contemporaries to die, a casualty of the
Yom Kippur war in Israel in October 1973.

Nick had been killed by an act of war; Francis Hope's
equally brutal end had come less than six months later in what
should have been peaceful, normal circumstances. One foggy
Sunday morning he had boarded a London flight from the old
Orly airport in Paris, thirty minutes' easy drive from the apartment, and within minutes the McDonell-Douglas DC10 had
crashed on the edge of a wood, killing all the passengers. In
one way the event seemed physically even closer. With his wife,
Mary, and Polly, their baby daughter, Francis had spent most
of his last winter in the flat in Rue de l'Abbaye de l'Epée, while
we had stayed in the south, first near Marseilles, then in
Morocco. The Hope family had only moved into what they

expected would be a permanent Paris home a few weeks before
the disaster.

There was a long studio room under the house's eaves where
I had my work place, and where Francis had also set up his
books and typewriter. Long after everyone else had gone to
bed on the first night I was still pacing restlessly around, filled
with a strong sense of waiting for something to do with him,
though with no idea of what it might be. My intuition proved
right: Francis *had* left something physically present in the
studio, but it didn't surface until the very last day of 1974,
while I was exchanging New Year's wishes on the phone with
Truda in Liverpool.

It wasn't one of our best-ever conversations – perhaps she
was nervous because on this night of all others there might
have been unexpected visitors to fracture her privacy. I had
also started badly by saying that my wish for 1975 was to meet
my sister. It seemed the inevitable next step, yet Truda's voice
instantly grew heavier with caution.

'It will be difficult because of the new baby.'

'I wasn't thinking of a long visit, just a meeting.'

'She mustn't be worried while she's pregnant.'

At this point my attention had been captured by an unfamiliar book tantalisingly out of reach on the high shelves beyond
my work desk. No author's name or title were visible on the
spine, which looked like a publisher's proof copy. It was bound
in heavy white paper and was apparently in mint condition.
There was something about it that looked unusual, a collector's item. I was almost certain that this strange new book
didn't belong to me and, by the time Truda was saying her last
words, nine-tenths of my attention had wandered. I was filled
with the excitement of imminent discovery.

The moment our talk ended with the ritual 'Happy 1975', I
reached up for the maverick volume. As I had guessed it *was*
a proof, a collection of articles by the critic Cyril Connolly
called *The Evening Colonnade*, his last book. Two sheets of
the squared graph-paper that French students use for lecture
notes were folded inside the back cover. They were covered in
Francis's unmistakable angular writing. He had been an ad-

mirer of Connolly, who had died very recently, so perhaps this
was a review copy he had worked on and left behind.

I held it under the light and saw that the notes were part of
a poem about packing up and going back to the cold north
after a vacation in the sunny Mediterranean. It had the sharp
edge present in everything Francis wrote and was called 'Fare-
well to the Villa Piranha'. The words were instantly familiar
because on the last occasion we had met, the last ever, Francis
had tried very hard to recite it all to me.

It had been at the very end of August. Francis was returning
from a vacation in Italy to Paris, where he would move into
the flat we had left empty with his family. As we were installed
in a vineyard only twenty miles from Marseilles, it was the
ideal place for the Hopes to break their return and also an
opportunity for them to find out about the peculiarities of the
Rue de l'Abbaye de l'Epée flat – to learn about the keys, the
concierge, the secrets of the Victorian central heating and the
neighbours.

After the burning drive along the coast he was filled with
nervous energy and we had walked around the hot, aromatic
garden. There had been forest-fires on the high ground that
summer. A sliver of glass or a cigarette-end were combustible
enough to account for hundreds of charred acres. There was
a tang of cinders in the air. Francis was dissatisfied with everything but the moment and comically distressed at the prospect
of his thirty-fifth birthday coming up. It was time, he thought,
to have fulfilled all that promise which had become a burden,
time to have written a substantial book or, at the least, a body
of journalism 'that would last'.

When he said this we were both struck by the humour of
the notion – our laughter drowned the sharp and regular rasp
of the cicadas. His mood changed instantly as he said with
sudden enthusiasm: 'I started a poem last night, can I read it?'
I said that I would prefer to read it for myself, an ungracious
response that he didn't mind. But before retrieving the text,
these same notes probably, from their estate car he went on to
recite some lines which I now recognise as the final verse jotted
on the graph-paper.

Chill in the morning air
Hints like a bad host we should be going.
Time for a final swim, a last black coffee in the square.
Leaving the palace and its park
We take our common place along the road,
As summer joins the queue of other summers
Driving towards the dark.

For some reason Francis had never retrieved the manuscript
from the car, though he had certainly set off to find it. Somehow he had been diverted. Soon after they were gone, rightly
apprehensive about the end-of-vacation traffic on the auto-
route, and keen to start the frantic drive 600 miles north to the
Rue de l'Abbaye de l'Epée before nightfall. I remembered Mary
rolling down her window to wave and the baby, Polly, looking
over her shoulder from her special seat in the back.

Reading the poem now was like receiving a message from
beyond the grave. What it meant I couldn't tell, except that in
some inexplicable manner he had been visited by an entirely
accurate foreboding that this Mediterranean summer was his
last.

Francis and I had never discussed death, though we had
talked of danger and I had several times discouraged schemes
he had to go to Vietnam, citing Nicholas Tomalin as an authority who shared my own view that the conflict had reached a
point of such futility and squalor that the only wise response
was to stay as far away as possible. Whenever Nick came to
see me while passing through Paris the late-night conversation
had invariably taken a morbid turn and we ended up playing
actuarial guessing-games about the life expectancy of war reporters who were no longer very young or athletically reckless.
As we often ate in the Rue St Jacques restaurant, a haven for
expatriates from Saigon, the train of thought was only too
predictable.

On the occasion of his last visit we had even agreed during
a late-night walk round the Place des Vosges that neither of us
would go to the wars again. There were family responsibilities
and age to consider – Nick's fortieth birthday was behind him:
I could all too easily discern my own on the horizon.

This discussion was a tribute to our good sense, but nevertheless as soon as war broke out in the Middle East, Nick had
set off as enthusiastically as ever, only to be killed by a Syrian
rocket. The *Sunday Times* London office had phoned me in
Tangier to break the bad news. When they first tried to get
through the line was cut before we could speak. It was twenty
minutes before they came on again – in the interim, assuming
that they wanted me to go to Israel myself, I had been working
out a Tangier-Tel Aviv itinerary. In the event the choice of
going or not was never offered. If it had been, then I would
probably have found it impossible to refuse.

So Nick had been the first casualty. At least there had been
a war on. When Francis's turn came, there was no such consolation. It was as if peacetime had turned against him.

The disturbing and saddening discovery of Francis's posthumous poem on the last day of 1974 might easily have obliterated all memory of my last talk with Truda in the year I finally
found her. Instead the effect was the reverse. For years I could
hear both our voices, mine tired and abstracted as I tried to
identify the maverick volume on the shelves, hers defensive and
sharp. The conversation had gone in desultory circles, returning always to my unknown sister.

At some point I asked wanly whether Margaret and her
husband wanted a boy or a girl. The answer held no interest
for me. I was merely going through the conversational hoops
my mother favoured. Truda was unexpectedly specific.

'A girl, of course.'

'Why, of course?'

'Because of Gillian.'

'You mean she'd be happier with another girl as a companion?'

'No, because of the clothes.' It sounded now as if she was
battling to contain her irritation at my slowness.

'Sorry, I don't see. What clothes do you mean?'

'Margaret's still got three cases full of Gillian's baby clothes.
Those she had when she was born. Pink. For a girl. If it's a
boy, they won't be any good.'

'Oh, that's why.'

'Yes, dear. Blue for a boy, pink for a girl.'

It was a trivial exchange which should have been forgotten
instantly. Yet for years the exact timbre of Truda's voice on
the subject of my sister and baby clothes echoed in my mind
whenever I tried to imagine what Margaret was like, how close
(or distant) we might be, whether we would get on with each
other. In two or three phrases Truda had 'characterised' my
sister for me – a narrow lady of thrifty disposition, convinced
that sex stereotypes to do with rompers were ordained by God.

I don't suppose she was trying consciously to steer me away
from Margaret. She was operating on a level of pure, unfallen
intuition. Some corpuscular sameness in our psychologies enabled her to transmit an image of Margaret that was exquisitely designed to ensure I lost sympathy with her. At a stroke
she turned me off, as people said then.

Truda's remarks convinced me not so much that Margaret
and I were different, but that she and Margaret were emotionally the same. My anger about my adoption was all the
stronger because Truda had behaved so logically, and was so
proud of her rational and pragmatic side. You have a baby
you don't want, so you find someone who does for the price
of a small ad. You hand the parcel across and it's all for the
best – demonstrably so, Truda was convinced. There were so
many demonstrably excellent reasons why she had done the
right thing. But this pink versus blue reasoning was meagre,
soul-pinching stuff set beside the sea of love that I persisted in
believing a child had every right to receive at birth. Its absence
in my own life had left a chill in the bone. The story of
Margaret and the baby clothes was one I was eager to forget,
yet it wouldn't go away.

At the beginning of 1974 I had, as far as I knew, no blood-
relations. Now, with the year ending, there was what Jill called
'a jostling crowd'. Via Truda I had learned of ancestors and
blood-links in great variety and yet they remained unreachable,
as if I were stuck on the wrong side of a frontier. The dead
were in fact more accessible than the living. They were closer
internally – Will Eagels, the dandified, incurably literary old
Jew who loved history and the sea, 'Ras' Madsen, ineffectual

devotee of churches, who spent an unassuming life vainly trying to capture spirituality with a primitive camera, Jack Chester, professional black sheep with an identity built on sand, a man so insubstantial that his very name shifted like the wind off the Mersey estuary, according to season, circumstance or whim.

As the year ended I found myself missing them all as palpably as I missed Nick and Francis, tribal brothers I had been compelled to invent for lack of other siblings, yet fine sustaining companions of a period when very little was impossible, and man had walked on the moon. Now there was a different kind of reality, economic growth was as out-dated as the music from Liverpool, and suddenly you could feel the capitalist societies shaking like dogs to dislodge the young and the poor as if they were unwelcome parasites.

The 1970s were leading us into a re-run of the 1930s, the period that had eroded both my natural parents and my foster parents, robbing them of their dreams. The century's second Jazz Age was now a past historic – no wonder the maternity wards were as empty as churches. My sister, this remote figure Truda had convinced me was so alien to her brother, was probably being no more than realistic when she planned to fit the baby to the clothes, not the clothes to the baby.

Over the years Margaret's supposed 'blue for a boy' vision of life was to come in handy. It went a long way to convincing me that by missing my sister I was not missing much, and that the artificial families you might be lucky enough to invent, thanks to the accident of meeting a Helen Hope or working alongside a Nick Tomalin, provided more emotional sustenance than could be found from your own flesh and blood.

But it was years before the chance image lost its sting. In the meantime I found it leading me back to my own unwelcome arrival in the winter world of 1937 when penury swept all other considerations aside. The only comfort to be found was from the hands of unhappy strangers, who were themselves as much victims of a callous age as Jack Chester, who for once said nothing, and Truda, who tried through cunning to walk away free.

IVY AND
DAVID

15

On 5 November 1937, according to Ivy in an oft-told tale intended to disparage my natural parents: 'You were ill with bronchitis because they looked after you so badly. They were poor, poor as mice, and no damn good. They didn't love you. They were ready to throw you away like dirt. They couldn't even get a bit of something to wrap you in. Your dad had to go out and find you a shawl to get you warm.'

It pleases me to think of David, the dad in question, casting around for a baby shop in the November streets – I hope that the Guy Fawkes' Night rockets and catherine wheels added a spice of excitement to his fatherly mission.

Knowing David, I'm sure he was ill at ease asking for this nursery item, and hard put to lay hands on one in an area where baby shops must always have been spread thin. Even so he did not, of course, return empty-handed: that was never his way.

Truda and John would have been waiting in the hotel room where they had arranged for their recently-born son to meet David Leitch and Ivy, his wife as everyone supposed, as well as some other potential adoptive parents. Ivy, in her furs, very likely treated John and Truda to a vivid breakdown of her own material and social superiority, while David prowled Bloomsbury.

He worked close by and in later years I acquired an intimate knowledge of his old shawl-hunting terrain, where Bloomsbury and Holborn meet and merge, with the dome of University College Library and the confident neo-classic façade of the

British Museum as border posts at the point where art, particularly literature, and the academic sciences, particularly med-
icine, give way to straight commerce.

As a schoolboy I often visited his office in the broad tho-
roughfare called Kingsway. Later, at 17, I was studying in the
British Museum library and we met almost daily, usually for
a quick lunch in Sicilian Avenue, an eccentric Edwardian arcade that still survives. He had been patronising two or three
of the local restaurants since before World War II – or plain
'the war' as we said then. Everyone greeted him and when he
introduced me as his son I benefited from a lot of kind attention. He had a gift for bringing out an un-English warmth in
people.

Often he would be too busy to spare more than twenty
minutes for coffee and a sandwich. 'Is it worth you coming all
the way down here in this weather?' he would ask. I always
told him 'Yes, of course it is', and so it was. The discomfort
of leaving the warm Reading Room on a rainy winter's day
was insignificant beside the pleasure of even a short meeting.
It is hard now to recapture the ease and trust and constant
amusement existing between us, even harder after so long to
recreate the lineaments of this man who was authoritative and
yet vulnerable, quiet to taciturnity and yet persuasive, trapped
within the home by a relationship always beyond his control
and yet as at ease in the hard, competitive world outside as a
salmon in the Severn.

Beside me there is a sheet of forty-eight 'Polyfoto' photographs, passport size, all of them portraits of David Leitch
caught in marginally different poses. There are now forty-seven
to be more exact, but number nineteen was neatly cut out long
ago for enlargement and reproduction elsewhere. It was probably used by the house magazine of the company he worked
for; perhaps when they announced his promotion to the Board
of Directors, though there is a chance that the missing snap
came in handy for a sadder purpose. It may have been used to
illustrate the obituary when he died, aged just 55, in 1959, not
long after he had reached almost the very top of the company
in which he had started, close to the very bottom, in 1934.

He had given them, he remarked on the day he died, 'A quarter of a century. Nearly half my life.' He spoke in a wry, distanced way as if recalling an error of his youth. As for me, he had given me everything he had, including his name, for my entire life, barring the first ten days.

The 'Polyfoto' system was designed to reveal a range of the sitter's expressions, from which the favourites could be enlarged. The forty-seven prints that have survived reveal an unusually handsome and strong face, the head habitually set slightly back, conveying immediate authority. I would guess that he was around 50 when he had this studio session – his high, broad forehead is accentuated by the melancholy fact that his once thick and wavy hair, combed straight back, was by now thinner, indeed almost flat, and receding as well as greying at the temples. Although he was not in the army, his sideburns are cut high in military style; he wears a formal suit, his habitual uniform. I am sorry about his lost hair, just as I am about my own. It has gone the same way as his – without benefit of blood or genes to collude in the pitiless process. I expect he would have found this funny, and I regret that he isn't available to share the joke.

You can see the humour in the photographs but the dominant characteristic is serious, even sober. The man exudes honesty, he is integrity made palpable. Here is the key to his success as a salesman, the only one probably, since on the face of it he lacked every one of the extrovert gifts you might think indispensable. Words seldom came to him easily, except, I think, when he was talking to me.

I served as test audience and prompter when he trained himself, learning each inflexion by rote with untiring stamina, until he could deliver effective public speeches. But the labour shone through. David's surprise expertise on the platform was to convey that he was only overcoming an innate reticence under the impulse of burning conviction. Otherwise he would never have managed to face an audience at all.

People trusted David and when they wished to form a political committee or raffle a turkey they looked to him as a natural secretary, or treasurer better still. For several years he

was active in local politics and won local elections on a true-
blue Tory ticket. His views were sincerely held and about three
decades out of date. It was an excellent base for a career in
Conservative politics. But his professional life was too demanding, his health was periodically bad, and there were other
problems.

The mini-photos reproduce a face that has borne a lot of
pain. His forehead is unwrinkled, certainly less than my own,
yet there are symmetrical pain-furrows, etched deeply from the
edge of each nostril and ending like duelling scars a couple of
inches on either side of his wide, humorous mouth.

He wears a well-cut three-piece suit of very dark grey with
a subdued chalk stripe, a white shirt and stiff cut-away collar.
The suit was in effect a uniform – he had half a dozen, one
theoretically for each day of the week, though he wasn't quite
as robotic as to put them on in strict rotation, as he did his
highly polished black-lace shoes. But he came close. By any
standards David had a hyper-organised personality. The suits
were cut for him by a small Kingsway tailor, whose clientele
consisted largely of Lincoln's Inn lawyers, and were both very
conservative (like David) and 'less than half the price of Savile
Row'. He prided himself, as a Scot and an accountant, on
thrift, or at any rate getting value for money. He was interested
in the quality of things – I can see him testing the broad
swathes of cloth between fingers that were immaculate and
well cared for (though never manicured), savouring the texture
like a wine connoisseur.

The only minor inconsistencies in this solid city gent ensem-
ble are a white silk handkerchief oveflowing from the breast
pocket somewhat flamboyantly, and the tie. Since the photos
are black and white all you can make out about this item is the
narrow stripes, and the fact that it is tied in a chaste, tight knot.

I can see David's ordered hands tentatively extracting this
tie, wrapped in its tissue paper, from a long narrow box embossed with the name of a fancy establishment in the Burling-
ton Arcade. His caution has been sparked by the monogram.
It speaks of a Mayfair luxury he would never have indulged in
himself. He approaches it warily, a man of Calvinist, low-

church sympathies who has detected a whiff of forbidden incense. The stripes are of alternating black and scarlet, and although they are very thin there is no getting away from their colour. I don't suppose scarlet was a colour he had patronised previously in his sartorial life.

At first he only wore it out of courtesy to the donor. In time, I guess, he grew to like it secretly. All the same, as I had forgotten until finding the 'Polyfoto', he always tied it with an even smaller knot than he employed normally, as if to counterbalance the excess. Deep down, David almost certainly felt that the scarlet required subduing.

I can remember spotting this item in a Piccadilly arcade one gusty night before Christmas – I still often see things in shop windows which he might like. When I write about him the cool narrative voice which is available for Truda flees me like youth. I got to know her bit by bit and from the outside. With David there can be nothing so neat – he was always inside me as if by osmosis.

To my continuing regret our lifelong exchange of various gifts came to an end one spring in my last year at university. David had spent his fifty-fifth birthday in hospital, undergoing the third major cancer operation in two years. He had made a noticeably swifter recovery than after either of the others. Within three days he was as well as he had been before the operation. During the only spell of optimism I had experienced for months a consultant told me the truth.

The recovery was due not to the success of the surgery, but to its almost total absence. The disease had spread so widely there had been no point in even touching it. They had simply cut his already much scarred abdomen open and then sewn him back together again. All he had recovered from was the anaesthetic.

At 20 I was proud to be consulted by this eminent medical man, perhaps three times my age. He asked what I thought about telling David the truth. 'He might last a month, two even. There are often minor remissions. But it could be a week. He may want to settle his affairs. He's that kind of man, I'd have thought.'

'As long as he thinks he's getting better I'll encourage him. But I expect he'll realise fairly soon – he's not slow.'

The consultant agreed and gave me a cigarette. We inhabited a world where no one had yet suggested a link with cancer.

David was cheerful and apparently optimistic that night and told me to go back to Cambridge and do some work.

'When you get a First we'll go off on a trip, just the two of us. You know, they've got a decent little golf-course in Mallorca, and the sun will do me good.'

Every night I phoned to check how things were with the night nurse. Every day I wrote a letter or sent a card that I thought might amuse him. On Thursday night the nurse told me he wanted to speak to me himself – he had had himself moved that day to a room containing a bedside phone. His voice came on, very thin but clear, and enunciated with the hard vowels of Lancashire and the rolled 'r's' of Glasgow. He spoke beautiful English: how I wish I had a recording of his voice.

He had arranged to leave the hospital to spend the weekend at home. After that he would return to the ward. In the daytime he had made appointments for 'meetings'.

'What meetings? Surely to God you're not trying to work already?'

'Oh no, that's over,' he said briskly. 'It's just the lawyer and accountant. Details really. I suppose you're working round the clock?'

The only round-the-clock activities I was putting in at the time involved nothing to do with work, but I lied: 'Amazing how much you can get done at the last minute.'

'I don't agree – it's always best to leave yourself a margin.'

He didn't wish to encourage my precocious tendency to flirt with deadlines. His voice was fainter, he tired awfully quickly. But I also detected disappointment.

'I could get down early on Saturday and pick you up from the hospital. Better than that ambulance.'

His voice lightened. 'As long as it doesn't upset your routine. You could be back in Cambridge by …' – I remember the pause – 'Monday some time. I'll be ready to go back then.'

'Then we'll have the weekend together.'

I picked him up in the hospital as planned, a pleasure as well as an ordeal, because it gave me a chance to drive his Jaguar, a company perk he had not enjoyed for very long. He was a fine, fast, safe driver. The car had a badge on the front with the figure 38 to indicate the number of years he had held a clean licence. It was called the Society of Veteran Motorists. Membership involved a reduction in insurance premiums. His were absurdly low.

It was ten miles from Harefield Hospital, famous later for heart transplants, to our home, and I drove it as if on an air-cushion: any jolt and his face went even greyer with pain. He was still in pyjamas and dressing-gown, a desperately frail figure. I suggested he might be more comfortable stretched out in the back seat but he declined.

The sound of someone trying to breathe with only one, diseased, lung involves a gulping, sobbing sound, close to what in Vietnam was called 'a sucking chest wound'. There was pressure to 'talk over' it, or put out a hand and touch his. The second alternative was impossible – he had so long instilled in me the cardinal principle that you never remove either hand from the wheel when driving, except to change gear or make a signal, that the solidarity of the gesture would have been annulled. Finally he was able to speak himself. 'They can take me back feet first,' he said, 'but I'll come home sitting up.'

There is no good way to tell your son you know you will soon be dead, particularly when 'soon' means within days, but I can't think of a better way than David's. Now that nearly quarter-of-a-century has passed, I have had time to acquire the knowledge that immortality is a concept with meaning, in the sense that he is as present now as he was then. He certainly knew this himself. All I could see then was his unremitting pain, the dreaded emptiness I knew would be left when the wheezing, gulping breath finally stopped altogether, and the horror of being left with Ivy.

When we got home he could not face going up the stairs to bed. Instead I settled him, supported by pillows bracing his back, in his own easy chair. He was as thin as a malnutrition victim, his ankles the size of baby oranges.

No memories of the weekend have survived. David, abetted by formidable medication, spent a lot of it asleep in his chair.

The memories start on Monday morning. I had to shave and dress him, even though he was astonishingly better than had seemed possible when he left the hospital. He remarked that I was the worst barber he had come across in the whole of his life. The word 'life' kept cropping up like an unwelcome guest. David's cheeks had shrunk, which made his smile crooked and also droll.

His laughing days were now past historic, but the grimace, a visual echo of the twenty laughing years I had experienced, served just as well. I was actually happy. It seemed that he had much more strength left than it had appeared. I was even beginning to think he could survive the summer.

The lawyer came first, at ten-thirty, and David apologised for not getting up to greet him before dismissing me to make coffee.

His fountain-pen (David was not a ball-point man) was ready on a side-table. So was his leather document-case which I had often seen, though never, as now, unlocked. Wearing one of his chalk-stripe suits, and a stiff collar, brother to the one in the 'Polyfoto', he looked like an acceptable caricature of himself in better days behind his desk. Since he was down to less than eight stone, the collar-size was three or four inches too large.

The accountant was expected at noon – between his arrival and the lawyer's departure David took a handful of pills. It was hard for him to swallow them. Once he had, the pain that led him to moan periodically eased surprisingly quickly. My impulse was to conserve this (largely illusory) vitality by postponing the second meeting.

'Ask him to come back tomorrow. He won't mind.'

'Tomorrow? All these years I've been telling you never to postpone till . . .'

The effort required for half a sentence, one that he had indeed repeated hundreds of times, caused another spasm. Helplessly I suggested a drink.

'What have I always said about mixing drink and work?'
His habitually soft voice had by now acquired a faintness
suggesting vastnesses of space intervening between the effort to
speak and the words themselves.

The accountant came and went, and so too did our family
practitioner, Dr Chambers, a man who prided himself on his
resemblance to David Niven and was said to be a bridge-player
of international class. His visit only peripherally involved
David – Ivy was his patient and she had called him because
the chest palpitations which had bothered her for years were
so violent she thought she was succumbing to a heart attack.
On the way out he 'popped in' to see David, who had always
disliked him and used another doctor himself.

'How are you feeling?' Dr Chambers began.

David's skin was stretched so taut it was almost transparent
and there was sweat on his forehead. Somehow, he summoned
the strength to make his last joke, a rather silly one of the kind
that amused me so much when I was 9 or so.

'I'm feeling like a drink.'

The suave doctor withdrew, I gave David quite a lot of
whisky, and he told me that he had handed over some documents to the lawyer to hold for me until after his death. After
that he smiled and we were very companionable, though without speaking, until the ambulance men came.

They gave him an injection and one of the worst moments
was his panic when he saw the stretcher. His breathing was so
disturbed that he couldn't say anything but he looked at me
and his tartan rug in a way which made it clear he wanted to
be carried.

It was very easy to do because he weighed so little. Ivy came
downstairs for the departure, aided by Dr Chambers. The ambulance was hard sprung and jarred David horribly at first. He
soon went off into a near doze, though his eyes were open, and
we rode all the way to the hospital with me holding his hand
and making sure the rug was comfortably round his bony
shoulders.

David felt the cold acutely at this time, even though it was
spring. Once the injection took hold and the pain stopped I

think he quite enjoyed the journey. We had always enjoyed travelling together and the silence was not unusual.

Silences were a feature of life in our 'nuclear family', the uneasy trio of David, Ivy and myself. They had a strange dense quality as if pregnant with the unsaid, and for this reason when young I liked either to talk incessantly, trying to divert my own attention from something awful that was always present, or turn off entirely, usually by reading a book. When David and I were alone, it was a different matter altogether. He was by nature taciturn. It never bothered me remotely. When travelling the one or other might break a long and harmonious silence with some observation often to do with a feature of the landscape, and not unusually we might find ourselves saying something identical at the same moment. We sang the same tune, whether we kept the melody inside our heads or aspirated it. Often this was literally the case. We might drive for hours singing music-hall songs, 'Roamin' in the Gloamin' was a favourite, so was the Jacobite song 'The Banks of Loch Lomond', or 'I belong to Glasgow'. They were all part of the repertoire of a Scots comedian called Harry Lauder. David had seen him often as a boy and the words and music had stuck.

This was the last journey and I doubt that he would have said much even if it had been possible. There was a sense of symmetry and rightness about it. We had begun with him finding the shawl, now we were ending with me arranging the rug.

When we arrived ambulancemen and nurses took over. The jolt as the ambulance stopped made David sigh, a mechanical, inhuman sound as if his lungs, or what was left of them, had been scraped with steel-gauze. It made me wince but his expression remained serene. He was looking straight into my eyes and he managed a thin smile. Had he been more mobile I think he would have shrugged. 'There's no more to be done,' he was indicating. 'You can't come on this trip.' He had been holding my hand very tight, his fingers now thin as claws. Quite suddenly he let go.

I kissed his forehead. It felt strange, damp and brittle at the same time. I wanted to carry him into the hospital and see him safe to his bed but they wouldn't let me. There were brisk, impersonal nurses all round like soldiers, entirely in command of an experience they probably went through daily.

The regimentation could not be denied. We were both of us part of a well-rehearsed and unstoppable process.

Somehow or another my father was bustled away for ever.

There was nothing I could do while David died except go to a quiet pub on a place called Batchworth Heath which we had visited in the past after amateurish games of golf designed to boost his convalescence. It was a way of putting off going home. There was a pond with ducks outside and I remembered a time when David and I had competed in a self-invented game, the object of which was to skim a flat stone right across the water to dry land on the other side. David was very skilled at it. I remember thinking that I'd never see anyone skimming stones for the rest of my life without thinking of him and experiencing heart-break. Part of the thought was true. Only in later years the stone-skimmers were always a reminder of childhood happiness, almost all of which David had been re-sponsible for.

When I phoned Ivy, her voice faint as if she too was not long for the world, she whispered that she was 'prostrate', and so it proved. She was distributed across their large bed like a beached whale. Trying to help move David had exhausted her low store of physical energy and also drained the high-pitched hysterical emotion that had served her for weeks as locomotive power. The hysteria and Ivy had wilted away in unison.

It would be misleading to say that she had arrived at some peace. Her state of fatigue had simply laid down a temporary border between herself and the pack of hysterical emotions that seldom left her long at bay. Now, as she lay on this big bed under this tent-sized eiderdown, a concoction in pink frills the colour of icing that echoed the 'gâteaux' she loved, I offered consolation with tea and cakes.

Contrary to lifelong habit, today the 'gâteau' was waved away with a gesture that might have come from Gandhi. I felt sorry because if cream cakes were no help then Ivy must have been really desperate. She stayed where she was until the phone

rang at about nine that night. I came in from the garden David
had loved. The caller was the night matron from Harefield.
We recognised each other's voices instantly. 'I'm sorry but
your father has passed away,' she began.

I pretended I hadn't heard: 'Hold on, you want Mrs Leitch.'
Ivy grasped the machine and addressed the absent nurse hum-
bly like a novice talking to the Mother Superior. She kept
repeating 'I understand, matron. Yes, I understand ...' like a
child awed by this official bureaucrat of death and wishing to
make a good impression. Ivy was always a great one for good
impressions.

Finally she turned to me, eyes popping and full of tears:
'Your father's gone,' she said, almost triumphantly. Death had
restored the energy sapped by the last stages of dying. Ivy was
no longer inert, half dead herself. As she busied herself with
address book and reading glasses she began to fizz with expec-
tation.

The leather book lived on a table by the phone but only on
special occasions was it consulted. Most of our calls were local
and to familiar numbers. Ivy enjoyed using the phone since it
gave her a chance to act one of her parts. She could be the
Great Lady calling the grocer to arrange deliveries, or, in as
common a vein, the Lady of the Camelias, close to death,
describing her newest symptoms to the ever-attendant Dr
Chambers.

Now she called number after number, 'friends' and 'relations', none of whom she spoke to from one year, or in some
cases decade, to the next. Each time she repeated the same
message, with awful metronomic precision, as she began to
develop her new role of grieving widow. 'David passed away
tonight. We were over thirty years together and we never had
a cross word. Never a single cross word.' Ivy was grieving
terribly and yet, so false was everything about her, she could
only turn to silly lies to express how she felt.

It is hard to imagine a sadder life story than Ivy's, a tale she
told me often when I was very small though scarcely ever

afterwards, for reasons which only emerged after her own death.

The narrative began characteristically with an account of sudden blood-soaked loss striking her father down, and thus by extension her own 10-year-old self, one quiet afternoon in the comfort of their large family house in Didsbury on the outskirts of Manchester. The time was not long after Queen Victoria finally died of an excess of years and glory. It was the Edwardian hiatus before the Great War, a period remembered as the apogee of imperial prosperity and confidence. Ivy's father, whom she loved with sharp and painful passion, was an engineer in Manchester, one of the aristocrats of high Victorian technology in an age where construction on a lavish scale was a yardstick of mercantile splendour. A 'beautifully dressed man', with a taste for silk hats and, reading between her lines, extravagant or even profligate living, he had 'injured his health' in some undisclosed and extreme manner. One afternoon his cab had drawn up outside the door and they found him dying inside. Although he was only 36 he had suffered a haemorrhage on so massive a scale that the cab had been swimming in his life-blood. Ivy's extreme and Victorian passion for cleanliness often expressed itself in a kind of physical assault on the domestic objects that surrounded her – she cleaned things to death, shattering and tearing them, in her efforts to eliminate any trace of dirt. It may have been that she spent a lifetime trying to remove every trace of blood from the cab where her father had died.

Afterwards his mother, her grandmother, who had a coach and horses of her own and was clearly the focus of the family money, 'took Ivy up' as she said, removing her from a large family of brothers and sisters, and a mother remembered as a disciplinarian, a martinet, and a demon for housework. In due course Ivy was sent to a boarding-school in York, an establishment where the girls wore blue cloaks and were subjected to the rigours of Quaker Christianity, leaving Ivy with a loathing of organised religion. The girls were taken for walks around the wall of the ancient city and once a year were treated to strawberries and cream for tea. But she was not happy at school – on one occasion, as a punishment, she was locked all night in an airing cupboard. These were the memories she passed on.

In York she also fell in love with a much older man called William Holliday. As with her father, she mainly remembered him in terms of the clothes that he wore – or, in his case, costumes. He was an actor-manager, performing in the elaborate melodramas which marked the transition between the decline of the Victorian popular stage and the bargaining popularity of the cinema. He was a fine rider to the point of appearing on stage with his horse, probably in the celebrated play *Derby Day*. His repertoire must also have included a drama of the Foreign Legion because I remember her showing me a photograph of him in the uniform of a Legionnaire officer. There was also a picture which he had painted himself with considerable skill – a portrait of his dog, his own name inscribed along the tag of its expensive collar.

The progress or otherwise of this love was never disclosed, though the accretion of souvenirs suggested happy memories – I hope this was the case because there were few ventures in her life which did not end in some disagreeable and even disastrous way. Certainly when she became a temporary nurse during the Great War, working in a fever hospital in the Lancashire resort of Southport which features elsewhere in this story, she herself contracted typhoid. It was one of the many occasions when she nearly died. Her hair fell out, though happily it grew back, and when she recovered she was so weak that she had to learn to walk again.

Ivy's biography in the years after the war until she met the young David Leitch consisted only of scantily remembered episodes. Later it became clear that the early 1920s comprised the span of her first and secret marriage to a man called Haber. He was in some way connected with both the Manchester cotton industry and also Cairo where she lived in circumstances of great unhappiness for some years. She told stories of 'working in fashion' and doing fashion sketches for the *Daily Telegraph*, an account that seemed unlikely since she apparently had no talent for drawing. She also worked as a cashier on a temporary basis during the Wembley Exhibition of 1923 – here the story was very detailed, including accounts of the exhibits and the fact that many visitors were so intent on getting in that they never picked up their change. There was also a period when she lived in an 'embassy' at 30 Palace Gate in London, where she met many distinguished European émigrés, including the pianist Paderewski, and a well-known French actress of the time called Ina de la Haye, a pretty dark woman whose photograph sat for years beside Ivy's bed, with an affectionate, stagey inscription.

Because she only told me these anecdotes when I was very young, I believed later that they were simply inventions or exaggerations. Yet in her very last years they were verified in strange ways. There was the tale of travelling in the Blue Train from Paris to take a boat from Marseilles to Suez and the Far East. During the night ride south, thieves entered her sleeping-compartment in search of her valuables. The felony was unsuccessful, though at breakfast other passengers were lamenting their losses. Ivy was cautious with her possessions and had concealed her jewels in her corsets, thus preserving them.

This story I had long forgotten but in the course of clearing up her affairs after her death, a number of rings and other trinkets were discovered concealed in a corset which itself was hidden in a wardrobe. The tale of high life in Kensington must also have had some specific basis of truth. Certainly, when my own address was 30 Prince's Gate in London she habitually addressed her envelopes to 30 Palace Gate, a memory trick from the past. And photographs left no doubt that she had lived in Cairo. There were snapshots of her, posing stoically under a sun umbrella, and on a camel by the pyramids. In each, a figure who had been standing beside her had been cut out with scissors. She told me that 'someone', perhaps the 'Haber' husband, had imprisoned her in a room there and burnt her with cigarette-ends. She also often repeated a tale of sailing from Tokyo to Suez, a voyage of which she recalled little because once again she contracted a virulent fever and nearly died.

Ivy's 'Life before your Father', as she called it, had been amazingly adventurous compared with the repetitive suburban years afterwards. Yet a similar thread ran through both: sudden reversals and disappointments, a series of vengeful illnesses which threatened to blow her away overnight, as her father was blown away, and also a hint of horrors, like the incident of the cigarette-ends, too terrible to be clarified or dwelt on.

Piecing the story together, it sounds as if some time in the late 1920s she had returned to base in Manchester to lick her wounds after her sorties into the disease-ridden and thief-inhabited world of 'abroad'. Having somehow got rid of Haber, she took up with David Leitch, the youngest of a family of five brothers, whose father had travelled south from Glasgow and struck it rich in cotton.

He was younger than Ivy and someone who 'knew nothing about the world outside Manchester' until she arrived to teach him, as she would shout accusingly when they quarrelled. The clan of brothers was thriving in a variety of business ventures to do with mills and shops and – a new departure – car show-rooms, and David's prospects must have seemed excellent. David may have been 'a bumpkin', as she said, but he was also young, good-looking, rich. As usual though, Ivy's luck was as bad as her health. Within two or three years of their 'marriage', in common with so many others obliged to live through the great slump of 1929, everything he had and more was lost.

Ivy's account of her efforts to stave off the disaster was a litany which accompanied my childhood as faithfully as the 'Nine O'Clock News'. To pay wage-bills she had sold 'my furs, my jewels, everything'. By the beginning of 1932 David was flat broke and banging on doors in the north-west of England with rain in his only shoes trying to sell cash-registers to shops whose stock was often worth less than the machines themselves. Somehow or another he succeeded: he was promoted to sales manager and they moved south.

They managed to fight their way back into solvency, or rather David did. But Ivy never forgave him for the lost jewels and never let him forget them. She was right probably in claim-

ing that he had lost the courage to cut himself free from institutional links and try to swim on his own in the entrepreneurial
world. On the other hand he rose slowly but steadily up the
company hierarchy and though never rich they were also never
less than 'comfortably off', as people said.

They stayed welded together through fear and habit and
their personal conspiracy, revolving round their non-marriage
and the illegal adoption. In their dissatisfied way they were a
very stable couple.

Ivy's underlying desperation was expressed cyclically in bitter, set-piece domestic battles. Her birthdays, which made her
mind turn to the diamonds and sables of yesteryear, were a
common pretext for rage and recrimination.

At least one of these birthday inquests ended in Ivy producing one of her 'fake' last exits. There was a set format for
these dangerous evenings, repeated a dozen times over the
years. A crescendo of quarrels, most of the verbal content
consisting of Ivy's hysterical sobbing accusations, would finally
exhaust itself in a throbbing, lowering silence. Waiting for the
next round to begin demanded a special intensity of listening.
It was like sitting under the path of a 'buzz-bomb', as the
German rockets were called, counting down the sixty seconds
that elapsed between the buzz cutting out, and the target,
which might be yourself, exploding under impact. They were
just big enough to destroy a house and family, like Ivy and
David's quarrels.

Ivy always ended the silent phase dramatically – by thump-
ing upstairs to pack. 'I'll never spend another night with my
head under this roof again, I swear,' she would scream on the
stairs. 'And nor will he,' with a finger pointed at me.

The nearest railway station was about a mile away. We had
to limp every inch, struggling with the huge suitcases Ivy had
loaded to the brim. My particular burden would be a hat-box
of Ivy's, covered with labels from exotic ports like Shanghai
or Port Said. The labels accentuated the cosmopolitan, somehow raffish life she had led before David's constricted destiny
had driven her to depths – and also heights – of rage and
despair.

These episodes always took place late at night. The station walk was a calvary, particularly for Ivy with her bad feet. David probably suffered no less, driving alongside very slowly in his grey Standard 12, a veteran of 1939, trying to persuade Ivy through the window to climb aboard – or at least let him load the bags up. Only on the station platform itself, with the train pulling in, would she relent, agreeing to return home 'for the last time'. Then there would be the problems of getting all the baggage back through the barrier. Ivy was not always able to obtain a refund on the tickets she had bought for the two of us a few minutes earlier. I remember more rows, this time between her and the ticket clerk. In the end we would return home in the same silence, unloading the Standard as if we were back after the annual holiday.

No matter how often this scene was repeated, I was never sure until we started for home whether this time would turn out to be a real departure or yet another charade. I would envisage a future marooned with Ivy, sole witness to her inconsolable despair, sole target of her unquenchable rages.

Ivy was a person of profound and strange passions, usually contained by monotony and isolation, and yet always present at the edge of her personality. There was a strangeness about her which contrasted with her conventional circumstances and I am sure now that she lived through a period of mental disorder which blighted her middle age. Her disturbance was expressed by acute misery which she went to some lengths to conceal from everyone except David and myself. Among strangers she affected a brightness and jollity which they accepted at face value. She was perfectly capable of spending a morning weeping inconsolably at a table, then rapidly controlling her fears should there be a visit of some kind, perhaps from a tradesman delivering or a salesman huckstering encyclopedias or bibles.

I prayed for such interruptions because she would dab her tears away with a powder-puff and rush to the door, a figure instantly transformed, with gracious smiles and English small-talk about the weather or the war. Once the interruption was over she would resume her sobs or, in another mode, a cold unstoppable rage, which she vented on the physical world, laying into domestic tasks as if the household objects which sometimes broke in her hands as she subjected them to a fury of cleaning and polishing were enemies on whom she was wreaking an impassioned homicidal revenge.

16

One of the souvenirs I preserved after Ivy's death was her favourite photograph, which was also much admired by Truda.

It shows Ivy and David together, attending one of the 'Ladies Nights' organised either by David's company or his Masonic Lodge or his Conservative Association, which took them off several times a year to some London hotel, usually the Dorchester or the Mayfair, and from which they would return in the small hours, David smelling of alcohol and cigars, Ivy giving off fumes of Sauterne or Château-d'Yquem, the sweet wines she liked, mixed with a generous dose of Chanel Number 5.

In the photograph, Ivy is seated, though her considerable bulk, encumbered in an enormous formal dress of a floral pattern, manages to conceal the chair altogether, giving an odd impression of great weight miraculously suspended. Her feet are concealed beneath the floor-length skirt (had she perhaps slipped off her shoes for greater comfort?). She wears white elbow-length formal gloves and holds against her stomach a small sequin-covered evening bag. Across her wide bosom no less than two flowers, one a chrysanthemum, the other now unidentifiable, have been attached, with safety-pins I would imagine. In her right hand, held dangerously near the line of the expansive skirt, it is possible to see a cigarette that has burned rakishly low.

Beside her, one hand disappearing protectively behind her back, stands David, looking amiable and elegant. Only a hint of ventriloquistic stiffness about his stance, an impression of being over-posed, betrays his shyness. They were both capable of a surprising ease when taking part in formal, gregarious events outside the home, though the notion of holding even a small party on their own turf never crossed their minds.

The only considerable gathering of outsiders that ever took place was for David's funeral – confirmation of my (previously untested) assumption that he had plenty of friends linked with his non-family life, 'business' as it was always called. It was a world totally apart, righteously so. Ivy used to boast that in all the years David had worked in central London she had never once phoned him 'at business'.

Many years later I wondered why this was so virtuous. At the time I accepted it was another example, among many, of Ivy's superiority to the army of those 'who don't know any better'.

In his lifetime the nuclear family trio formed by Ivy, David and myself remained almost proudly inviolate, as if living in an isolation ward gave you points for virtue in some rarefied ethical league. David never said as much. Ivy, however, often used the phrase 'keeping yourself to yourself', accompanied, very likely, by a contemptuous sniff, so that I recognised it as one of her commandments or moral maxims.

She was not simply expressing a temperamental preference for spending most of her time on her own at home – in Ivy's eyes this was the only virtuous course. 'Virtuous', in this as most other Ivy contexts, meant non-proletarian. Ivy was the priestess of a bourgeois Victorian cult of class, a religion that transcended mere churches, transposing ethical and social imperatives so the two became identical. Virtue was 'middle-class', which in turn exemplified individual striving and conscientious industry, though of a kind where the intelligence was employed always, and the hands (manual labour) never.

This work you did on your own, and never in groups. It enabled you to save, as opposed to squander, and it meant that you would pay cash for something when you could afford it, as opposed to buying it on hire purchase, thus incurring heavy interest charges. According to the same commandments you owned property, as opposed to renting it, wore semi-formal, as opposed to work-clothes, and avoided promiscuity in every form. Thus Ivy would never enter a pub, partly because she disapproved of pub drinking, partly because they were crowded and she regarded proletarian crowds (as opposed to a crowd of, say, Masons in dinner-jackets) as intrinsically and literally unhealthy. They gave you diseases.

In Ivy's lexicon of morality, no entry was more potent than 'privacy'. Thus, 'talking to the neighbours', an apparently harmless activity, was frowned on, because it shattered the boundaries of privacy, but also, like all the other prohibitions, because that was how They lived.

But this was Ivy and David at home in their family personae. Their public selves were markedly different, indeed they involved a change of personality so extreme as to be tantamount to disguise. What is so striking then about the photograph is its misleading quality – just the element, very likely, that Truda was so pleased by. The forgotten photographer, a journeyman specialist probably in weddings and anniversaries, has managed with some expertise to capture Ivy and David's public face, one I myself saw very seldom.

Truda and John saw a younger version of it during the adoption negotiations and no wonder they were deceived. They wanted to be, of course. In desperate pursuit of a couple to take the baby off their hands, in haste and without too many questions asked, they were in no position to scrutinise the applicants' credentials.

Forty years later it is not surprising that Truda grew restive, her attention filming over, the only time I began to explain some of the bizarre surprises, including the fact that emerged with inconvenient consequences after Ivy died – David and Ivy Leitch were never married at all.

'Not married,' I remember her saying. 'There must be a mistake about that, I'm sure.' It was not a subject that she pursued, and nor did I. Truda was far too stuck with her Hollywood vision of an ideal couple – derived from the brief encounter in the Russell Hotel – to take another version on board. She was no humorist, unfortunately. Otherwise she might have appreciated the broad irony of the role reversal –

as things turned out, she, and not Ivy, had been the 'respectable married woman' after all.

But it was dangerous territory. Truda's moral position *vis-à-vis* my adoption stood four square on the premise that Ivy and David, thanks to age and circumstances, had been demonstrably preferable as parents to John and herself. That was how they had rationalised their decision, or how Truda had, and it was true as far as it went. It followed that any awkward truths about my adoptive parents, of which there were many, looked uncomfortably like an indictment of the adoption itself, and of her effort to care for the child.

In the circumstances this would have been bitterly unfair. For Truda and John were by no means alone in accepting Ivy and David's plausible façade. There is a reassuring aspect to the photograph – it speaks of custom and stability. In Ivy's eyes there is a yearning quality, which is moving, and very likely moved Truda. She believed that Ivy's dreams, so like her own, had been realised.

The two women had a lot in common, though I only realised it bit by bit. One year, for instance, Cambridge University won their annual boat-race against Oxford, an event in which I invested little emotional capital. I was astonished to receive a long, extravagant phone call from Merseyside offering congratulations. Truda had seen the race on TV, and spoke as if I had been rowing the Cambridge boat single-handedly myself. This was the purest Ivy.

My adoptive parents had no intimate friends, no one who dropped in for a drink or a meal, let alone to stay for a night or weekend. But there were people who had known them outside their domestic scene for many years: their assessments would have been close to those made by Truda and John. Here was a fine couple, an impeccable couple even, Ivy 'warm and jolly', David intelligent, responsible, a figure of some moral weight, a natural leader.

These quasi-intimates would have been astounded to learn of the screaming exchanges, the near homicidal attacks, the suicide attempts they both made. That their life together was an exercise in self-destruction, a union which worsened as it

lengthened, would have been even harder to credit. Like everything else that was intimate, they kept their misery to themselves. When I wrote about them in *God Stand up for Bastards*,
I advanced the view that they had adopted a child in the hope
of improving their relationship and that my arrival had at any
rate made things no worse. A decade later this verdict is less
convincing. The child in the house probably lightened the
atmosphere sometimes. When it turned out that my school
career was successful, they both derived satisfaction from these
boyish achievements (just as Truda did in retrospect). But the
effect of having a child was to keep them together when the
only hope for their lives had been to make a break and start
again.

'I was young, only 32, when I first saw you in that hotel,'
Ivy was accustomed to say when the subject came up – always
at my behest. 'The moment I saw you, I knew you were going
to be mine for ever.'

Then she went on to explain how the young couple had
soon disappeared – Ivy and David were left holding the baby.
This was the 'I couldn't have gone on living if they'd taken
you away' stage of the story. For, as Ivy would explain, tears
playing havoc with her make-up while I watched in awe, since
the 'couple' (or parents) were lost for ever, there was every
risk that I might now be incarcerated for life in some heartless
institution for orphans.

She would ask if I remembered the film of *Oliver Twist*. I
did indeed.

Then they had thought of a wonderful solution – like a
miraculous escape in a fairy-tale. 'We got rid of the dog, Rex.
He used to drive us nearly mad with his barking, and then
there was the maid. Irma was German, she was the one who
taught you to say "Heil, Hitler", so she didn't know anything
different, and so – hoop-la, we packed everything in a big van
and disappeared too! Overnight we were gone.'

After that everything was easy, as Ivy told it, and from this
point on my own internal doubts about the story were resolved. I had always known that some important element was
wrong or simply untrue. As a child I had no more than gut

feeling and knowledge of Ivy's truthfulness in other matters to go on. Even now, with the accumulated information of decades, far more than I could ever have dared hope for short of miraculous intervention, there are still mysteries to do with Ivy's life which will never be explained.

The story of the midnight flit with Irma and myself, but without Rex, fits better once the fact that Ivy and David were unmarried is added. They did not normally do anything with intense precipitation: they were a couple for long-drawn-out processes, where change is infinitesimal. But no unmarried couple could hope to undertake legal adoption in 1937. Their only way was to snatch the infant and light out.

'I told the new neighbours you were my little baby.'

Ivy, perhaps sensibly, had wanted to give an impression that there had been a choice between having a child of her own in the normal way and adopting me. She had chosen the second course because she loved the unwanted baby on sight – specifically more, she always insisted, than she could have loved a natural child of her own. By telling the story in these terms she may have intended to offer reassurance to an obviously insecure and 'highly-strung' only child of a couple who were themselves abnormally insecure. They suffered mentally and physically – David from what were called 'peptic ulcers', a classic stress disease, and Ivy from a bewilderment of illnesses.

Where domestic tension took its toll of David's stomach, scarcely any part of Ivy's body from head (a lifetime of migraine) to toe (rheumatoid arthritis) was spared painful symptoms. During my childhood her illnesses suffused every room of our various residences like acrid smoke – indeed when I think of them now I recall the asphyxiating and deathly taste in the throat that derives from contact with tear-gas or the polluted wind from an installation containing gas or oil that has been shelled or bombed.

Ivy's illnesses were not restricted to home – they became more acute and harder to handle whenever we travelled. During the war, we seemed to be constantly on the move and I remember a succession of waiting-rooms outside surgeries of unknown doctors in obscure communities where we had been washed up in order to continue our fugue-like escape from the raids on the big cities.

Later, in peacetime, when life was back to what was called 'normal' and we went on vacation for three weeks each year, her illnesses and their variety posed insoluble problems. They reached their apogee – what in later years people would call 'Catch 22' or a 'double-bind' – when we set off for Penzance, the Cornish resort, during the endless hot summer of 1947.

Ivy had been suffering from 'heart trouble', which led to palpitations and fears of imminent death, combined with a thyroid condition which caused her throat to swell and led to extreme shortness of breath. Her rheumatism, later diagnosed as arthritis, had always made walking difficult. Sadly, at this time and for many years after, she was also afflicted by an injury to her heel, which necessitated specially designed shoes, one containing a special pad of foam rubber designed to min- imise the pain.

Walking more than a few yards was purgatory, and she often had trouble standing up at all. The plan had been to stay by 'the seaside', but it had to be aborted because her thyroid condition immediately became very severe. A local doctor diag- nosed the cause as the ozone content of the sea air. The symp- toms only disappeared once we had moved some twenty miles inland. But here, in the country, there was the problem of walking. Her heel hurt too much for her to hobble more than a few yards. By the sea she could have sat on a bench and enjoyed the life of other holiday-makers along the promenade. 'What are you supposed to do in the country when every step's like a red-hot knife going through your foot?' she demanded.

What we did in the end was both farcical and sad. In the morning, accompanied by a taxi, we drove to a local 'beauty spot' where Ivy, equipped with sandwiches, thermos and rug, was installed for a few hours. Although she couldn't drive, she insisted on having the car to sit in and, I suppose, provide a sense of security. Accordingly, David and I would then take the cab to the most accessible beach, commuting back to Ivy's picnic spot later in the day.

Although she behaved like one, Ivy was not, strictly speak-

ing, a hypochondriac. Her illnesses were real, not invented –
the 'spur' on her heel was a case in point. After many years of
doctors and specialists, all 'useless' as she finally decided with
bitterness, she happened on an osteopath. Thanks to some
ruthless manipulation – 'The agony was terrible. I could hear
the bone click,' Ivy often recounted, miming the noise by rap-
ping on a glass surface with her wide gold wedding ring – the
'spur' was cured, and gave no more trouble. The thyroid condition, too, improved with time, finally vanishing. She always,
as she said, 'had a heart', but though the palpitations were
scary, she survived, in fair health, during the years after
David's death, to the age of 77.

Her inner demons, too, seemed to subside once she was
widowed. By some compound of deception that only she could
have catalysed after a lifetime's commitment to the science of
the untrue, she transmuted rage for what ought to be into
nostalgia for what never was. She talked of 'when my husband
was alive' with a built-in 'of course'. 'Of course, then everything was very different. . . .'

'Of course, we never had a cross word in thirty years. . . .'

Late in her life, making a visit, I came into the room as she
was speaking this sentence to an unsuspecting outsider – a
kindly neighbour who often helped by shopping. The reluctance of modern stores to send delivery vans was one of the
yardsticks by which Ivy defined the world's decline from the
ampler days of 'marriage'.

There was, finally, no hate in me for her – we had agreed to
communicate via an edited past, and in the present, since
neither made undue demands, we managed a shallow amiabil-
ity. I no longer felt guilt when I left – I knew she no longer
wished to keep me. I was hers in the past, secure as a studio
portrait. She had no taste for updated versions, with wrinkles
and grey hairs replacing the expectant empty canvas of myself
aged 20 (such a study, expensively framed, occupied a position
of some prominence in her domestic stage set).

But the relief I felt when she died in 1972 was tempered by
a number of astonishing surprises and revelations. It was then
that I discovered that Ivy and David had never been married.

For over forty years Ivy's marital status had been 'legal separation' from someone else, which led to a legal imbroglio of weird and long-drawn-out bureaucratic extensions. Also she was nine years older than she had said. This accounted to some extent for her illness, and also for the succession of illnesses, mental and physical if such distinctions can be made, that had always haunted her and our tiny triangular family.

I had believed she was in her middle sixties: a couple of years earlier she had made quite a fuss about qualifying for and drawing the old-age pension. Was it 'charity', she wondered? Was she justified in taking the money when 'there are so many others much worse off than me'?

Only when I pointed out that it was a statutory right, one David had paid for by a lifetime of contributions, had she made up her mind with a great show of reluctance to accept state money. 'I can always donate it to some good cause,' she decided.

Despite her reservations over the pension, she had been drawing it equally for well over ten years. The arguments were not about whether she had received the money or not (she indubitably had), but whether she had any right to do so. An official finally told me that had the affair been discovered while Ivy was alive his department would have prosecuted her for fraud. As a result of the 'legal separation' she had received a small fixed income since the early 1930s. As David's 'widow' she had drawn a large executive pension since the late 1950s. Over the years she had made innumerable false declarations of different kinds.

The deception went back a long way, long before the meeting with Truda and John and the illegal adoption which had already led me into other blank encounters with officialdom, there being surprisingly many occasions when it is indispensable to possess a birth certificate in one's own name. Now I understood for the first time that this illegality (the result, Ivy had always said, of her overwhelming attachment to me as a 10-day-old baby) was only one of many. It was not an isolated act out of character.

I discovered that more than half her life, certainly the

forty-five years from the age of 32 until her death, amounted to what popular melodramas used to call 'a living lie'. David himself, the man everyone trusted on sight, had also been involved in the ruse. The story began well back in the 1920s and any of the people who might have known how it came about were long gone.

When in due course I managed to learn enough about my natural father to have a sense of the man it seemed a shame there was no way of passing this news on to him. Of all the people involved he was perhaps the only one who would have appreciated the irony.

What a quartet they comprised, those four parents of mine, and what a comedy of manners and appearances they played out, trying to size each other up under the Russell Hotel's crystal chandeliers. The red plush and gold Edwardian flash, the architecture bordering on folly, was the perfect setting for a meeting of four strangers, none of whom was quite what he or she pretended to be.

17

'Write it down or you'll forget,' Truda said in the premonitory, mildly bullying tone that came easily to her on the rare occasions when she was mellow enough.

I assured her that there was no danger of forgetting how her baby grandson's toes were arranged, and she rubbed her bare foot sensuously across grass that had taken on a rusty tinge from prolonged absence of rain. She was pleased at her own audacity, removing a stocking in public, in Hyde Park. She had endowed this surprising act with a distinctly naughty aura, as if playing Eve in the garden.

We had taken sandwiches and a thermos of ice for a picnic and now we were lolling in the green shade of an enormous lime, all wearing little sun hats like Australians, three generations of us.

It was August 1976, and London's hottest summer for a decade, the dryest for a century, and the heat had gone to everyone's head as if the burning cloudless days were some unexpectedly strong and addictive foreign liquor the natives could neither handle nor leave alone. A Minister for Drought was appointed, as if the government distrusted this excess of weather. At night the cool streets were unusually crowded, and people played music.

Before lunch we had fed the ducks and gone for a boat ride on the Serpentine. She had held Luke, who was docile with content about the novelty of water, well away from her slightly over-elaborate park-visiting outfit. After lunch Luke had ambled up crab-wise to sit in her lap. She settled him on her

knees in a way designed to prevent him making her skirt bag.
In recent weeks he had taken up walking and used it for short,
slow journeys. When in haste he would revert to crawling, an
art he had developed to a more advanced state. It was his
equivalent, since he was a rapid crawler, of breaking into a
trot.

Truda watched him perform as if it were all for her benefit
– she had come to wear the role of grandma as if it were a
well-deserved decoration conferred for rare merit. She accepted
her important position in the general scheme of things with
seamless confidence, especially now, thriving like a lizard.

She placed a finger and thumb on his big toe, which he took
for a game, and demonstrated that her second toe, like Luke's
and like my own, was distinctly longer than the so-called big
or great toe. 'It's a family sign,' she said. 'Ballet dancers often
have them,' she added, with the complacent throw-away air of
a retired Pavlova. 'Everyone has it in our family.'

It was one of her longest visits and as perfect days passed
she established her family place unobtrusively like a cat. Every
day we took a short drive to the park, leaving the car and
plunging in among the trees as if it were an oasis.

She was relaxed enough to remember London summers in
her youth. The first was clearly in 1936 and Truda at 24 must
have been conducting her affair with my father, perhaps delicately encouraged by the great royal love affair which was just
breaking surface. The Harrods staff were better informed than
most – Wallace Simpson, the beautiful American divorcee who
was the King's mistress, naturally patronised the store.

Truda and John had jobs and (so far) no responsibilities.
They lived in a Harrods approved and subsidised boarding-
house at Barnes in west London, and they would walk along
Barnes Terrace, past the old South Western Railway cast-iron
bridge, watching the boat crews training for Henley. It was an
area dominated by the Thames and dedicated to brewing and
rowing – they used a pub called The Rose, another called The
Sun, and went to dances at the store's sports club, also at
Barnes. Briefly, they were young and free and members of the
aristocratic employed, thriving in the midst of a Third World

comprised of their fellow citizens. Some of these would stake out Harrods' canopied entrance twelve hours a day, hoping to find a bag to carry, or even a cigar-butt.

That had been the first summer, and clearly the best. The next year she had been pregnant with me, they lost their jobs in turn, and John had written job applications, to no avail, next to the statue of Peter Pan in Kensington Gardens. The night before she left I learned by chance of a third summer, this time in wartime. She had been looking through old photos and had found the study of Ivy and David I have already described, Truda's favourite. 'I remember she said she liked ballroom dancing like me,' Truda observed. 'They were probably out dancing the night I came.'

'When was that?' I enquired, only half listening.

'I don't know when exactly, during the war. I'd been dancing myself as a matter of fact, with a friend, at a lovely ballroom in the Strand called the Lyceum. When the dance was over, they wanted me to go on somewhere but I decided to come out to that place, where they lived. Where the school is.'

'You mean Harrow?'

'Harrow-on-the-Hill, of course. Where Winston Churchill used to visit and sing songs with the boys. Did you go to school there?'

'No, but we lived there when I was very small. Before the war. You mean you went right out there on the train?'

'Yes, it must have been the last one. There weren't any more when I tried to get one coming back.'

'You went to see them?' I was amazed at what she was saying and that she had never mentioned it before.

'They weren't there. You weren't there either, no one was, that's if it was the right house. I thought I might have got the address wrong because I was, well, I'd had a couple of drinks and it was enough to make me wonder. I rang the bell and knocked on the door but nobody came. I didn't want to wake the neighbours. It was hard to see – I had a torch but it was still hard.'

'What did you do?'

'I went back to the station and it was closed. They'd finished for the night. I had to wait until they started up again in the morning.'

'Poor you. Was it cold?'

'I was tired mainly – it was summer, but not like this.' It was too late to continue the story that night and there was never another occasion when I could persuade her to add to an anecdote I knew instinctively was true. Probably she had been in London for some reason she did not care to elaborate – it sounded like an excursion away from John, maybe in 1943, the year after Margaret was born. All the same I was very pleased she had tried, when a little tipsy, to see how I was getting on. Her reasonable self had given way to an impromptu diversion dictated by maternal regard. She had probably got the house right too – she wasn't to know that Ivy and David had long since paid off the maid, ditched the dog and moved quietly on.

'Write it down or you'll forget.'

MARGARET

18

There was never another summer so dry, so hot, so foreign, in London again. Later on, this season, when we inhabited Hyde Park like aborigines, came to be remembered like a successful vacation trip abroad, a substitute for those we planned but never made in reality. Truda's Cunarder had long set off up the Mersey without her and except for one final visit to Denmark, home of her paternal ancestors, she stayed close to base. The Copenhagen visit, unfortunately, was without me because by then I myself was far away – first in Australia, then America, then Australia again.

We 'kept in touch', but many of the ambitions I had cherished never came to pass (to Truda's relief, I am sure). So we never made contact together with the Danish relations, nor did we ever sit down at a table with Margaret and her family. There was markedly little news of my sister and the two children, Gillian, usually called Gill, and Richard David, always called Richard. In the course of a phone call, Truda might mention that she had just seen them, or was planning a visit to the Welsh borders where they lived, but that was all. I tacitly acquiesced with her desire to let the matter of meeting Margaret drop.

Truda and I met in Liverpool early in 1979 when I told her that my marriage to Jill had ended, though there was a plan for Luke and his mother to return to England from the Sydney beach-front apartment where they currently lived. Truda asked almost nothing at all about the divorce but referred to 'that hot summer before you left' several times over a weekend. In her mind, and mine too, the time of comparing toes and her memory of the lost night journey, when she had tried in vain to find me in the unfriendly wartime suburbs, had set a seal on our family connection.

By the beginning of 1981, where I started this story with the phone call from the unknown woman, I suspect that our relationship had settled down into something that could be called normal. I was slightly worried about her health. She was almost 70, the steepness of the stairs leading to her flat and the 'senior citizen' fixtures which she had demonstrated with a smile when she first moved in were no longer a subject to joke about. She was getting feebler – what was going to happen when she was too old to look after herself? If Margaret had to take over, how could the secret of my existence be preserved?

There was no chance at all of persuading her to anticipate some situation like this by bringing my sister and I together. As my mother grew very gradually weaker and older, she also became stronger when it came to having her own way. It was impossible to imagine insisting on anything she didn't want.

When the phone rang in the house by the canal I didn't think it could be Truda.

Nowadays she was a much later bird – midnight or after was her time to call. I don't know how many hours we had spent talking across how many thousand miles. It had become a habit, a process I hadn't seriously thought of coming to an end.

'Hullo?'

Caller: 'May I please speak to Mr David Leitch?'

'Yes. Speaking.'

It's a strange voice, a woman's. She sounds nervous. Mysteriously, she is completely taken aback.

He says, prompting, 'Who's that calling?' and wishes she'd get to the point.

Caller: 'My name's Margaret Parkin. Does that mean anything to you?'

'No I don't think so. Should it?'

Caller: 'I'm not sure. I live in North Wales ...'

Again she hesitates and by now the man is relieved, not irritated, by the delay. Belatedly, he has grasped where the exchange is leading, and where it will end. He is terrified by the unwinding of a process which he has no power to arrest. A few more words, three probably, and then ... There is no point in putting it off.

'Have you a daughter Gill and a boy called Richard David?' he says finally.

Caller: 'Yes.'

'Christ. Then you're my sister, aren't you?'

Caller: 'Sister? Am I? I don't know.'

'Truda's dead, isn't she?'

'Yes.'

At which point recall dissolves, as I found myself dissolving in grief for Truda, my dead mother, mother after her fashion. At the same time I was writing down Margaret's, my sister's phone number, which turned out to be in Flintshire, North Wales.

I said I needed a bit of time to collect myself, then I'd call back.

Later, astonishingly, she was to tell me that if I hadn't phoned again, which she half expected, then she would never have summoned the courage to contact the strange London number, found in her, our, dead mother's address book, a second time. It showed me how little this sister of 37, speaking for the first time to her brother six years older, understood him. And vice versa.

For a long time after putting the phone down I didn't move, but sat where I was, staring out of the window at the vile night, the spirit-eroding London rain bothering the dark surface of the canal, a ghostly, blanked-out yellow from the sodium lights. Nothing passed, no cars, not even a last nocturnal barge with the faint chug-chugging that caused visitors who wished to indicate their familiarity with the city of Venice to say the sound reminded them of a *vaporetto*.

I have been almost everywhere in the world, or everywhere
I want to go, and some places I certainly didn't, but never to
Venice. Deliberately really: there had been many opportunities.
From my youth it had been a special symbol for me: of arriv-
ing. It was the place I would go when everything was right.
Some time in the previous four or five years, I had discreetly
dropped the boyish notion. No Venice for me, I thought, and
now it's even too late for La Venezia.

Time to call Margaret. How must she feel? I had lost Truda,
the mother I'd truly lost at birth. But she had lost 'Mum', as
she would naturally think of her, someone entirely different.
Truda, whom I'd never called 'Mother', let alone 'Mum',
had given the strong impression that I wouldn't like my sister! – Margaret: nor she me. 'Your backgrounds are
so different. She's always had a very ordinary, normal life.
You . . .'

She had never divulged Margaret's married name. She had
made me promise I would never try to find her. Once I had
phoned Truda, from Los Angeles airport, while Margaret had
been present in the flat. The anxiety, close to panic, had come
through all the way across the Atlantic and the North American continent: half way across the world.

'There's someone here. I can't talk now.'

Periodically, when Truda said something about my sister or
her family, I had suggested, casually and always without pressure, that the time might have come for a meeting. She was a
big girl now, after all, with two children of her own. Truda
had resolutely declined to rise to the bait, even though it had
been cast so reassuringly and on a silken line. 'Not yet,' she
had always replied. 'Later – perhaps.'

She must have left a will, telling her secret. By 'later' she
meant 'when I'm safely dead'.

I experienced yet another dissolution of grief at the reminder. She was gone, it had taken a lifetime, or most of one, to
find her, and the superhuman effort, abetted by extraordinary
luck and coincidence, had yielded . . . what exactly? A friendly
but strictly circumscribed relationship lasting almost seven

years, without notably progressing. The answers to a number
of questions, most of which I had divined for myself, known
really, all along. In most cases it had been sad, more than
anything else, to have these intuitions verified, particularly
those to do with my father.

Many people who, like myself, had been adopted, had written to me asking advice. Advice – what could I tell them? That
finding a lost parent might easily turn out to be a discovery
you were better without? They knew this anyway. Most of
them suffered from the sometimes buried fear that they were
monsters begotten of monsters. In the case of pregnant women,
who featured quite often among the correspondents, especially
those from the USA, that fear surfaced in the form: if there
was something wrong with me, and my parents, will there be
the same something, or worse, wrong with my own child? Am
I forging another link in a chain that goes back to primeval
slime, and may continue until Armageddon?

Dialling my sister's complicated number, I realised that I'd
been mentally testing the word 'sister'. The more I tried the
word out, the better it sounded.

Best of all, she had found me. I'd thought of winkling out
her full name and address somehow, by searching through
Truda's address book while she was occupied in the kitchen,
for example, and then turning up on Margaret's doorstep,
using some ploy – a census check, a vacuum-cleaner sale, whatever – just so I could have a look at her, and even, with a bit
of luck, snatch a look at her children: my niece and nephew.

But it had come about in the rhythm of things. Without
guile, without any techniques of private detection or investigative journalism. Instead of searching and finding, I had been
sought and found.

Waiting for her to answer, my spirits began to lift. The story
had finally been completed. There would be the answers to a
few more questions, another comfortable accretion of family
minutiae, all the high drama was in the past.

How wrong I was.

*   *   *

'Hullo. Sorry it took so long to call back.' And then, hesitating, 'That *is* Margaret?'

It was only when I heard her say 'Yes' – and picked up the depth of her confusion, a quality of being taken aback that was close to the state of being in shock – that the human dislocation implicit in the exchange fully hit me.

And also the extent of my own disturbance. For a start I had no idea how much time had passed. I'd lost the sense of it. There had been at least two other incoming calls, neither of them important, or important enough for them to have left an imprint on my memory. They may have been wrong numbers. I have no idea. I had moved elsewhere; time had elapsed. And now here I was talking to my full sister, a woman in her mid-thirties or more, and I, at the age of 43, knew her so little, our acquaintance was so scanty and new-born, that we lacked even the capacity to recognise each other's voices with certainty.

There seemed no precedent for the experience. It was like suddenly not knowing how to tell the time, or what direction was north. There was no compass, no map, no path, no blazes on the trees to say someone else had been here before. The sense of helplessness, of simply not knowing how to react or what was expected, bridged the long time-gap back to early adolescence, even to childhood. It was overwhelmingly strange.

We were the rawest of recruits in the unknown world of brothers and sisters – it was like being a 'rookie' in the army, not only were the reflexes untutored and unacquired, we didn't even know what the vocabulary signified, let alone how to use it. Naturally, we began out of step. As we talked I felt increasingly dizzy and disorientated. It was like being adrift in an unknown element, space perhaps, and trying to adapt to it without any foreknowledge. A process of trial, error, doubt. The nearest I had been to this before was during a time of incessant travel in the late 1960s, waking in an at first unknown bedroom in an unknown country – too hung-over, or jet-lagged or exhausted for the mind to pinpoint where in the name of God one had geographically fetched up. Meanwhile, it was necessary to go through the motions of groping for the light switch, by no means sure that once located, the light it shed would provide sufficient clues to establish what one needed to know.

For a change, this wasn't happening to me in total isolation. I realised that she was undergoing the same experience, except for her it must be much worse. Almost at once she said something that made me understand how extreme her predicament was. I'd been assuming that Truda, whom I'd seen before Christmas, had left a message, in her will perhaps. It wasn't so. Not at all. The only clue was an entry in an address book. And intuition. My sister – I began to feel proud of her astuteness and courage in calling this stranger in the middle of her grief – had backed a hunch. And also possibly a childish memory of some overheard conversation. Or an apparently unfounded fantasy of having an unknown sister: 'I'd always thought something had happened when I was 7 or 8, around 1950,' she said later.

'But don't you realise? I'm your *elder brother*.'

'Are you?' She still sounded doubtful.

'Of course. I was born in 1937 – when they were working at Harrods in London. Before you were as much as a twinkle in . . .'

And though I went on, almost without hesitation, 'their eye', it was hard to know how to refer to 'them'. 'Our parents'? 'John and Truda'? 'Father and Mother'? 'Mum and Dad'? I had known Truda, after a fashion anyway, but always as 'Truda', never as 'Mother', let alone 'Mum'. As for John, my father, I had never known him at all, never met him, except perhaps in the cradle. I didn't know whether he had ever spoken to me or touched me.

I'd had a little time to take in, quietly on my own, in familiar surroundings, the death of a mother whose motherhood was really only technical. My sadness was acute, but more for the life Truda had lost than what I had lost myself. It wasn't frankly very much. Occasional, often somewhat stilted, and – if it was on her home turf – clandestine meetings. A voice on the phone at night very late. Her punctilious anniversary letters, birthdays, Easter, Christmas: 'Love to Luke'. She wrote

briefly and very conventionally – any attempt to progress beyond the conventional, semi-formal exchanges and she would
withdraw, prevaricate, evade. It was several decades too late
for intimacy. Often we had enjoyed light, companionable times
together, but when it came to my father, or my sister, her
reticence had driven me almost to despair. Sometimes the awk-
wardnesses, the stilted quality of the relationship, made me
angry.

'How did you find me?' I asked.

Margaret's voice, still tremulous, said that my name, and
that of Jill Neville, my ex-wife now, plus some addresses in
Paris and London, had been in 'Mum's' address book. And
also 'Luke: 18 October'.

I explained that it was my son's birthday and also, coinci-
dentally, as the name had been chosen in advance, St Luke's
Day. 'How did she die?'

She explained that it had been a coronary arrest – quick and
sudden – in bed. A neighbour had found her body the next
day. The police had called Margaret. Her voice was shaky and
I realised again how different our grief was. Hers was an
expression of her own deep loss of 'Mum', the mother she
had always known, not a stranger whom she had laboriously,
tediously tracked down, only to find the 'natural mother' was
indeed a stranger.

Margaret was now close to being the same age as me when
I had first met Truda. Was she about to experience a similar
frustration? That of finding simultaneously a close blood-
relation – and a stranger? Worse, an uncomfortably intimate
stranger, one who shared a close physical resemblance, a set of
closely connected, sometimes eerily identical characteristics,
the same reactions and tastes, the same deep prejudices or
passions. Would my sister feel this discomfort when we met?

I didn't want the conversation to drag on, even though it
was getting easier. There was an embryonic sympathy developing. It was like gaining confidence in a foreign language. But
I wanted to see her face to face, not talk via a machine.

'Why didn't she tell me about you?' Margaret felt hurt,
excluded; it was in her voice.

'We must meet face to face, dear,' I said. 'Spend a day
together. She thought that if you found out about me, it would
spoil her relationship with you. I tried to persuade her. She
said "perhaps later". She was very excited when your son was
born – Richard David. I wondered if the "David" was pure
coincidence. I said to her once, "Are you sure that Margaret
doesn't somehow know more about all this than you think?"
She looked frightened. But she said she was sure. Didn't John,
our dad, ever say anything? He sounded so indiscreet. And
drunk.'

'He said something, or hinted something, about 1950. That's
why I always thought Mum might have had, might,' she hesitated, 'have had a baby then.'

'And had it adopted?'

'Yes.'

'Well, maybe we've got another brother.'

'I always imagined a sister.'

'She'd be more likely to be a half-sister, I suppose. As they
had separated by then.'

'Yes. Dad always wanted her back.'

'What was he like?'

'He was such fun. He kidnapped me from school and the
police chased us all across Wales and half way across England.
Then they caught me. But it was the most fun I ever had in
my life.'

This was good to hear. Truda had not made John sound as
if he had been 'fun'. Not for her, anyway. Least of all for
Margaret. 'I've got his cigarette case,' I told her. 'A silver one.
Mum [I almost said Truda] gave it to me. The first time we
met.'

'Have you? I gave him that. I've got a lighter of his. It was
in Mum's flat with the other things.'

'Did you find my letters? And cards?'

'Two cards, that's all. Signed "David". One from France,
one from New York.'

'That's strange, I sent her a lot – and letters. Wasn't there
a book called *God Stand up for Bastards*, inscribed from me?'
Mysteriously, there hadn't been. Except for the two cards, and

the entry in the address book, there had been no trace of my
existence. Somehow all the rest had been obliterated, or hidden, or given to a third party – a bank safe-deposit? I enquired
– for safe-keeping.

'No, she closed her bank account over ten years ago. I
phoned them and they said she didn't have a safe-deposit
either. And Bob searched right through the flat looking for
things. He looked everywhere.'

'Why was that?'

'I had a feeling that she'd left something for me. A message.
Something.'

'What did Bob think?'

'He thought I was crazy.'

'But he did it anyway?'

'Yes.' It was the first time that we laughed at the same time.

'You thought you might find something about a sister?'

'Yes, something anyway.'

'Well, you found me. I'm very pleased.' And so I was. I was
delighted to have been found, almost as delighted to hear that
my father was not, in Margaret's eyes at any rate, the ogre
Truda remembered.

We made arrangements for me to attend the funeral in just
under a week's time and Bob, my newly acquired brother-in-
law, came on the line to exchange a few incredulous friendly
sentences. Margaret had carefully sent him out to the pub
while she made the first call. He sounded like someone still
uncertain that he wasn't the victim of an elaborately set up
practical joke.

I said I was sure that we would all become close friends.
There were other things too, but my recall becomes sketchy.
I was astonished by what had taken place already that evening,
but left with a sense of still unexplained mysteries. How, for
instance, had the traces of my correspondence with Truda,
photographs of Luke, other objects, been removed? She had
not been anticipating death. A medical check not long before
had led the doctor to say her pulse, blood-pressure and heart
were those of a woman twenty years younger.

Margaret and I together would probably manage to find out

– my sister had the curiosity of an investigative reporter, that was clear. Perhaps that was why Truda had been so anxious to keep us apart. Now, as in a fairy story, the truth, or some of it, had been told. But too late.

Late into the night, long after the phone call had ended, I sat writing, just as I had been earlier in the evening when I had suddenly become aware that it was nearly ten, thinking I'd need to hurry to be in time for dinner. Now, however, I was working on something new – an account which became *Family Secrets*, partly for Margaret's benefit, and partly to clarify the confusion in my mind. I began with a description of a man sitting by a window overlooking the canal. It was in the third person – 'He', not 'I' because it was more like a novel than a factual account. And, although I had the evidence before my eyes, including Margaret and Bob's phone number on my notepad, it was hard to think of it happening to me. It was the kind of thing that happened, if it happened at all, to somebody else.

19

The morning of Truda's funeral broke blowing an easterly storm and long before dawn I was poking my head out of the window to sniff the weather.

The wind gusted and roared along the canal, ripping into our skeletal midwinter trees. There was a sharp sodden edge to the gusts, as if they had started off in a latitude where ice-floes slept. It was a classic south of England winter storm: blasting straight in off the North Sea, and cold as an old ache.

The conditions made the drive to Liverpool abnormally dangerous. Lines of articulated trucks from Holland shimmied skilfully along the fast lanes at 80 miles an hour, trailing slipstreams which broke every so often across my windscreen, obliterating any forward visibility.

It was hazardous enough to keep at bay all thoughts unconnected with immediate personal survival. For this, crouched over the wheel in my black duds and rough, pre-dawn shave, I was grateful enough.

Slowing down on the outskirts of Liverpool, it came over me that for some time I had been talking out loud to the empty car. The monologue was being delivered in a tone someone very simple might employ for jollying along a fretful toddler on an awkward journey.

'My God, Mum, you're not missing much today,' was what I seemed to be saying in this silly, coaxing voice. 'Nothing but cold and misery from start to finish. Raining, too. You're far better off where you are, all cosy and snug, and with a nice warm drink I wouldn't wonder.'

I don't know where this voice came from. It was an aber-
ration. But I had no doubt about the way Truda would have
reacted to the day and the occasion. She would have loathed
it all, just as she had loathed going to Leicester to pay grudging, obligatory respects to my father. I remembered her saying
the church had been full of men 'like a football crowd'. That
sounded pure Dad. You could bet that there would have been
a beery, genial undercurrent on the day they put him under the
sod.

It was a pleasure to think how comfortably she had arranged
to make her exit, just when she was getting uncertain about
her health, more noticeably out of step with the way the
world around her was changing. Down, down, down, as she
saw it.

'Nobody's ever going to be bothering you again,' I continued, delving down towards the belly of the tunnel. 'Not Jack
Chester, not me, not the dockers in the pub, or the weather in
the streets, or any damn thing at all. No more having to go
through the motions. Peace at last.'

Truda had apparently taken the easy way. Now we would
see what ogres she had left behind. Bad ones for me, and far
worse for Margaret, the sister I was finally going to meet. The
thought excited and terrified me – but the element that rejoiced
in the prospect of the new connection was stronger than any
other.

There was something dream-like and extra-real about the
meeting and it had a comic streak as broad as a music-hall
punch line. I wondered if my sibling would smell it too. Not,
for sure, if she was like Truda, who never countenanced inappropriate laughter.

Somewhere between the death-dealing intercontinental
trucks and the Mersey Tunnel exit, I found myself wondering
how I was going to be accounted for. What had Margaret told
the other mourners about this unknown stranger in Truda's
life? Had she, perhaps, ducked the issue (that's what I'd do
myself) leaving the elements to grind out their own anarchic
happenstance without human intrusion?

I concentrated on finding Laird Street as I drove out of the

tunnel. The anxieties to do with arriving were lost in more
acute ones about getting there late, as in the old joke.

In the end I drive up no more than three minutes after the
time Margaret had appointed. No time at all to spare, up the
two flights of stairs to Truda's flat running hard. Plenty of
voices from the other side of the door.

When I ring the bell with the musical chime a tall blonde
woman appears at once. She looks smart in her mourning,
welcoming, somehow knowing.

There is something attractive and close about her but none
the less I never for one moment mistake her for my sister.

'Are you David?' she says. And then, without waiting for
confirmation – can that mean she somehow recognises me? –
'I'm Lois. Margaret asked me to show you ...' and I don't
hear what my sister thinks I'd like to be shown. A big drink
most of all. Lois says that Margaret's in the kitchen making
sandwiches.

She's hiding from me, and I don't blame her. I'd be doing
precisely the same, only with bottles and glasses. Sandwiches.
Shades of Truda. Will they be ham and cucumber, cut into
long-based triangles?

Lois smiles, and says friendly things I can't catch in what
I'm surprised to find is a hubbub of people, all squeezed like
tube passengers. At least I hadn't begun by embracing the
wrong relative.

The flat had never been so full of people, the men in dark
suits and black ties, the women equally sepulchral. Everywhere
strange, usually old faces, old with knowing each other and
the emotion of the occasion. But I didn't know any of them.
If they knew me, or knew who I was, they certainly didn't give
any sign.

The crowdedness changed the place completely. I had been
visiting Truda's for seven years minus a few months and in all
that time I had never seen another human being inside the
premises. It had been as if she had lived in a vacuum or, like
some domesticated fish, in her own well-accoutred bowl. There
had never been any outsiders or intruders. Now, hearing an
even later-comer than myself ring the bell and set off the

shorthand chime octave, I was struck by this further novelty. There had never been anyone admitted in the past. No one had ever got as far as trying. Truda had inhabited her own total silence.

Had there ever been such a crowd on her premises in her lifetime? There hadn't I suspected. Jill, my ex-wife now, but still an inveterate giver of large and chaotic parties, once mentioned to Truda that there had been around 200 guests at some occasion. Truda had looked thoughtful. I detected a flicker of revulsion at such social promiscuity, a feeling I shared myself when it got to be past the time for people to go home. Afterwards Truda had asked me: 'What does she do with her *things* before those big parties?'

'Things?'

'Her china and ornaments, the things that get broken.'

'She takes a chance they won't, I suppose.'

Truda didn't comment but looked even more thoughtful. Those were precisely the kind of chances that she would never consider.

Lois, the door-greeter, cleared my way through so I finally entered the kitchen. Several women were busy cutting sandwiches from large plastic packs and distributing cups of tea. Here, in Truda's particular domain, where my visits had always begun, usually with some meal involving salad, tea and similar sliced bread, I met my sister for the first time.

She was dark, I saw with astonishment. Truda's own colour spectrum had been fair to blonde, her face dominated by glasses which accentuated the size of her eyes, their pale blueness, but diffused their perspective giving an impression that they were caged. Margaret's eyes were also blue, bluer than my own, but stronger than either mine or her mother's. There was humour in them, and laughter lines which splayed out faintly and, under different circumstances, might have endowed her with a puckish and even mischievous look.

Her overall shape reminded me at once of Truda, and also of my son Luke. But where Truda had been built on a tiny bird-like scale this person looked more solid, strong even. There was more texture to her, rich contrasts and unexpect-

ednesses implicit in the darkness of her colouring and the intelligent blue gleam of her eyes. Thank God, this woman – my
sister – isn't a fool, I thought. By no means. She's smart, a lot
smarter than me probably.

The knowledge that she was also going through the worst
day of her life and that there was absolutely nothing I could
do about it followed at once. She was pale and her face had a
tautness that suggested she probably hadn't been sleeping
much. She was also very nervous. The feeling communicated
itself to me. I can't remember what words were exchanged,
except that she said she hadn't told anyone who I was except
for Lois, her step-sister, who had let me in, and Bob, her
husband, who appeared looking simultaneously immaculate in
his dark suit and full of a kind of animal verve.

Bob gave a tethered impression – he looked as if he would
welcome something specific to do. We moved into Truda's
bedroom, where I had often slept, she insisting that she was
fine on the sofa, and we already seemed to be drawn into a
conspiracy.

In the rushed, stormy departure, I had mislaid my black tie.
There was a welcome discussion about where I might find a
substitute. To my relief Bob said he would take me to a shop
down the road. We went out into Laird Street, where it was
no longer raining, though the gritty air was damp on the skin
as if distilled through water. It was also very cold. Jesus, what
a day for a funeral.

Disconcertingly, Bob produced a cackle of pure liberated
laughter, as if he had just heard the punch line of a new,
maybe indecent, joke.

'I don't see what's so amusing,' I said. Bob had ginger hair
and eyes of a caramel brown which I was later to recognise in
both his children. He didn't look a natural wearer of dark
suits, though he carried it off with a certain flourish, a hint
of Special Occasion or Saturday Night swagger that wasn't
entirely appropriate. He had zest and a natural quality of
savouring things that I associated with some other environment
I couldn't specify. Perhaps it was to do with the countryside
or men in groups.

'You wouldn't,' he said.

'Why?'

'Because it's you.'

'Me? How d'you mean?' I found myself looking sideways at my own reflection in one of the damp shop windows.

'Your hair. The way it sticks up. You're the spit image of your Aunt Edna, who's in there sitting on the sofa, and hasn't the faintest idea who you are. Margaret's told her you're a friend of Truda's from London.'

'Jesus. Will she recognise me?'

'We'll see.'

By the time we were back in the flat, my black tie now in place, the guests were preparing to leave for the funeral parlour. Margaret looked paler than before. I was able to identify Edna at once, a more solid and less glossy version of Truda. Her hair, like my own, did indeed show a tendency to stick up, and blow around in the slightest breeze. Her eyes met mine and moved on without undue curiosity, or any sign of recognition. The tall blonde, Lois, also caught my eye. I thought I detected a restrained flicker of the same amusement that had engulfed my new brother-in-law.

The guests made their way through the tight little front door out of the flat, their feeling of occasion manifesting itself in tiny needless courtesies, elaborate indications that someone else should precede them or be helped on with a coat. I felt a strong desire to stay alone in the flat but it would have been out of the question. A breach of the protocol of the thing.

'A friend of Truda's from London', my not very convincing label, would not be expected to be deeply affected. Coming from such a distance was itself a sign of respect, a surprising one maybe, as except for Edna, who lived in Leicester, and Lois from Birmingham, they were all Liverpool locals. I had to avoid any excessive show of ... any excess at all. I had to remain a secret, which meant I had no proper place in the events, and no rights, not even that of a son responding to his mother's funeral.

I wondered how the others were feeling. In the few minutes I had been there, several of the women had confessed to being

'quite upset' in tones that might have been used to describe the
after-effects of consuming some novel food, or perhaps watching an over-realistic programme on TV. They hadn't directly
referred to Truda's death or even used the term 'passed away'
which was to crop up later. Apart from the clues provided by
their clothes, a stranger would have no way of telling there
had been a death. Could it be that the women in their black
straw hats kept special funeral 'outfits' in their cupboards? Did
Truda possess one too, now an unnecessary luxury, in her own
wardrobe where the boxes lived?

Were they 'upset' by Truda's death bringing intimations of
their own mortality? Or was it that any disruption of normalcy
was threatening, an intrusion of bad form or unseemliness
which needed careful handling? It was all beyond me. Except
that these mourners were poorer, I might have been back over
twenty years ago at the funeral of David Leitch. I recognised
an emotion, dominant all those years ago, and now instantly
resurrected and remembered like a scent of vines.

It was all to do with escape, an urge to take off southwards
away from the northerly emotional weather. This was what I
had done almost at once after David's funeral twenty years
before, escaping to Rome, far away from Ivy's human climate.
Now I had to find another way to deal with the overwhelming
desire to weep and scream and generally behave in a way that
was impermissible.

I felt uncannily close to something in my great-grandfather,
the cocky nonagenarian preening himself in a photographic
studio in Oxford Street, freezing himself into a sculptural pos-
ture for posterity. Old Will Eagels looked quite deft enough to
know a way of circumventing it all in the first place – he was
palpably capable of a day's prefabricated flu, spent in bed in
a discreet hotel with a cheery lady and a bottle. His reputation
as a lady's man, again perhaps intentionally, had somehow
been preserved quite graphically. My own similar variant on
the family theme might also have included bedroom, mistress,
a wood-fire, an absence of deadlines. Perhaps, blessedly, it was
for some Truda-tailored equivalent of my own philistine Eden,
one equipped with Ovaltine and Dvorak and pearls and em-

broidered water-bottle holders I would bet, that my small,
ungiving mother had lit out.

The funeral parlour was on Laird Street, five minutes' walk
from the flat. Outside, a couple of ancient hearses waited, their
bodywork an intense black with age and incessant polishing.
Evidently the funeral people took care of their rolling-stock.
At this moment the door opened and Truda's coffin was
brought out.

The men carrying it were of average size, yet it looked like
a toy, so tiny it might have been a matchbox or a joke item
made of papier mâché for amateur theatricals. Because she had
a small person's sense of pride in her own diminutive physique
Truda had not, in life, given an impression of being as short
as she was. She always wore very high heels for her London
jaunts. Only in her lambswool slippers and dressing-gown at
night, in Laird Street or London, had I sometimes been struck
with protective amusement at her lack of stature, her dinkiness.
Now the coffin, which might have been a child's, brought that
back. Also her qualities of endurance and the refusal to be
vanquished. Life had always been a battle and in all likelihood
from cradle to grave she had scarcely ever met another human
who was not easily capable of dominating her physically. Perhaps this explained her lack of resources for people outside,
except of course for Margaret. She was standing by the decre-
pit hearse with an expression on her face as if she had been
struck. Truda had needed to fight harder than other people
just to hold on. There were no reserve funds to draw on in
emergency; survival had been the limit.

In all the years I'd known her and all the others I had
imagined what she and John must be like, I had never felt such
sorrow. There was no sense of the amputation I had experienced when David died, or the nagging restless guilt that Ivy
bequeathed. It was heart-rendingly sad of itself that this puff
of life, once so full of importance and dignity, had blown away
like a change in the weather.

From then on it became a true ordeal. The cold began to
grip as we stood around the hearse waiting to leave. There
were more politenesses about who should sit where on the

road to the crematorium. I hovered grimly on the edge of
Margaret's entourage, opening and closing doors and probably
merging with the funeral personnel in the minds of any mourners who noticed my unfamiliar face.

It was all unremittingly slow. There was a sense of killing
time. The pace was appropriate to a vacation in the sun – as
if a long pleasure-filled day lay ahead and rushing would have
been an inappropriate intrusion on the luxury of the moment.
I could see Margaret was trembling with cold; only Bob, like
some ruddy country animal, seemed unaffected, full of energy
and a kind of driving blitheness. My sister, evidently, had made
a successful marriage.

It was finally time for the small cortège to move. The car, I
now saw, was a Humber, a model as dead as the dodo or the
Edsel Ford. At the very last moment, just before this
museum-piece coughed into motion, I clambered aboard unceremoniously. There was a spare seat in front, normally used
by the assistant to the driver. Happily, the driver told me, this
figure, deterred by the weather perhaps, had failed to appear
for the morning shift.

'Do you need him?' I asked. 'What's his job?'

'Help carry the coffin – no problem with that today. You've
seen it – it's no bigger than a kid's.' He shook his head backwards in the direction of Truda, an odd twitchy gesture as if
he had a luxuriant growth of hair obscuring his vision. This
wasn't the case – he was almost completely bald except for a
few strands combed straight back and brilliantined flat to his
pear-shaped skull. He covered it with a greasy black cap and
started up.

There was an immediate complicity between us. He clearly
assumed I was an adjunct to the main party rather than a full
member. From his driving-seat there came the odour of stale
beer and a rawer whiff of spirits, presumably his breakfast
eye-opener, employed to top up the level achieved the night
before and lost during sleeping hours.

He spoke of his work with pride and satisfaction and never
stopped during the twenty-minute journey to the crematorium
which, it turned out, needn't have taken so long. 'People like

to have a bit of a ride,' he said. So he chose a circular route, partly to give us our money's worth like a kindly roundabout operator, partly to avoid arriving too soon, and getting our party confused with the one ahead. While we drove at fifteen miles an hour, he told me about the travails of the previous day. He had been obliged to drive to Bristol and collect a corpse from a coroner's office. It had been a demanding task. There were several morgues in the city and he had fallen into bureaucratic traps establishing the one housing his client.

The idea of corpses being left around, waiting for the satyr-driver to collect them between pub stops, was disturbing. I said something to this effect.

'They should worry,' he replied with a professional's lack of sentimentality. 'I'm the one as has to find 'em and sort it all out. It's the forms as bothers me. Fillin' 'em in, signin' for receipt of deceased, counter-signin', drivin' cross-country with a twenty-five-mile limit on the old hearse ...'

The appalling conversation cheered me up distinctly. I had a feeling that it would probably have cheered up my father John as well. Poor Truda, no doubt, would have done her disapproving look and pretended that she hadn't heard.

Our cunningly circuitous route took us past the Birkenhead Library where Truda borrowed her books about the Romantic poets and other subjects, often historical, which captured her imagination. It was the library where she had ordered my book. When it arrived two weeks later she had carried it out-side with the others she was borrowing, only glancing at it on the broad neo-Classical steps. Seeing a baby picture of myself on the inside jacket, poor diminutive Truda had fainted away like the nineteenth-century heroines for whom she nurtured an adolescent taste.

There was something worrying about this story. How could she have been so surprised by the photograph? She must have been uncertain whether the book was by her son, even though she had read reviews of it and seen me on a television pro-gramme – the seductive flies which, as I intended, had sum-moned her from the bottom of the stream to take the hook.

Why, then, had she reacted so extremely and been ill, as she said, for days afterwards? Surely she must have known what was coming.

There were several explanations. I knew there had been an element of uncertainty in her mind at least until the time she had received my first letter, just as there had in mine, despite detailed evidence in her own letters, until I actually saw her on the doorstep in Birkenhead. In her case it was to do with the possibility that a third party, via Ivy or David or myself, had learned the story and written about it as if it were his own. It sounded crazy, but it was true. A reunion of mother and son in this way after thirty-seven years was simply too unlikely an event for it to be credible until the moment when it took on a palpable physical reality. I had wondered, even on the train, whether she could be an imposter, a relation or friend of Truda's who now wanted to pass herself off as my mother for reasons of craziness or gain. I had even entertained this fantasy despite the evidence of handwriting, which I clearly recognised, even though I no longer possessed samples of the originals to verify the new letters against.

Now I was aware that Margaret was uncertain – was I real, was I an invention? It was Bob, pointing out my physical resemblance to the innocent Auntie Edna, seated composedly in the back, who had verified me. An unbiased witness, he had seen the point at once.

The thought led me to glance back into the body of the hearse where Margaret, Bob and, I now saw, Edna herself were sitting. I felt highly vulnerable. Had Edna, looking at the back of my give-away head, finally detected the resemblance for herself? Certainly she was wearing a strange look.

My eyes caught Margaret's and, as I turned quickly forwards, I could not censor the beginning of a reflexive grin. There was just time to catch the birth of a similar smile on my sister's face. The ghost of a grin more than the real thing.

It was in this instant that the understanding between us began.

20
Margaret's Story

Wavertree, Liverpool in the late 1940s, was a suburb in due process of repair and renovation. Hitler's bombs had left many terraces badly mauled. The large, once fashionable houses looked shabby and dilapidated. Everyone seemed eager to dispel the myth that Liverpool had suffered badly from the air-raids. Now that materials were becoming available, everyone had enthusiastically started to rebuild and clean up the mess.

But not, however, at 21 Sandown Lane. There we rented the ground-floor flat with its enormous over-run garden containing a heap of rubble that had been the air-raid shelter used by ourselves and the other occupants. There were two flats above us. Olive and Terry, a newly-married couple, lived on top. He was in the merchant navy and Olive was often on her own for long periods.

She and Mum became very good friends and she would look after me when Mum had to go into the Liverpool jeweller's to collect and deliver the strings of pearls which she made up at home.

Dad was definitely not the handy-man type. So the back door, so awkward to open, remained permanently shut; the leaking window-frames were stuffed with newspaper: the enormous crack in the living-room ceiling gaped wider all the time.

Dad's talents were many and varied but they didn't stretch to house maintenance or landscape gardening. If he was worried at the prospect of the place collapsing around him he certainly didn't show it. He was the most genial of men, apparently without a care in the world.

Mum's own world was nothing like as contented and carefree. She would spend hour after hour at her work-table, rethreading her pearls and repairing jewellery. My territory was the garden where I played for hours in the destroyed shelter.

Twice a week, a cleaning-lady arrived to scrub the long passage-way and the big stone steps outside the front door. She was a large, remarkably cheerful presence who even let me ride on her back while she was performing her unenviable tasks. She was also a good friend to Mum – quite often she didn't get paid for weeks. At one stage when finances were critical, Mum suggested she might find another job. She not only worked for nothing, she brought us black-market food parcels.

This lady called me 'Queen'. She always had sweets in her pocket, she always smelled of carbolic and, there is no doubt, she always spoiled me. For some reason I never did understand, her attitude to Dad was identical. She was devoted to him. Whenever he was in 'bad books' she would sing his praises and do her best to restore him to favour.

Dad was quite often in 'bad books'. As soon as the evening meal was over he would jump up remembering that he 'just had to see' a man about a new house or a job or a vitally important business deal that wouldn't wait, no sir! Mum would spend the rest of the evening at her work-table, sometimes chatting to Olive, waiting for the warrior's return.

He would often arrive in the small hours, invariably by taxi, and there was every chance that by then he had taken a couple of cronies on board. I remember they often seemed to have whisky, though God knows where they acquired either the drink itself or the cash to buy it. Mum always hustled them in double quick, knowing that in the morning the old lady upstairs would complain bitterly about being disturbed in the middle of the night. Dad was always hearty in manner, even in the mornings. When the late-night sessions were running, his lovely cultured voice (impaired by a dreadful stammer) would take on plenty of extra volume.

On occasions I would be brought down from the bedroom

for cuddles, beery kisses, and the odd half-a-crown. Mum remained tight-lipped – it was when she was called on to provide food for the revellers that her control often snapped.

Food was still rationed. It must have been difficult to produce a meal for three or four hungry men without notice, even allowing for Dad's contributions. He would delve into his briefcase and come up with oysters, smoked salmon or even steak, unheard of luxuries in postwar Liverpool. Even aged 5 or 6 I was old enough to notice that Mum was a long way from sharing my own delirious excitement as Dad complacently unpacked his items of treasure trove, triumphant as a pirate who had run the gauntlet, kept his Jolly Roger flying, and somehow made it home to port again. Where these goodies came from remained a mystery. But Dad's friends were often involved in black-market deals. He was not above the odd transaction himself.

At one stage we had a bedroom filled with cartons of glucose in flat grey tins. Another time hundreds of ladies' powder compacts were stacked neatly in the old wardrobe. Then he bought a consignment of net curtains from a dubious contact and foolishly sold them to one of the biggest stores in the town.

Twelve months later he had to appear in court, luckily escaping a prison sentence but faced with a hefty fine. This misdemeanour was duly reported on the back page of the *Liverpool Post*. Mum was mortified. Dad seemed to think it was rather amusing – he congratulated himself for surviving the episode relatively unscathed.

He had even managed to keep his latest job (how he had managed to get it in the first place was strange enough). He was currently the advertising manager of a large car manufacturer, quite a coup for a self-educated man.

When he was a small child a doctor had diagnosed a heart defect. From then on he had been treated as a semi-invalid – too frail to attend school. He read every book he could lay his hands on and was very knowledgeable about a wide range of subjects. He was a brilliant man, supremely confident, able to charm the birds from the trees and talk his way in or out of anything.

In 1939 he had been called up for army service. Strangely the medics failed to detect any heart problems. It wasn't until Dad discovered how uncomfortable army-issue boots were that he reminded them of his long-standing illness and was promptly discharged.

Dad's drinking caused serious financial problems. He never drank alone, and loved an audience. Publicans from miles around welcomed him. Their patrons treated him as a local celebrity. He was a marvellous raconteur and the company could look forward to an evening's entertainment with Dad footing the bill. Domestic bills were another matter. He boasted that he collected threatening letters as some people collected cigarette cards. If Mum hadn't been able to contribute to the family income I'm sure we would have been homeless.

I remember an occasion when Mum and I had been 'out' (that's to say hiding behind the door) when the rent-man called. With his impeccable sense of timing, Dad staggered into the hallway carrying a present for me – a very large doll's house. He came face to face with the collector and after a few convincing words the man went on his way, happy but empty-handed. Dad thought it was terribly amusing.

On reflection I can see that Mum must have been very unhappy. Her family were all so respectable and secure and law-abiding. Yet there she was, married to this charming rogue. Whenever there were family gatherings, the disapproval became apparent. Dad often absented himself from these occasions and if he did grace the company with his presence it was a safe bet that he was well fortified in advance. He would recount shocking stories that had everyone in the grip of outraged and embarrassed silence.

Truda often withdrew into herself, working late into the night to pay the most pressing bills. Perhaps she welcomed the hard work as a distraction.

There was a stage when Dad was obviously between jobs and we seemed to spend a lot of time together. He loved to take me out and show me off to his friends. There were frequent trips on the Mersey Ferry, excursions always ending in some little coastal pub on the Wirral peninsula. Dad was totally at home in these tough communities with bad reputations – the shore-line abounded in caves, and smuggling had always been a way of life in the area. There was still an illicit feeling about its pubs which went beyond their habit of staying open 'after hours'. The locals talked in low voices, a sly confidentiality between them, in which Dad always shared as if he was one of the gang. For him, it was his second home after Liverpool. I would often sit in the bar, happy with crisps and fizzy drinks, listening to Dad and the landlord setting the world to rights.

Years later, when Dad was living in the Midlands, he would say how much he missed the Mersey. He could never visit Liverpool without a trip to the Pier Head. I have inherited his affection for the place and can never resist a chance to sniff the same peculiar ozone.

Because of a dispute with the education authorities, I was not attending school at this time. The two local schools were deemed 'unsuitable' by my parents because of religious and social differences – one was too Catholic, the other too rough. The establishment they preferred was full – so I stayed at home. Mum and Dad undertook the responsibility of teaching me to read and write themselves. They did an excellent job and were very annoyed when they received a summons because of my non-attendance at school. It was decided that I would enrol at a smart private academy nearby. How they intended to pay the fees I'm not sure. But Dad went along to see the headmistress.

The interview went very well until the unfortunate woman asked him to bring me for an interview. Dad was furious. He told her in no uncertain terms that if his money was good enough then his child was good enough too. I think it must have been a time when Dad was 'in funds' and very much riding high. Certainly he took Mum and myself to the Wirral by taxi, itself a great extravagance, and we visited several picture-book Tudor houses surrounded by yellow gorse and purple heather, because Dad (in high, expansive mood) was 'thinking of buying a property'. All this was an adventure for me but I suppose poor Mum couldn't think of anything except the taxi-meter ticking. She didn't have the alcohol in her to take any pleasure in his dreams any more, and she took little notice when he admired the sunset over the River Dee and claimed you could see the Welsh mountains along the horizon. Unlike me, she knew that no matter what great scheme Dad currently had 'in the pipeline', when it came to paying the rent or school fees we would end up as usual – skint. The day of the court hearing was drawing perilously near when suddenly the favoured school rang to say that they had managed to find me a place for one term only. So my formal education began a bit late – I was just over 6. The school was a bus ride away and Mum would deliver me at the gate. Afterwards she would often visit her sister Hilda who lived nearby.

Hilda's house was modern and semi-detached with a pleasant orderly garden, bright paint and a tranquil atmosphere. Mum must have felt so envious. There was no tranquillity in our house. Auntie Hilda's husband had a share in a florist's – he worked long hours for what was probably a meagre return. To help out they took in a 'paying-guest', a recent widower. He had a young daughter called Lois – most of the time she was away at boarding-school in Southport, the Lancashire resort down the coast.

When she was home for the holidays the two of us got on very well. So apparently did Mum and Lois's father, Jim Bucknall. He was convalescing – all his life he had suffered from serious illness. His family were butchers and had a string of shops in Liverpool. While he recovered, his own shop was being managed by his brother-in-law. Jim spent much of his time in bed or, if the weather was good, sitting in the garden with a rug wrapped round his legs. Mum would often keep him company. Hilda must have approved of the relationship. She would bring drinks to them outside and the atmosphere was always convivial.

Dad's 'brother' lived in an almost identical house in the same area but in very different circumstances. Flo and Willy owned a fish and chip shop and four greyhounds, one of which belonged to Dad. The place smelled strongly of pickled onions, stored in every available spot in the kitchen. The dogs had to be exercised regularly. Dad and I would take them to a local park called The Mystery for hours.

Dad adored these animals but I was never so enthusiastic and kept my distance. One afternoon I was bitten, not a serious wound but enough to make Mum furious. She decreed that I was never to go there again. I was secretly relieved. Dad and Willy continued with the dogs and went on working at a variety of enterprises which they believed would make, if not their fortunes, at least a fast buck, to free them from their constant financial difficulties.

They were manufacturing ice-cream in Auntie Flo's kitchen for instance. They'd hired a van and took me to Thursaston Hill, a local beauty spot on the Wirral. My role was to stroll among the day-trippers enjoying an enormous cone and informing the 'punters' where they could buy the same thing. Business would not have been so brisk, I guess, if they could have seen the kitchen where the stuff came from, with the pickled onions and the resident dogs.

Then came the time when Dad and Willy went into floor coverings. A small green van arrived outside the flat. I dashed out for a ride around the block. Alas, there was no room for me – the van was packed solid with rolls of linoleum, yet another commodity in short supply at the time. Dad was jammed in the driver's seat. The passenger seat had been removed. Uncle Willy was crouched on the floor, lino above, below and all around him. They were going to Birkenhead market for the day, in pursuit of a very quick turnover.

Their merchandise, as so often, had been acquired from someone they had met in the pub. Mum begged them not to go as she was sure they would be arrested. They had no licence, either for street-trading or the van. Still they set off, undeterred.

Mum was anxious all day but they returned in high spirits. The van had broken down in the Mersey Tunnel but business had been excellent. Mum was instructed to find a baby-sitter at once – she was to be wined and dined on the proceeds. It was one of Dad's most successful ventures, a rare one.

One afternoon I came home from school and was surprised to find the flat almost bare except for some cardboard packing-cases. We were moving. The car arrived and off we went to Auntie Hilda's. Mum somehow omitted to mention that Dad was not included in the accommodation changes. We stayed there over Christmas and, if Dad failed to arrive, the seasonal festivities were a great compensation.

Soon we would have a new house by the seaside, I learnt. I was very excited. I didn't take it in that all these future plans were to exclude Dad, even when we moved to Southport with Jim and Lois. It was a beautiful house that had been rented quite near Lois's school. She was to continue there, as a day-girl now rather than a boarder. It was marvellous living so near to the sand and sea. Uncle Jim, as I now called him, was still not fully recovered: life seemed an extended holiday. Lois and I spent all our spare time on the beach, but I was homesick for Liverpool – and Dad.

Years later Olive told me what really happened on Christmas Eve while we were elsewhere. Dad had returned to find that his home of several haphazard years standing had been picked clean to the bone. Lavishly equipped with gifts probably, if they hadn't been forgotten in the pub, he had arrived noisily and late, coming home for Christmas, only to find nothing at all. Olive, their neighbour of so many hard years, had her ears cocked and heard the characteristic John Chester entry. She had wondered whether to go down, and decided not to. Perhaps he would come up? Instead: 'He stayed for half an hour, walking about. Then he just left, slamming the door behind him. He really banged it as loud as he could. I felt sorry for him. He was a man who had lost everything.'

Ignorant of all this, I knew only that I had lost Dad. He would be coming, I was assured, but no one seemed to know when. As I had so little previous schooling, the holiday could not last and it was settled that I should go with Lois. I was taken on at Farlee High School and, for reasons I could never quite determine, we were enrolled as boarders. The rented house was within walking distance of the school. Yet this did not mean that we had many more home visits than the other

children. It was quite exciting at first. Lois had been there for
two or three years already so I was quickly accepted. But there
was still no sign of Dad. Mum thought that he probably had
a job abroad and would see me during the holidays. I later
learned that he had no idea where we were. To find us he
hired a private detective. Mum had covered her tracks well. It
took him three months to complete the mission and we were
only eighteen miles away.

My eighth birthday arrived. Instead of the expected visit
from Mum, the head called me into her study to give me
presents and a card from home. I was totally mystified. Mum
was only round the corner. But the highlight of my birthday
was still to come.

Dad arrived unannounced one evening soon after, demanding to take me out for supper. The head could not allow it
without previous permission but we went anyway. I was overjoyed to see him as well as upset and a bit tearful at Mum's
absence. This was too much for Dad and so we boarded a
train for Leicester, the Midlands town where he had been
staying for the previous fortnight or so. When we arrived, he
rang the head to inform her that I would not be returning. The
poor woman became hysterical, screaming that she would have
to alert the police. Dad seemed unconcerned. I would be well
looked after, he said, and put the phone down. I think that
later he came to regret this impulsive move.

I settled in to his rented digs with no possessions other than
the clothes I stood up in. My gypsy life had begun. When he
made the trip to Southport I am sure that he never intended to
return with me. If he had given the matter a little thought he
would have realised how impractical it was to have me there.
He had only been there a short time himself, he was working
full-time, and as yet had not made his mark on the unsuspecting Leicester populace. This was to come later.

The next two or three weeks were spent staying the night
here and there with people I had never seen before. They knew
as little about Dad's long-term plans as I did. Dad was his
usual buoyant self. One night a policeman knocked at the door
asking for him. Once he had established that I was at the same

address he set off on his bike to inform the local Welfare
Officer. They would return to sort out all the problems, he
promised. In Dad's mind there were no problems, except the
ones 'They' would create. So we packed our bags quickly and
made for the local bus station. I have wondered since if Dad
knew exactly where we were making for that night or if he
just picked a name at random. But before long we were en-
sconced in a large country pub on the outskirts of Leicester.

This village inn must have been Dad's idea of heaven. It
soon emerged that we could stay, but I didn't like the look of
the lady behind the bar who I was supposed to call 'Auntie'.
We moved off to stay with an old lady who had a tiny cottage.
She was kind and I liked her but this too was to be a very
short stay. The cottage was basic. That is to say it had no gas
or electricity. The candles and oil lamps must have been very
charming in the summer months. But during what seemed to
me a dreadfully severe winter, the place was abominably cold.
How the old lady had survived these conditions year after year
was beyond me. On the night we arrived there was a particularly vicious snow storm and we were literally snowed in.
There was only one inadequate coal fire so we spent three
shivering, sleepless nights waiting for the snow to melt. Since
then country cottages have held little or no appeal for me.

Our next port of call was much more comfortable. This
time we had been offered accommodation by a young couple
in a new, warm house. We stayed there quite a while. I even
went to the village school for a few weeks and I made friends
with a boy whose father was the richest man in the village.
They owned a farm and, much more impressively, a television
set. One afternoon I was invited for tea. Later the gentleman
farmer opened the double doors of the mahogany cabinet to
reveal this marvellous acquisition. No MGM epic was ever
received with more excitement and pleasure.

However, my viewing days were numbered. The education
authorities had alerted the social services. One morning I was
whisked off unceremoniously to a council-approved foster
home. From there, for the first time in twelve months, I spoke
to Mum on the telephone. Dad ranted and raved but the autho-

rities were adamant. They placed me with yet another 'Auntie' and there I stayed, enjoying it, for seven months.

Mum now came and visited me several times. Dad had moved into a lovely flat nearby. I think by now even he admitted that this was by far the best arrangement – even he couldn't run for ever. He had started to work at an army barracks in the Leicester suburb called Glen Parva. I was in another school and stayed (unofficially) with Dad at weekends. He had a flat with french windows opening on to a beautiful garden. More importantly it was next to the local concert hall. In the summer with the doors open we were treated to our own private recital. My love of orchestral music began then. That beautiful flat and the music held very special memories, but as ever I had to move on.

Dad was now on the receiving end of some kind of case instigated by Mum. I was never officially informed but as usual I picked things up from conversations that ended abruptly the moment I walked in. Words like adultery, enticement and custody seemed to feature strongly. I didn't know what they meant but I did know that for the first time in his life Dad was worried.

When the case was heard Mum won custody of me – Dad was to have reasonable access. I felt like a lifeless trinket and wondered if everyone had forgotten I was a person. Years later somebody said I should have been called 'the suitcase kid'. It fitted me perfectly at that time. I was off again, this time to Liverpool and Mum.

There were many journeys like that in the years to come, always alone. I invented a travelling companion. He was a good friend, agreed with my decisions, and was always ready to eat and drink when I was. If any problems arose, I consulted him and we worked out a solution together. He didn't have a name or even a face but he was there and that was a comfort. He went his own way when I reached my destination, but always arrived promptly on the train for the return journey.

Mum and Jim met me in Liverpool and we went off to his house behind the shop in Admiral Street. I wasn't impressed because the shop and the living quarters above and behind

were old and barn-like. Jim was a quiet, reliable man but I felt
somewhat cool about him. In my eyes he was a very pale
imitation and replacement for my charming, ebullient, extravagant father. I made no effort to get to know him even though
he was very kind and treated me exactly the same as Lois, his
own daughter. Looking back this must have been very painful
for Mum. I think she loved Jim very much but her attempts to
create any bond of affection between us failed miserably. The
situation became intolerable. I hated the smell of meat, hated
the cold house, and was at best indifferent to Jim. Mum got in
touch with her old friend, Olive.

It was decided that I should stay with Olive's mother for a
little while as Jim's health was declining rapidly. I stayed there
for a 'little while' that lasted eleven years. Almost as soon as
I moved in with the Williams family, Jim went into hospital.
He came back a very sick man, and though Mum looked after
him devotedly, he died that summer. She was devastated. The
thriving business had long since become a liability. Mum was
left with nothing but debts. While Jim had been ill, the shop
had been supervised by a succession of managers. Mum
worked alongside them for periods but she didn't know enough
about the business to prevent what profits there were from
being diverted into their own pockets. She became very bitter
and withdrawn but, in the end, helped by Jim's younger brother, she managed to sell the shop and the house. She was left
with some furniture, but little else. She found herself a bedsitter
in the area and went back to the jewellery trade again.
Although she worked long hours in one of the city's largest
shops, she was poorly paid, and seemed unable to accept her
loss. Dad's maintenance payments for me were as irregular as
ever. She must have felt her problems were immense.

Although I was living on the other side of the city I did see
much more of her and we became much closer. I felt I had all
her affection and devotion now and didn't have to share her
with an outsider. I was blissfully unaware of her money trou-
bles. To her credit she never told me that she walked to work
to save money so I could have the extras I needed. The
Williams family were very close-knit and kind but they found

me something of a puzzle. My idea of heaven was to retire to my room with an armful of books, rather than play with the local children. In twelve months I had exhausted the library. The Williams's efforts to get me to join clubs and make friends came to nothing. 'Only child, lonely child,' they said, shaking their heads wisely. It was true that I didn't make friends easily – I'd never stayed anywhere long enough to learn how. But I was happy, spending the school holidays with Dad and seeing Mum every weekend.

The holidays were marvellous. Dad ensured that every day was busy and exciting. We went to London and he took me on a guided tour of Harrods, which was wonderful enough, though I had hoped to see Buckingham Palace. He said I could have anything in the store as a memento. I chose, instinctively, something cheap – a box of carbon paper. There was another adventure in Nottingham. Dad insisted on going to a restaurant called The Black Cat, which he knew from 'the old days'. He began reminiscing with the owner, and soon Dad's mind turned to buying the place himself. I remember them doing drawings on the menu, because Dad was planning to change the kitchens around to make them more efficient. He had a lot of friends in Leicester who were actors, touring the working men's clubs that were so popular then. We would travel to Northampton, Coventry, Nottingham and spend the day sightseeing, then meet up with the 'theatricals' for the show in the evening. They made a great fuss of me and allowed me to go in their dressing-rooms to experiment with the stage make-up and admire the sequins and feathers.

It was an ideal arrangement because Dad could drink happily all evening, I was being entertained by his friends, and they would take us back to Leicester in the early hours. Heady stuff for a demure 12-year-old. I very soon learned, however, that Mum didn't approve of excursions to the Midlands 'night-spots', so I played up the visits to art galleries, cathedrals and exhibitions. The evening adventures I conveniently forgot. Why not? Mum was happy, Dad was happy, and only I knew that my censored accounts saved ugly situations from developing later.

I also played the same game the other way round. Dad was always furious whenever I mentioned John, Jim Bucknall's younger brother. He had a beautiful house on the outskirts of Liverpool with stables and a big, landscaped garden. Mum and I often spent weekends there. He and his wife made us very welcome. They would have a night out while we baby-sat and could be together enjoying the luxurious surroundings that Mum found so impressive. We stayed there one Christmas and I was foolish enough to tell Dad how the local church choir had come to sing carols in the reception hall on Christmas Eve.

Dad's sour response was that John must have paid well for this privilege, so future visits went unreported. I didn't lie about them but simply neglected to mention them. It became quite fun hood-winking them both. I congratulated myself on being so astute. For once I was in control of the situation which was very satisfactory.

School work had never presented any problems, considering my formal education had been so limited. There were gaps in my knowledge of the most elementary subjects but I got by on the strength of reading so much. I was also a master of bluff. In due course, I delighted everyone by winning a scholarship to the local commercial college. It took me only half a day there to realise that these children were extremely intelligent. They didn't need to deceive anyone, and if I was to keep up things had to change dramatically. I started working very hard, though I had always been lazy, and when the exam results came out, my self-imposed regime paid off.

Dad was so pleased that he sent me a watch. Mum was also delighted – and so I had another watch. I never mentioned to my fellow pupils that I was fostered: the very word stuck in my throat. My friends thought I was a spoilt and over-indulged child, my smallest whim being indulged by one doting parent or the other. In a way it was true. Although my parents were not even on speaking terms, they seemed eager to outdo each other with expensive gifts, very often duplicated. Apart from the watches I acquired two sets of luggage, two signet rings, two portable radios. I would gladly have exchanged the goodies to see both of them sitting in the Philharmonic Hall for the annual prize-giving, instead of Mum alone, or on rare occasions just Dad. Even for me they would never come face to face.

Later that year one of Dad's friends lent us a holiday house on the coast. We were to spend a week there and another week in Leicester. Dad may have thought that as I had done so well at school I was mature enough to understand how badly Mum had treated him. I had to listen to example after example of how she failed to understand his ways and needs. It may be that I had grown up more than even he had thought. For the first time in my life I began to think that living with Dad might be less than ideal, and to sympathise with Mum. Dad was morose. The visits to Harrods and The Black Cat had been ways of keeping close to Mum through me – whatever had happened he still loved her, adored her. He had always believed (or dreamed) that they would get together again in the end, and they had never divorced. But finally I think he had come to accept that the two of them would never be reunited. By now Mum had found a good new job, was enjoying a better standard of living, and had come to terms with Jim Bucknall's death. Dad, I think, had given up the fight. I don't know why he chose to burden me with his bitterness but it upset me so much that I returned to Liverpool at the end of the week instead of going on with him to Leicester.

I never told Mum why, but I think she knew. It was the start of a very lonely period. There was no one I could confide in. I was depressed by the momentous change in Dad's outlook on life and his letters were full of the same bitterness. My school work suffered very badly, I had no energy, and I think I just gave up. I was dreading the next visit to Leicester.

The one bright spot during this miserable time was acquiring my first boyfriend. He was old beyond his years and never probed into the problems he must have known I had at home. I never volunteered any information. We got along very well. He did my homework, went to the library for me, met me in the morning and took me home in the evening. I think he saved my sanity. The close friendship, which lasted until I had left school and found a job, made life bearable – my solid, reliable friend was also a model for choosing friends in the future.

My first job and the taste of independence that went with it
was particularly sweet. Dad's irregular cheques had been a
cause of trouble for as long as I could remember. He should
have carried out the transaction with Mum. Instead he made
a point of sending the cheques to me, a reminder probably that
he was my sole provider. Mum always bought most of my
clothes; the cheques led to tension, the sense of exaggerated
relief when they came, the fear of future rows when they
didn't. I always felt he resented paying for me. Very likely this
was wrong and he simply forgot or felt like rebelling against
the system for the hell of it. But I shouldn't have had to feel
so grateful when he fulfilled his responsibilities without a fuss.
That first wage packet freed me from being a burden to either
parent ever again.

I hated the job, the antiquated office, the bitch of a super-
visor who taught us the intricacies of very early computer
programming. It paid well for a 16-year-old, but though I had
shown an aptitude for figures at school, computers were not
for me. Being able to support myself more than compensated
for the dreary surroundings – I was determined to stick it out
and I did. My contemporaries mostly earned less than me and
were envious of my 'good job' – I looked smug and never
admitted that I hated every minute.

Now I was independent my relationship with Dad became
easier again. He was pleased about my job and I felt within
my rights to make my own decisions without consulting anyone. My rebellious years had begun and it gave me a sadistic
pleasure to announce 'I have decided ...'. Dad admired the
new me. His bleak period had long disappeared – now he was
genial, optimistic and very generous again. The expensive gifts
came regularly and he took particular pleasure in shopping
trips. He liked announcing grandly before the impressed assist-
ants that I could have anything I wanted, knowing full well
that I would choose something within his budget. I think he
was relieved that I had finally grown up and we could communicate much better. He had been brought up without sisters,
he had no previous experience with children, and it must have

been hard to cope with a young daughter. His natural charm
had always endeared him to women and I was no exception.
An evening out with him was something to remember – only
the best was good enough for his beautiful daughter.

I never was a beauty – but it was nice pretending. Our last
holiday together was probably the happiest time we ever had,
and I thank God that my last memories of my beloved father
were such good ones. He was in high spirits. Things were
going well and his various outside interests were keeping him
very busy. He was also able to combine business and pleasure
in his favourite way. A friend of his had started a small cater-
ing firm and Dad had taken on the responsibility for ordering
the food and drink for various functions. For many years now
he had lived with a couple who also had an interest in the new
venture. Things were hectic, but Dad loved every minute of it.

On the last trip I felt like a visiting dignitary. I was introduced to innumerable people and had to look interested in all
the many different projects he had in mind. I managed with
sufficient aplomb and returned from Leicester with a gold bracelet, my last gift from this generous man.

Mum's life was very busy too. She was the manager of a
small but busy jeweller's on the Wirral. The owner suggested
that it would be easier for her if she moved across the water.
Travelling every day was tiring, time-consuming and expensive. With his help, she found a flat and was preparing to make
the momentous move – for a Liverpudlian – to Birkenhead.

She was thrilled with the flat and her boss was paying the
moving expenses. I helped her with the packing and preparations but because I was working she had to make the move
itself on her own. The van was pulling away from her new
address, leaving her surrounded by cases and tea-chests, when
a policeman arrived. They had been trying to catch up with
her all day.

Dad had suffered a fatal heart attack at work that morning.
Mum arrived at our place in Liverpool looking only slightly
dishevelled, but one look at her face told me all. In their usual
calm and efficient way the Williams family managed to get us
on the evening train for Leicester. I stayed for a week with

Dad's friends and remember very little about it. My mind has a safety-valve that switches off completely when the going gets too rough and that week it worked well. Mum had to get back to the new job but returned to Leicester for the funeral. She was in a terrible position. Everyone knew that she and Dad had been separated for years but she wouldn't let me face the ordeal alone. She could hardly play the grieving widow – and it seemed all of Leicester wanted to pay their respects.

The crematorium was packed, mostly with men, and it crossed my mind that it could have been a football match. Everyone was good to me but I couldn't get back to Liverpool quick enough. The first thing I did was to call the office and tell them I wouldn't be coming back. They thought I must still be in shock and said they would hold the job until I was better, but I knew my days as a junior trainee were over and felt mightily relieved. I never wanted to see the place again.

After a holiday in Italy the old combination of bluff and good luck worked again. I found a job with ICI which required concentration and precision and left no time to dwell on the past. I was still in touch with friends from the old job and we spent many hours in a tiny club in Hayman's Green, close to where I lived. It was owned and run by the mother of an old friend and consisted of three small basement rooms smelling of damp and decaying wood with a tiny stage in one corner. Mrs Best appeared only briefly to collect the entrance fees, her son Pete played the drums for the resident group. If I turned up with a good crowd he would often let me in for nothing. The focus of attention was the juke-box and his group had three or four 'spots' in the course of the evening. Towards the end our coins often ran out – 'The Quarrymen' would experiment with unrehearsed numbers to fill the gap. They were terrible. I remember people imploring others to feed the machine and shut them up. In due course 'The Quarrymen' both improved and changed their name to 'The Silver Beatles'. The juke-box was redundant. John, George, Paul and Pete sang themselves hoarse without anyone complaining. Soon they became just the Beatles and acquired a contract to play in Germany.

Since Dad's death Mum and I had become much closer. For the first time in my life I was able to give affection wholly to one parent without feeling disloyal to the other. I spent most weekends with her. When I went out whoever was taking me would drop me back to her flat. Just before my twenty-first birthday I moved in to her flat in Birkenhead, the first time we had actually lived together since the summer at Southport when I was 7.

It was a wrench leaving the Williams family who had taken care of me for so many years. But they understood that the timing was right. Mum was overjoyed. We found a lot of pleasure in living together but, after Liverpool, Birkenhead took a lot of getting used to. I made many new friends but still crossed back over the Mersey whenever I could to visit my old haunts. By now the Beatles had returned from Germany and were playing regularly in Mathew Street. The Cavern was probably the worst appointed club in Liverpool but they generated more excitement in one lunch-time than all the rest of the places in town could muster in a month. The queues outside were themselves a source of entertainment. There wasn't much choice. Despite our impassioned claims to the doormen that we were friends of Pete Best (true) and Brian Epstein (we bought records from his shop) they kept us waiting with the ever-growing hordes of fans.

This was hardly Mum's territory. But when I started to go out with the son of someone highly influential in Liverpool she was very enthusiastic indeed. 'He's just right for you,' she insisted, and made a great fuss of him when he came to the flat. I'm sure she had hoped that his visits would continue indefinitely until we ended in front of the altar. But it wasn't to be.

One night at a folk club I met a particularly good-looking young man wearing the regulation duffel coat and Ban-the-Bomb badge. He didn't stand a chance. I knew as soon as I saw him. Incredibly, his background was very similar to mine. He too was the child of a broken marriage. He too had been brought up by a succession of 'aunts' and had been moved around all over the country. His advantage over me was that

there had been two of them – his sister had accompanied him
and they were very close. I envied them their obvious devotion.

Mum's social ambitions for me were thwarted. Bob was a
butcher and a very down-to-earth person, and he lacked the
social graces she had admired in my previous suitor. But this
did not stop us getting married within the year. We started life
in an attic flat, only a stone's throw away from her. Our new
home was five flights up, draughty, and had a leaky roof and
a thriving mouse population. We stayed there for twelve
months, working and saving for a proper place of our own,
and we both agree it was the happiest year of our lives. Mum
may have been disappointed but she soon conceded that I had
made a wise choice. She and Bob got on so well in fact that I
sometimes felt the outsider when they were huddled together
over one of their shared passions – crossword puzzles.

She came to stay most weekends when we finally moved to
our new house in North Wales about twenty miles away. In
1970 our first child, Gillian Wendy, was born. Mum retired a
few months later and then she was able to spend even more
time with us. Gillian, whom she spoiled unashamedly, was the
main attraction. Mum had also begun to enjoy her unaccus-
tomed leisure. For the first time in her life she was able to
indulge herself – reading, listening to music, visiting exhibitions and staying with friends. She was also able to travel
abroad – Denmark, where we had relations, became a great
love.

She still stuck to her trusty pearl-stringing at home. It kept
her in touch with friends in the trade and when they tried to
get her to go back to work she was always delighted. Because
of her years of experience as a jeweller she was in great demand. Her only problem was accommodation – the old lady
she had shared a small house with for so long was becoming
worryingly senile. Mum badgered the local council to find her
somewhere else to live but to no avail. She had to sweat it out
on the waiting list.

We wanted a second child but it didn't happen. By now
Gillian was 4, and with my own memories of being an only
child uppermost I consulted a specialist. His parting words

were: 'I don't think you'll ever conceive again but I hope you prove me wrong.' I certainly did. Exactly twelve months later our son was born. Naturally we were delighted, and so was Mum – I remember how particularly pleased she seemed when we decided to call him Richard David.

It was an exceptionally good time for her. After waiting so long she had been allocated a modern apartment of her own. Bob and she slaved to decorate it, and I was worried that she was doing too much (she had also allowed herself to be persuaded into taking a part-time job). But nothing was too much for her at this time. She had never been so optimistic and full of life. She called Richard David's birth 'the icing on the cake'. I took this as a reference to her new home.

To my surprise she began going up to London to see some exhibitions and to stay with 'an old friend' she had known many years before but for some reason had never previously mentioned. It was a plausible story and I was so immersed in looking after the new baby that I didn't think anything about it.

Gillian had been an easy baby. Richard turned out to be the opposite. By the time he was 6 months old, I was physically and mentally exhausted, so low that I was almost suicidal. Mum moved in to help and though she was sympathetic I realised that my illness totally mystified her. She simply couldn't understand my depression because she could see no reason for it. Perhaps there was no reason in the sense she meant, but I was still acutely ill. With the help and care of a sympathetic doctor and an understanding husband I recovered completely. But even writing about this awful period gives me nightmares.

Richard had been a difficult baby and he grew into an impossible toddler. This inquisitive, hyperactive, irrepressible child required constant attention. I would often catch Mum looking at him with a strange expression. Was she thinking how strange it was that Richard should be so unlike his sister Gillian? I assumed so but how wrong I was.

When we went on Sundays to visit Mum in her new flat I was always surprised at how calmly this house-proud person accepted Richard's chaotic activity. Far from being worried about her prized possessions, she found his romping very funny. One of these regular occasions provided a glimpse of Mum's 'other life', as I now know existed.

I noticed something strange about the *Sunday Times* she had been reading. A small square, which must originally have contained a head and shoulders photograph of the author, had been cut out of the book reviews page. I asked her who was in the photograph. Mum was never flustered or stuck for words, so I was amazed to see her composure crumble. She produced a story about burning the page with a cigarette-end – such an obvious lie that I looked around to see Bob's reaction. Inevitably, he was dealing with Richard and had missed the whole episode. She scuttled off, leaving me to read the text. The subject was not one that Mum would have been interested in under normal circumstances. The photograph, which she had so carefully cut out, was of someone called David Leitch.

The name meant nothing to me but I was curious.

I bought my own copy of the *Sunday Times* the following week. Almost immediately I found the same name on the same page – but this time the photograph was there too. It was only a tiny photo, and I was disappointed. I would like to record that it struck me as being familiar in some way. But it didn't. It was just a face. But there were a few words underneath saying that the writer was himself married to a novelist called Jill Neville.

I pondered this information for a time. Then it struck me. Could Jill Neville be the sister I had imagined existed all those years before – the daughter of Mum and Jim Bucknall? The reason, if that's what it was, why Mum had missed my birthday, as Dad had pointed out? All kinds of niggling, irritating questions crowded my mind, but there were no answers. In the meantime I read David Leitch whenever I could. I reached the conclusion that he was certainly not the shadowy figure I had always felt must exist somewhere on the edge of Mum's life. I did not see how someone of 25 – and that was the age the missing person had to be – could write so confidently on a variety of matters, international ones mainly, in such an illustrious paper. I learnt that he lived in Paris and that he wrote very well. In time, since there was no information forthcoming from Mum and I didn't want to cross-examine her, I stopped thinking about this mystery.

Our lives continued as before. For New Year's Eve 1980, according to a pattern that had developed over the years, Mum looked after the children so that Bob and I could go to a late party. The next weekend we visited her. She seemed well. There was a plan to visit South Africa, where her younger brother lives, but she was nervous about making the long journey alone. I tried to persuade her to buy the tickets – her health had been exceptionally good for someone of her age, and I told her she should make the most of it.

Four days later a policeman arrived on the doorstep while we were having supper. He told us that Truda had been found dead in her flat.

I felt so alone. Friends told me how fortunate she had been, no suffering or long illness. They were probably right, but it was no comfort. I went through the motions of arranging the funeral in a haze of misery and disbelief. One of the worst jobs was packing up all her possessions. It seemed like an invasion. She had been such a private person. Papers and documents had to be found which wasn't difficult because everything was in perfect order. We found nothing revealing, nothing secret, and as far as I remember there was no thought in my mind that we would – the suspicions about David Leitch and Jill Neville were now some years in the past and I had other things on my mind.

But all the same, going home one night the idea came to me that there was someone else who should be told what had happened. I didn't know who, but I was convinced there was somebody who should be given the news. I found myself reading through Truda's address book later that evening. The children were asleep, I had suggested to Bob that he go and have a drink, and the house was unusually silent.

The address book was one I had given her and like everything else it was meticulously neat. In due course I came across something unusual – instead of a name the initials 'D.L.'. I realised at once that this must be the same David Leitch.

There was no address but three different phone numbers –
two obviously abroad, the other starting with the London
code. I decided to try it – even if he wasn't there someone
might know his whereabouts. When he answered himself I was
stunned. I am not often at a loss for words. In this instance I
found myself struggling for breath and could hardly get anything out.

The next few minutes will be engraved in my mind for ever.
I had a brother. Not a half-brother, or step-brother, but a full,
complete, total male me. We were both in a very emotional
state – he noted down my number and promised to call
back.

Bob reappeared and when I told him the news he was as
astounded as me. We sat at opposite sides of the kitchen table,
a rapidly diminishing bottle of whisky in the centre. It was
hard for either of us to take in this revelation.

David soon called back. An hour or so later I knew for a
certainty that I wasn't the only child of my complicated parents. This stranger with the lovely voice shared the same dis-
tinction. That night I didn't even bother to go to bed. David
had been very distressed. He had guessed at once that Mum
was dead. She had made him promise never to contact me. He
supposed that she had left a note or explanatory letter. He had
had seven years to get used to the idea of having a sister. I had
lost my mother and found a brother in less than forty-eight
hours. As I sat waiting for the dawn I wondered time and
again: why had Mum gone to so much trouble to keep his
existence a deep secret? Surely she must have known me well
enough to guess my reactions, to know how pleased and excited I would have been? The more I thought about it, the
more depressed I became. I felt that her motives were something I'd never understand.

It must have been six months after Mum's death and the
discovery of my brother before I could begin to make sense of
the story in a fairly balanced way. As far as I could make out
it was simply inconceivable that Mum had been conducting a
secret and private relationship with her son, my brother,
somehow resurrected after thirty-seven years. I felt all the more

excluded because their relationship had begun, however briefly, in an era before I was born. Discovering I had an older brother forced me to accept that there was a very important side of Mum's life from which I had been entirely excluded and about which I knew nothing.

She had often talked about her pre-war London life. Now I saw how carefully edited her accounts had been. She had confided part of the story to me – the trouble was she had left out the essentials. I'm sure she was telling the truth when she described how amazed she was, coming from a virtually Victorian family in the provinces, to discover how differently people behaved in London. She was very proud to have worked in Harrods. Her favourite story was about the old Queen Mary asking her advice about a piece of silver. In the mornings, she recalled, all the sales staff had to line up for inspection. The head buyer lifted each skirt hem to make sure that the regulation white slips were newly pressed. She scrutinised their uniforms for straying threads or missing buttons, and even uncovered their bra straps to see they were freshly laundered.

Another of her stories was to do with her landlady who was in charge of the Richmond house where the Harrods sales staff had digs. Mum, this kind lady thought, needed 'building up'. So every morning she produced a double helping of greasy bacon and eggs. Mum's idea of breakfast ran to a cup of tea and a cigarette. So she worked out a scheme which depended on the landlady turning her back. Then she would dispose of her man-size meal thanks to the good offices of a fellow lodger with an unusually healthy appetite. For the first time, it struck me that the breakfast eater was only too easily identifiable as Dad!

The first conversation with my brother that night holds very special memories. Some parts are unforgettable. Some have gone forever. It was all highly emotional – and bewildering. After I put the phone down, and took some time to compose myself, I began to realise that there was another aspect to it apart from the unbelievable news I had received. Something else very significant had taken place during the talk. But what was it?

Then it came to me. The lovely voice saying: 'My dear girl
– don't you realise I'm your older brother?'

It was twenty years since anyone had spoken to me in those
tones. The voice was so like Dad's it could have been an echo,
but amazingly I only made the connection after the conversation was over. The similarity of the voices had added to my
confusion when David answered the phone.

At that moment I lost all lingering doubts about whether the
revelations were authentic. My first reaction was: 'Poor Mum'.
She must have recognised the voice too. It must have been so
painful to remember and go through the experience alone.

She mentioned Dad very rarely. When she did, I always
thought that she immediately regretted it. If an occasion arose
when she introduced him into the conversation, she always
seemed to choose her words very carefully. My impression was
that she was making a special effort to give me an unbiased
version. To her credit, she never criticised him to me. I was
very conscious of her effort to play according to the rules.
They had never been stated or discussed, these rules, but we
both knew she was abiding by them.

But this time she just hadn't played fair. I had a brother. I'd
always had a brother. But there had been no hint of his existence, no mention, no clues of any kind.

Over the next hours I was so involved with my own pain
there was no time to think that David must be suffering too.
His reasons were slightly different. But it was the end of an
era for both of us. Perhaps, more optimistically, it might be
the beginning of a new one, but I'm not sure whether that
thought came to me then, or whether it took longer to surface.

Even the word 'brother' was difficult – I still expect someone
to correct me whenever I say: 'My brother ...' But on that
first night it was impossible to connect the eerily reminiscent
voice with a concrete image. The nearest I could get was Dad
when he had been young. All I had to focus on was his voice.
When we started talking it had been confident, polite and
pleasant – but he certainly had the advantage on me. At least
he knew I existed. He must have anticipated talking with me
at some time, even if he didn't know when. But I knew nothing

about him, even that there was a 'him'. I had to be the one
asking all the questions. He was trying to provide acceptable
answers.

Quite early on in this incredible exchange he said: 'I know
everything there is to know about you.' I tried to digest what
he had said calmly. But really the more I thought about the
situation, the more I found it unbelievable. I was quite unprepared, for instance, when he suddenly asked if I would like
him to attend her funeral. I had hesitated for a moment. Only
because at this point the funeral was still miles away from my
thoughts. He misinterpreted the pause, and added hesitantly:
'I'll only come if you want me to.'

I did want him to. He added these words without the same
confidence there had been before. I knew then that he was as
unsure of me as I was of him. This was the moment when I
knew we had something in common, even if it was only the
same uncertainty.

We had two or three further conversations in the next few
days. They were easier each time. I felt I was talking to a
friend – but not to a brother. I didn't know how you talked to
a brother. We had no memories or reminiscences of family
treats or disasters in common. Just his experience or my experience. Nothing shared.

The voice was a comfort. I began to look forward to my
'London calls'. A bond was slowly developing, a fragile relationship was building up – and at a pace I could control. As
the day of Mum's funeral came closer, the prospect of meeting
my brother for the first time filled me with trepidation. After
all, we were strangers with seemingly little in common. Except
the – possibly dubious – privilege of sharing the same blood,
same origins, same roots. I wondered whether he was feeling
nervous too. But at that time I couldn't bring myself to ask.

It's difficult now to imagine that we were ever so far apart.
Less than a week before, my first impulse would have been to
ring Mum for advice and reassurance. But she had left me to
face up to this alone and unprepared. My selfish streak could
not help a feeling of resentment. It was unfair and I found
myself thinking that she had been irresponsible. Surely in the

course of the seven years she had known him there must have been a moment when she could have told me about my brother?

The day of the funeral arrived. I'd hoped it would never come. As the clock crept round and it was five a.m., I was overwhelmed with the desire to run away – to run anywhere. Anything was preferable to facing the ordeal of the day.

How do you bury a dear mother and meet your brother, a brother you have only learnt exists at the age of 38, on the same day?

There were no guide-lines. I didn't know what to expect – or what was expected of me. I had never heard of anyone experiencing such a thing.

Bob, as usual, appeared very calm. I knew it was for my benefit. In a way it seemed he had no help to offer. But in reality I knew very well that his strength and stamina could be relied on to get me through to the end.

After a lot of thought we had decided the best thing to do was to introduce David to the other mourners as 'just a friend from London'. It was far too soon to begin long and complicated explanations ... I wasn't by any means sure that the right time would ever come to tell anyone this story or whether they would believe it if I did.

LINDA
ELIZABETH
CHESTER

21

Having a sister, it now turned out, was a great consolation in times of trouble. We got on so well and so fast in the strange new relationship that only a fortnight after the funeral I wrote in a diary: 'Impossible to think of a time when I didn't have a sister.' After a month had elapsed, the two of us were already well advanced in our long dialogue of 1981, most of which was conducted by phone. I remember it as a time when we were always enquiring how the other felt, trying to ease sadness by either sharing it or assuring the other person that it wasn't going to last. Margaret seemed to understand me remarkably well, responding to the Jack Chester in me probably. I don't know how much I understood my new-found sister but I recognised her instantly with delight, like a forgotten flavour, the favourite of another time or place. Truda had insisted long before that we had nothing in common. Now it emerged either that her judgment of her children was wildly amiss, or (much more probably) that she had only said it to put me off.

I soon learned that Margaret believed in her own intuitions with unmovable stubbornness, even though she usually preferred to keep them to herself. Every so often though she would reveal what she was thinking, partly because she enjoyed saying something that would take me aback.

In the course of one of our first talks on the phone after the funeral she announced: 'There's another one of us still around you know.'

'Another one?' I was astonished and I could tell that she was enjoying the fact. 'What do you mean? Someone not

accounted for? A relation of Truda's, or a confidante, who's
not come forward?'

'I'm not sure yet.'

Margaret did not seem finally to have made up her mind
and she was certainly not going to commit herself further. But
she sounded sure that she was right. It was something I didn't
understand, and was happy to shelve for the moment. It was
too soon for me to take the idea of 'another of us' on board.

In February 1981 a lawyer friend, Elizabeth, lent me her big
house in west Sussex because I wanted a break from London.
The book I had been writing on the night Margaret phoned
for the first time was shelved. Instead, far from sure that it
would end in a book, I had begun a memoir of Truda, which
led to John, and would soon be leading to David and Ivy. In
due course, if I persisted, I would arrive at Margaret and
maybe even 'the other one' my sister sometimes gave an
impression she was expecting daily. I still had no idea what
she meant.

It was a season of rain and sharp, blustery winds which kept
the temperature a few degrees above freezing. I went for long
tramps through the hushed, sodden countryside thinking about
the past as I hadn't before in my life. I also thought about
Truda and the close relationship we might have enjoyed but
which had somehow managed to evade us. This was the sad-
dest thing.

Margaret was in north Wales, and I was 200 miles south in
Sussex, but we kept in constant touch. Even so, despite what
she had said about 'another one', I didn't fully understand
what was going on up there. She believed that under the
floor-boards, in an old store-room, behind the fitted cupboards, somewhere, anywhere, her 'mum' had left a clue, one
meant specifically for her. She thought that the entry in the
address book with the London number, and my name and
Jill's, was only the first clue, and that there would be others.
At the start she thought in terms of a specific personal message.
As time passed she mentally downgraded the notion of a personal testament and simply continued searching in the hope
that she would find something, or indeed anything.

The search turned into a major operation, most of it under-taken by Bob. He stripped carpets and underfelts: then labor-iously relaid them, speaking silently to himself while he laboured. He tapped walls for hollow sounds. He sieved through the contents of Truda's store-room after going to much trouble to obtain the key. His actions were all the more virtuous as he had never for an instant believed that anything would come of them. On several occasions I spoke to him on the phone when Margaret was out and though he was reticent I gathered that he was anxious about her mental equilibrium. Her conviction that, against all evidence, there was something waiting to be found, had become an obsession. My own posi-tion was difficult. Bob obviously felt that the preoccupation with Truda and her secrets went far beyond the bounds of what might be called reasonable or normal grief. It was hard for me to judge. Largely because of Margaret's intuitions about her mother (which had led her to call me originally), I had considerable faith in her judgment and instincts. On the other hand I was quite sure that Truda had not left anything that could be called in any way a deliberate clue. If there was something waiting to be found it would be *despite* Truda, not because of her.

It worried me that by talking to her constantly, often late at night, and by writing letters about Truda and John, I might be encouraging an obsession which was bad for her. Apart from the fact that they made me feel better, these conversations were a great help with the story I was now getting on paper quite quickly.

Sometimes, I thought that the work was being done at Truda's behest. I could hear her saying that afternoon in Hyde Park: 'Write it down or you'll forget.'

At other times, when Margaret wrote to me or spoke on the phone, passing on some piece of information that Truda had lied about, or omitted, or told me in another form – one that was more flattering to her usually – I felt that my tentative efforts to establish the truth of the affair were made in the face of Truda's opposition from the other side of the grave.

Why else had Truda tried to wipe out all traces of me and

my family before her death? Except for the entries in her address book, and here I was identified only by initials as if she had deliberately used a code (which I was sure she had), it was as if I had never been. We had only been out of touch since before Christmas, a matter of three weeks, and I had sent her a card, just as she had sent me one. Yet there was no trace of it in Truda's apartment, or any other evidence that might have led to me. There was a parallel with the events of my adoption. Three or four weeks after I was born everything had been rearranged in such a way that it was as if I had no existence at all.

'Could she have confided it all to a third party?' I noted on 24 February, a month after the funeral. 'Margaret suggests she did, and is sure something will turn up. But she doesn't know what and she's tired of waiting!' Three days later I added: 'Bob and Margaret haven't managed to find a last letter, a will, any more references to me. Yet something has happened to verify that a deliberate job of concealment has taken place fairly recently. Richard (Margaret's son) noticed *God Stand up for Bastards* on his mother's bedside table and said "That's the book I found under Granny's bed . . .".'

The new book was now seriously underway. I had settled down to a daily routine at Elizabeth's big Victorian table, a solid mahogany object built to last, looking out across a valley beyond which I could see the Sussex Downs. Beyond them, invisible but exercising a magnetic pull all the same, was the Channel. For once, the desire to stay put was stronger than the prospect of setting off on a new journey. The process of embarking on the new project felt distinctly different from the early stages of other books I had written. There was an additional dimension. The story was not a static thing waiting to be unfolded but elusive, and growing, changing as I worked.

At crucial points the facts failed to hang together, the connections were not made. Margaret was as dissatisfied as I was myself. I laboured on, wondering if winter would ever end. The empty house, a haven of peace when I had started, began to be oppressive. I felt not so much lonely as impenetrably, eternally isolated. Margaret's calls were the high spots of each day, even though they resolved nothing and usually ended with a new set of unanswered questions. She usually chose to ring when Bob had gone to the pub. We seldom had a conversation in the course of which she didn't remind me that it had been a sister, not a brother, she had hoped to discover by giving in to the impulse to phone the number in London on that first night. It was as if her imagination had been primed in the past to accept the idea of a sister, but not a brother. Now a brother had turned up, without benefit of premonition, it surprised me that she wasn't satisfied to let matters rest.

I couldn't believe in this hypothetical sister, though the possibility, remote and irrational as it was, filled me with excitement. I told myself that what had come about already was spectacularly beyond all computable odds and when we talked I tried to indicate that there was a hint of what in the high 1960s people had called 'bad karma' about her train of thought. It was as if prayers having been answered, the beneficiary promptly demands a second helping.

She always responded in the same way, defensive now, but not conceding that her instinct could be wrong. 'I can't believe she went off just like that leaving nothing but a dead end.'

In fact, Truda must have known, somewhere in her mind, that when she died, I would inevitably learn of it and, just as inevitably, make contact with Margaret. I was secretly sure that Truda had washed her hands of the future – after all, she herself was not going to be involved. Very likely, she didn't much care.

Whatever Margaret believed of her 'Mum', I couldn't see my Truda leaving any clues, except inadvertently.

'Do you think there's a full sister, John's child, or was there another marriage we don't know about, or did she have a child by Jim Bucknall? She took his name ...'

Spelling out the various possibilities I became all the more convinced that my sister was following a false trail – in any case by the end of February a point was reached where Margaret herself wasn't prepared to speculate further.

'Has Bob come up with anything yet?'

'Only a lot of old junk.'

That's all they would find, junk not clues, I thought to myself. Truda's last impulses, the evidence suggested, had been to try and block future connections between her children, not prepare the way for them. She had wanted to take all the family secrets with her.

March began with a snowfall and the house was so silent it might have sunk beneath the frozen lake in the village. The sense of there being something missing did not diminish. It was as if Truda had bequeathed me the human equivalent of one of her crossword puzzles, only with some clues destroyed. Puzzle over it as long as you liked, there was no solution. The frustration was so acute that some days I would feel ill with it, like a disease that wasted.

One night Margaret excitedly told me about a new find – she had discovered a Christmas present list written by Truda which contained the entry: 'Buy Baby-gro ...' This had been enough for her to construct a plot involving an unknown woman, who was somehow our sister, and who had a small child. She was, so Margaret's fantasy went, in clandestine contact with Truda ... 'I've asked all over and we can't think of a single person she knew with a young baby. Who could it be?'

She never made any progress at all in finding out. But within days she was confiding another discovery, with caution because I knew she suspected that I might laugh at her, which in the circumstances I wasn't prepared to do, any more than Bob was. She had found another address book entry giving a name and phone number of a woman in Cheltenham. Truda had never mentioned such a person, she was sure. Margaret wasted no time in producing a theory to do with this unknown – Cheltenham was within convenient range of Birmingham, where Truda had gone quite often to visit Lois, Jim Bucknall's daughter, the smart blonde figure at the funeral and Margaret's own school companion at Southport before John had taken her on the night train to Leicester.

After a week Margaret phoned sounding distinctly sheepish – the Cheltenham entry had been accounted for quite innocently, and with no suggestion of an unknown sister. Again there was a suggestion hovering around that I might make fun of her conviction – which was beginning to sound truly ob-sessional, and her detective work, which was progressing not at all. I carefully made no jokes. Even though I was sure she was wasting her time I was as disappointed as she was.

By now I was absolutely certain that there would be no revelations. The view of the South Downs through the high windows of the drawing-room had been replaced by a wall of mist the colour of barrage-balloons, a dirty foreboding grey – these gas-filled devices intended to make low-level bombing impossible had been part of my childhood skyscape. Inside the blank pages, outside an enveloping colour of war. Page after page was handwritten, corrected, typed; the narrative moved forward, but had I got it right?

There was something about the story which resolutely eluded me. I dreamt of following a woman's figure along a moving staircase, trying to catch up because I was convinced that it was someone I knew very well. Yet every time I came close enough for recognition the face turned away, and was obscured by shadows.

22

Soon after I was driving up from Sussex to meet Margaret at Euston station. She came briskly off the 10.14 through the platform five barrier, we kissed on the cheek, and we set off across the arcade. She looked pale as if recovering from illness but also perfectly sturdy, even strong. The blue look in her eyes was full of an excitement that I quickly caught – her presence instantly raised my spirits. She carried her luggage in the well-organised, military kind of way of someone who knows how to get on with things, and we instinctively hurried.

Walking in step we worked our way rapidly through the floating station population. We made much faster progress than when, with Truda by my side, I had negotiated the identical route many times over the previous seven years. Truda had a way of inviting protection and pampering: you took her arm prepared to shield her from something or another. The natural gesture with my sister was to link arms as if preliminary to some shared effort. Margaret's physical feel was robust, yet emotionally volatile and run through with subterranean energy like the current in an underground river. Suddenly everything was unusually enjoyable.

The day was bright and blustery beyond the protection of the plastic roof, and we set off like a brother and sister in a children's book ready for a day of adventure.

We drove home along the north side of Regent's Park past the zoo, the same route I had always taken Truda. Margaret's attention, like her mother's, was caught by the hanging, asymmetrical shape of Lord Snowdon's aviary. When we got to the house she might have been there many times before. She was much more at home than Truda had ever been, some edge of self-consciousness that had kept her mother always firmly in the rank of visitor was absent in the daughter. Margaret went firmly for wine in preference to coffee – she was obviously set to enjoy herself. She was also eager to show me the contents of her bags.

'Can I chuck these things out on the floor? It's all so tightly packed I can't deal with anything unless it all comes out, if you see ... You wait till you see what I've brought you.'

The first item she produced was a small silver-plate cup of Dad's, awarded presumably for prowess at sport, yet with no inscription to indicate whether it commemorated a memorable performance at table-tennis or bezique, gin rummy or cricket, bar-billiards or darts – the homely games at which he had been reported to excel. I was delighted to inherit this typically equivocal tribute to a certain kind of predominantly indoor sporting life.

Then came the first photograph I had ever seen of my father as a young man. He looked about 26, and was wearing a look of earnest, almost scowling, determination. It was not quite 100 per cent successful. The glint in the corner of his eye, which conveyed the suggestion that honest toil was not his idea of man's highest destiny, both gave him away and redeemed him. I found myself smiling affectionately. Margaret laughed out loud over my shoulder as if she had been with him the previous day. 'His hair was dark and long', she said, 'terribly long for a man. It went into tight soft curls, and you could pull it like that – it would go swoosh like a silk curtain.'

She knelt amid a cornucopia of family icons. Some of the contents of Truda's boxes. 'You wait until you see ... just wait.'

For an hour we sorted through photos and pieces of jewellery, many of them made by Truda herself. Margaret gave me a porcelain mermaid from Copenhagen, a souvenir of Mum's I fancied, and I returned to her the cigarette case which, it now turned out, she had once given to Dad. I remembered the noise it had made snapping shut when I had returned drunk and

wildly confused from the first meeting with Truda. Naturally,
she had omitted to mention that it had been a gift from Margaret. The act of restoring it was satisfying in a way I couldn't
describe.

Margaret, sniffing around the house and among the books
like a natural-born reporter, made two finds – a packet of joss
sticks and a catalogue of the Tutankhamun Exhibition held at
the British Museum some years before.

'Oh, you're not into these terrible things too, these terrible
sticks – that's where she got them from. I wondered why we
had these wretched horrible things burning away everywhere.'

'I think I brought her Vietnamese New Year incense from
Paris once.'

'She told me she found them in Birmingham when she stayed
with Lois and I knew it was wrong, I knew. And this.' She
held up the gold catalogue of King Tut. 'I sat listening to her
story of Tutankhamun and the Carter exhibition and I knew
very well she hadn't gone on her own. I was listening to this,
and that, and she told me where she'd stayed, and who with,
and I didn't believe it, and she knew I didn't believe it, and
yet . . .'

'And yet you never got it out of her?'

'No, I thought when she's ready she'll tell me.'

'That's what I thought.'

'She wasn't ever ready, was she?'

Margaret gave me one of her deep cunning looks, an impressive sight with the dark hair and blue eyes, a reminder of
the Jewish blood and the Danish melded together, and no
doubt of John's own enigmatic genetic contribution, of which
we knew as little as he had done himself.

'If it had been the other way round . . .' she began.

'How do you mean?'

'Well, if I'd suddenly found I had a brother then I could
never have resisted . . . in a moment of downness, or perhaps
in a moment of gladness, I might have suddenly found that I
had to, you know? I'd have had to come and see for myself. I
couldn't have resisted it.'

'I phoned once when you were there.'

'Did you? So if I'd picked up the phone we might have met seven years earlier?'

'If I'd had the brains to say "It's your big brother here." '

'Mum usually answered the phone when I was there.'

'I bet she did. But what waste, all the years. We could have met normally like brother and sister when you were born in 1942 if it hadn't been for something proud and conventional in Truda. In 1937 they had a choice between turning up at home to face her mum without a job and saying "We've got married and had a kid" or doing what they did, announcing the marriage but leaving the baby out. It wouldn't have made much difference, except in terms of what Truda's mother or neighbours or whatever thought about shotgun weddings as opposed to run-away marriages. I know conventions were much stricter. All the same ... imagine being offloaded for reasons almost of etiquette, if you like, as if I was the wrong fork.'

'Do you think they could have managed to look after a baby? Wasn't it too much of a burden?'

'For them on their own it was, I'd expect. By 1942 when you were born it might have been easier, in spite of the blitz. They both had jobs. Standards of living were higher on war-time rations than they had been for the unemployed in the thirties. Not to mention our outgoing Dad meeting men in pubs with things that fell off trucks ...'

'Mind you, I was still a burden,' Margaret said. 'Let's not kid ourselves, because neither of them was able to look after me in the way I should have been looked after. After Bucknall died she went into a bedsitter. There was a court case. She was given some kind of custody. I had to be near her in Liverpool, and not in Leicester where Dad was, but only on condition I stayed with the Williamses, this family who thought I was so odd for reading.' Margaret's love for her mother did not stop her dispassionate judgment working. 'It suited her not to have me, it suited her way. It wasn't just that she always worked, which she did. She was a romantic. She wanted a little doll at a distance. You know, she wanted to call me Pearl, which Dad said sounded like a Piccadilly prostitute. She settled for Margaret Sylvia. Why Sylvia? Some kind of ballet music she liked, of course. *Les Sylphides*. She was so romantic. And bitter. When we went to see *Dr Zhivago* I cried all through, but she was like stone. When I mentioned it afterwards she said, "I've already wept all the tears I'm going to in this life." Every illusion had gone. I remember the way she looked when Dad died and she found he hadn't put any stamps on his card so she couldn't get her widow's pension.'

I thought of Ivy and her bitterness about old betrayals and sacrifices. 'You'd expect her to have had at least one spell living with you and looking after you, between 6 and 21, wouldn't you? You know, she never told me that. I always assumed she brought you up herself, except when Dad "kidnapped" you. Why didn't you live together?'

'Lots of reasons, lots always. She lived in bedsitters. Her work hours. She couldn't manage. She didn't really want it. She left it to others.'

'There were lots of good reasons for others to bring up her kids. Like Ivy and David Leitch. She was sure others did it better. Truda wasn't what's called into maternity,' I said, and we both laughed, though this was the plain truth of it.

There had been a half-plan for my friend Elizabeth to join us for lunch but she rang to say she was too busy. We walked to the Italian restaurant down the road and ate the pasta and liver with sage I had missed by the accident of answering Margaret's message-in-a-bottle call from Wales. I was about to say this when she beat me to it. 'I waited that night until Bob had gone to the pub before ringing you in case I made a fool of myself. After we spoke the first time and you said you'd ring back I sat in the kitchen and I thought he either will, or he won't, because if he doesn't I'll never call him. I've done what I had to do. And then the next thing Bob arrived in. I said something strange's happened. Sit down while I tell you. He said what on earth have you done? Mind you, I'd had a few whiskies.'

Even though I was beginning to get to know Margaret, many of her reactions still amazed me. The idea that I wouldn't have rung back was incomprehensible. In some ways she was less self-confident than I was. On the other hand she retained a stubborn commitment to feelings or hunches that I could never have sustained without evidence to support them. When I began to talk about trying to write a book she announced: 'The story will be hard to write because it isn't all over, is it?'

'You mean the part about "the other person" which hasn't come out?'

'Yes. For years, always really, I've known there was someone else. When I found the *Sunday Times* clippings I thought Jill might be the one – it had to be a girl. That's why it was so fantastic when after a couple of minutes I said: 'You were born in 1950, were you?' And you said: "My dear girl, I'm your elder brother." That's what really got me. I realised then that you were my father's son, that was the main thing, by far the most important thing to me. That really knocked me for six.'

By then it was later in the afternoon and from the way she drank her wine and smoked her tipped cigarettes and put her considerately shoeless feet on the sofa it was clear that the subject had been taken fully on board. It was no longer knocking her for anything at all. I filled her glass and she took a measured swig. 'I'd never thought for one minute, it had never crossed my mind even, that Dad had another child. Never.'

'You knew all along she'd had another?'

'Yes, that's what I thought.'

'Well, you were right.'

'I was, and I still am.'

'You mean, the other one – this girl?'

Something stubborn came into my sister's face. 'All I know was that Mum didn't come and see me on 9 September 1950 for my birthday when she should have come, and I was terribly upset. Then next weekend Dad turns up, announces to the head that he's taking me out for supper, and I tell him what a terrible life I'm having. He says if you don't want to go back to that bloody awful school you don't have to and off we go to get the train to Leicester. I didn't even have any clothes.'

'And you believe she had another child, a sister, about then?

Why not another explanation? Flu, there were epidemics every
so often. I mean –' And then I burst out laughing, because my
thoughts had run ahead of the arguments. I was thinking –
supposing it's true? Another one she never as much as referred
to?

My sister was unshakably certain. The discovery of my existence seemed to have done no more than whet her appetite
to add to the family circle.

'So when you first phoned you thought that I might be ...'

'I thought this was who you might be. That somehow it
hadn't been a girl but a boy. But I was on the right track –
that's the marvellous thing about it all really.'

'Why are you so sure?'

'There was a reason why she couldn't come round the corner
to see me. Either she was very pregnant, or having a baby, or,
I don't know.'

I still couldn't see why pregnancy had to be invoked to
explain the birthday absence. But Margaret's conviction half
convinced me, and I started calculating. 'So if we say five
months would be pregnant enough to show ...'

'It means the end of 1950, or the start of '51.'

Margaret had obviously done the arithmetic already.

'Your birthday was 9 September. If we checked files from,
say, August '50 to, what, January '51?'

'If you can find them from Somerset House I would like to
know very much and I'll tell you another thing: if you find a
name it will be a girl's.'

'What name?'

'Elizabeth.'

'How on earth can you know that? That can't be intuition.
Did you hear something, or overhear? Perhaps as a child. Perhaps from Dad. It sounds so specific.'

'Dad would say things at the end when he had his Black
Moods. I was a teenager, but very naïve I think, not like a
teenager now. He never actually said "Your Mum was pregnant." But he would go, "By gum, only lived on the corner but
never came to see you on your birthday. That's a funny thing,
isn't it?"'

Supposing Truda had been pregnant, this seemed to exclude any possibility that Jack Chester was the father. But how could it be? I didn't want to disappoint Margaret by telling her outright what I felt. Truda had me at 26 in bad circumstances, Margaret aged 31 in times that weren't very much better, and she had only managed to bring Margaret up by general recourse to 'aunties', paid and unpaid, and finally with Margaret in a formal foster family, with visiting at weekends. Surely, at 38 with this history, the last thing she would have done was get pregnant? And even if it had happened by mistake, how could she have concealed the fact? Presumably, by adoption, unless she was around incognito, disguised as one of the innumerable Ivys and Olives and Ednas and Mollys who overlapped in the rich Merseyside matriarchal stew. Yet Truda, I sensed, was excluded from the sorority: at best tolerated. They would have backed her up without respecting her. They kept their kids. Her act implied a general female failure according to the sexist code that prevailed. For a woman to give up her children voluntarily put a barrier between herself and the herd. Luckily for Margaret, the sorority didn't take it out on the kids. They had stayed around to add support.

'Truda didn't have many women friends, did she?'

'There were a few, not many, who she said had done wonderful things for her and she'd never forget.'

'I suppose there was never a week when she didn't have to earn the rent, and some cash for food, and for you. She had to be the man. No time for sentiment and hard to run a one-parent family then ...'

'You have to gang up,' Margaret said. 'For support, strength. Truda didn't like it, not like Dad.'

We were being half-critical, half-defensive of our dead mother. As usual, she got most of the blame for failing in the madonna role she hated, while John's responsibility was assumed to be diminished, as if he were a child or defective.

'But Truda had no really close friends.' The thought came back to me – there had been past benefactors, women who had mothered or protected her, but not people who were close. Instantly I thought of Ivy. Two friendless women who told

lies. I also suddenly wondered whether the 'other', the hypothetical third child Margaret associated with the name 'Elizabeth', whoever it was, could still be on the Liverpool scene,
even now secreting Truda's will and the signed framed photo
of Luke aged 2.

All day the arguments ran through my head in an unsatis-
factory circle. Just before my sister climbed aboard the train
home I said: 'You know, it still doesn't necessarily follow that
she was pregnant in the first place.'

She came back strong. 'I know it doesn't, but I'll damn well
bet she was.'

23

Margaret's visit had convinced me that before the story reached its end we needed to discover one more major piece of information, or possibly another character who had been there all along but somehow or another had remained hidden. Unlike my sister, I was a long way from being convinced that 'Elizabeth' was the answer. It was too neat and too cynical. Now I had managed to reach an emotional peace with my natural mother, the last thing I wanted was confirmation of another adoption, the prospect of trying to reach yet another mental accommodation.

This was probably why I didn't immediately try and trace entries at Somerset House after my sister's return home, though I planned to the next time I was in London. Meanwhile, I stayed in the country at my friend Elizabeth's house. But one day I woke to find the temperature had fallen again and on impulse I decided to drive to the local station and spend the day in London. It was 17 March. I dropped in at Elizabeth's flat in Redcliffe Square, a cluster of eccentric Victorian blocks between Earl's Court and Fulham. It was as if something had yielded – the sky was hard blue, sun I hadn't seen for months filled her white sitting-room at the top of the house. I had promised to phone Margaret, and while I dialled her number, I admired the castellated façades and grey-slate roofs which reminded me of mornings in Paris.

Margaret's voice was different. In our brief history I had never heard this note before: eager, triumphant, unusually hard. I felt a response in me to the hint of ruthlessness I heard in her voice. It was like being reminded that an ally is carrying some muscle.

'Get ready for a shock,' she said, without preliminary niceties.

Something had bowled her over, overwhelmed her nearly. She couldn't wait for me to share the experience.

In the instant between her command and the news itself I realised that she relished a certain bomb-shell technique on the phone. Truda liked her calls conventional – the weather, how much things cost. My sister, closer to me, savoured surprises and oddities, the unexpected or, as in this case, the astonishing. She was taking some pleasure in setting me back on my heels.

As she started to explain, one thought kept going through my head: 'There is another one of us. There is . . .'

'Auntie Ivy says there is something. About Mum. Olive knows, but she's very reluctant to divulge it.' The hunter's eagerness sounded in my sister's voice. She had kept probing all Truda's friends and acquaintances, among them Ivy, of all names, and Olive who had served time as honorary 'aunties' when it came to bringing up Margaret.

Margaret was going to talk to Olive later in the day. It was likely that whatever she learned, whatever the secret was, would introduce new elements that could be painful. The heavy word 'divulge' indicated that the 'something' might be discreditable. Still for both of us, as I noticed from my sister's impatience, the impulse to find out was stronger than any desire for ignorant tranquillity. There's my girl, I thought. It was impossible not to smile with affection into the empty room.

'There's no way I can get hold of Olive in less than six or seven hours,' she said. 'Call me back around nine after the kids are in bed and there's some peace.' I said: 'Good luck.'

There followed one of the longest – and slowest – days of my life. In the course of it I had to deliver some work to a typist, do some shopping, meet a friend's children after school. The thought of what Olive would have to say, what news it could be, beat in my head like a pulse. At five in the afternoon it was dark. The only way to destroy the remaining hours was

to go to bed. I slept for two hours and woke in the grip of
wild impatient excitement.

When I finally got Margaret she said at once: 'There *is*
another one.'

'Meaning . . .?'

'A sister. She was born in a nursing home not far from the
school. It was about the same time that Dad came and took
me away.'

'Were the two connected? He wasn't the father, was he?'

'Oh no, he and Mum hadn't seen each other for nearly a
year. But he may have heard something.'

'Where is she now?'

'Olive doesn't know. She was adopted before Olive saw
Mum. By the time she visited her the baby had already gone.
It sounds as if this adoption wasn't like yours at all. It had
been set up in advance and was done very fast.'

'How was Truda?'

'In a terrible state. Very depressed and ill.'

'Did Truda see the baby again?'

'Olive doesn't know that either. She doesn't think so. Mum
never talked about it, never referred to it. They never spoke of
it again over all those years.'

'Thirty years. The baby would be about 30 now.'

'Thirty and a half. She must have been born in August or
the beginning of September – about the time I started at the
school. Around the time of my eighth birthday.'

'We ought to be able to find the names they gave her. Truda
and Jim Bucknall, who must be the father. Shall I get on with
that?'

'Yes, I suppose so.'

'Have you told Lois? "Elizabeth" must be her half-sister
too.'

'Not yet, but I will.'

'It doesn't sound as if she's still on the scene in any way,
does it? I mean, as someone Truda was in touch with?'

'I don't know and I can't work it out now.'

'Yes, that's how I feel too.'

After the initial excitement, a new link of blood, new poss-

ibilities, everything had gone flat. We agreed later that we had
both been touched by the same wave of cold depression. It had
taken us since the funeral to reach an unspoken agreement
about Truda, which came down to making the best of it all
and not blaming. But there was something very chilly about
this news which destroyed the balance. My adoption could
easily be put down to youth and inexperience, Margaret's upbringing to the hardness of circumstance, but to have a second
child adopted when she was 38 was something else again.

Later that night I noted:

So there is another of us, Margaret's long-held fantasy of a sister
is true. When she phoned me out of the blue that night, thinking
to find a sister, perhaps one called Jill who had been married to
me, she was achieving literally what she set out to do, only at one
step removed. What a strange story – I can't take it in. Truda did
it twice. That's what is painful. It really leaves me full of despair.
It's inhuman, having a baby and giving it away, coming close to
selling it. When you're young and in terrible trouble, it has to be
seen as the kind of thing that could happen to anyone. The world's
oldest joke and oldest nightmare. Inexperienced, far from home,
desperate – you may feel inclined to blame a mother or a father,
especially if you're the baby that gets dumped, but at least you
understand how it came about. When she said it was for the best,
a way for me to acquire these magical 'advantages', there was even
an element of truth. Even if from the point of view of the child
who had to be got rid of, the 'advantages' won't ever count as
much as the losses, the childhood emptiness of knowing your
parents have gone away and won't be coming back no matter how
much noise you make to remind them you're waiting.

It's now obvious that she was so against my meeting Margaret
because she didn't want me to know that my sister's upbringing
had been uncomfortably close to my own. That is to say, she had
her fostered but kept in touch. When she was old enough not to
be any trouble she was able to live with her. At least that was a
bit of progress, but 'Elizabeth' got exactly the same treatment as
me, only in a more professional manner, and legally.

There is little point trying to make reason out of an event with
so much emotional pressure. Margaret sounded far worse than I'd
ever heard her before. I wonder if she had an outbreak of disagreeable memories, like me.

While she was talking, after she had confirmed that this sister, half-sister, really was born in that funny seaside place I went to with Ivy at some time during the war, when we were evacuated from London, I kept hearing Ivy's crazy voice saying hysterically: 'They were no damn good, can't you understand? No damn good. They just didn't want you. All they could think of was how to get you off their hands. They said they'd come back and see how you were getting on. But they only came once. Then they disappeared completely. We were pleased because we wanted a lovely baby boy. They didn't. We loved you much more than they did. They didn't love you at all . . .'

That episode must have been when I was 12 or 13. I had just mentioned my real parents because I was curious. I thought there was something about them I hadn't been told. That was what Ivy said. I don't think I went near the subject again for years. When I did she said the same thing again, identically. Tonight I could suddenly remember every word and inflexion. It is strange to find yourself at the age of 41 being filled with rage against two old women. One for speaking like that about the other, and the second for filling me with shame because Ivy had a kind of spurious moral case going for her, a rare experience I suppose. Imagine being so angry about two people both of whom are in the grave!

Finding a name for 'Elizabeth' is the first step. She could have been registered under Bucknall or Chester or Madsen (Truda's maiden name). Tomorrow Elizabeth will send a clerk who knows her way around Somerset House to make a search for the names between August 1950 and January '51. It sounds certain that this time Truda did it legally. The sister, most likely half-sister, as Jim Bucknall must be the best candidate for father, very likely knows that she was adopted. She may even have been trying to find out who her real parents were herself . . . It's going to be a while before I can take all this in. Margaret sounded like death.

The diary entries over the next few days read as follows:
Friday 20 March:

We are three-quarters there! There is a certificate recording the birth of Linda Elizabeth Chester, mother Gertrude (Truda) Chester, née Madsen, born in Southport, Lancashire in August/September 1950. We won't get a copy of the document, which contains the father's name, given presumably as John, until next Tuesday. When I phone Margaret with the news of Linda Elizabeth she accepts it very flatly as becomes someone whose prophecy has been fulfilled. She must surely have overheard some reference to the child, as well as the name, when she was small, probably from John. Even though she isn't surprised, she's none the less very down. She said: 'Now I know for sure, I feel I'm not sure I want to find her, I feel frightened about it all.'

It's contradictory, after a month when she's thought of nothing but tracking down 'Elizabeth', that now we establish for certain she exists, Margaret draws back. The funny thing is I entirely understand part of the reaction, I feel fear too, and tenderness, for this unknown sister. I don't want her harmed or upset but I'm entirely committed to making contact. You can't not.

Margaret sounds as if she distrusts Linda E. Is this because she thinks Linda Elizabeth could have been Truda's accomplice or confidante? Has she been *watching* us? Might my half-sister be the custodian of a suitcase, a variation of Truda's boxes, with instructions for it to be opened in the event of Truda's death?

Could she have been in contact with Truda for all these years? Could Truda have told her the whole story and given her all the stuff to keep in case Something Happened? Something certainly has.

By the end of the call I could hear the side that's in me, the inquisitive itch to know, overcoming the fear. I think she knows very well that the day will come when we'll all meet. For her this must be some kind of nightmare to do with Dad and Mum coming true, as well as a dream, both long-held. 'I've always hated the name Elizabeth – it makes me go cold inside,' she said. I tell her my friend Elizabeth is called 'Liz' by almost everyone except me. From now on I must remember to call her 'Liz' in front of Margaret.

Sunday 22 March:

A letter to Margaret passing on the fruits of family law researches from 'Liz', confirming what we suspected.

The system is so devised that we are totally cut off from her. There is one way, just, that she could get to us, but it wouldn't be at all easy.

Under the new legislation, Linda E. can get to see the names of her natural parents. In this case, where the name of the father is almost certainly false, Truda using it because she was still married to John though living with Jim Bucknall, this isn't of much use.

And, of course, they're both dead anyway. What she could do, however, is check the names of her natural parents against births. I wouldn't appear, but Margaret would. It would need quite a lot of sweat and understanding of how the information can be retrieved. Otherwise, she's stuck, and unless a legal loophole can be found, so are we. Possession of her name and date of birth (and consanguinity!) gives us no access to the adoption documents. It seems a dead end. The winds blow at gale force as I drive down to Sussex to work on the book. It may turn out like *God Stand up for Bastards* – the only route there is ...

When I wrote that entry in my diary in the early spring of 1981, I half expected a different outcome, despite the legal barriers. Margaret and I had been inhabiting a world where the unlikely or unbelievable happened. Nothing seemed too wild to be possible, past hunches had come off, and I secretly suspected that the streak would continue because the cards were still hot.

When Margaret's fears, like my rage, proved short-lived, I was even more confident. She had established that Lois, who had never suspected Linda Elizabeth's existence, had no objections. Lois greeted the discovery with her habitual air of slight scepticism. She wished Margaret's researches well without herself feeling deeply involved. My sister obviously took this as a challenge.

She was soon writing to say that she had gone through Truda's address book yet again and found there two entries which were unaccounted for. She pursued the Cheltenham number very optimistically, having resurrected the theory that Truda visited Cheltenham when going to see Lois in Birmingham, and that Linda Elizabeth would soon be revealed in this genteel colonial setting. It took the best part of a month to establish that the Cheltenham connection didn't exist. It was six months or more before we learned for certain that the same applied to the second name, the man in Yorkshire, as well. In the meantime there had been approaches to various agencies dealing with adoptions and Margaret had become well known to the officials in charge of Southport's filing departments. The registrar told her that such enquiries were common. Unless it was a matter of parent and child, the chances of making contact were remote. Informally, he advised her to turn it in. One adoption organisation assured us that the local registrar would invariably co-operate to the point of informing us on one point: whether or not the person we sought had even attempted to investigate the files. This proved wrong, at least in the case of Southport.

I don't know when or how this passion to find Linda Elizabeth instantly cooled, but it did, and there grew up an unspoken assumption that though one day we would surely meet, it was going to take time. A year after Truda's death, we had given up making enquiries: there were no more leads to follow. It was apparent that there was only one method available to attract her attention. This one.

Margaret wrote her account, and I gradually worked through my own. Three years passed.

Truda had opted out some way down the line but she had left enough, and given enough, to open up the possibility that the three children she had given birth to might one day sit in Hyde Park and picnic with their children, and maybe even compare toes. Tribal links could be created and restored, more connections made, or so we believe.

Margaret's intuitions and dreams must never be underestimated. A week before I finished the manuscript she rang to report a dream of the two of us on a porch waiting for Linda Elizabeth to answer the door-bell I had just rung. She wanted to run, but I had persuaded her it was worth waiting.

What, I wonder, will Linda Elizabeth be like, and in what circumstances will the door open? There will be enough of sister Margaret in her for the late night phone call, enough of me for the fuse of patience to be short. I doubt that she will be able to resist responding to our smoke signal. But who can tell? The story is so strange that, ending it, I feel myself shiver again, as I did when I began.

MORE ABOUT PENGUINS, PELICANS
AND PUFFINS

For further information about books available from Penguins please write to Dept EP, Penguin Books Ltd, Harmondsworth, Middlesex UB7 ODA.

In the U.S.A.: For a complete list of books available from Penguins in the United States write to Dept DG, Penguin Books, 299 Murray Hill Parkway, East Rutherford, New Jersey 07073.

In Canada: For a complete list of books available from Penguins in Canada write to Penguin Books Canada Limited, 2801 John Street, Markham, Ontario L3R 1B4.

In Australia: For a complete list of books available from Penguins in Australia write to the Marketing Department, Penguin Books Australia Ltd, P.O. Box 257, Ringwood, Victoria 3134.

In New Zealand: For a complete list of books available from Penguins in New Zealand write to the Marketing Department, Penguin Books (N.Z.) Ltd, Private Bag, Takapuna, Auckland 9.

In India: For a complete list of books available from Penguins in India write to Penguin Overseas Ltd, 706 Eros Apartments, 56 Nehru Place, New Delhi 110019.

A CHOICE OF PENGUINS

☐ *The Complete Penguin Stereo Record and Cassette Guide*
Greenfield, Layton and March £7.95

A new edition, now including information on compact discs. 'One of the few indispensables on the record collector's bookshelf' – *Gramophone*

☐ *Selected Letters of Malcolm Lowry*
Edited by Harvey Breit and Margerie Bonner Lowry £5.95

'Lowry emerges from these letters not only as an extremely interesting man, but also a lovable one' – Philip Toynbee

☐ *The First Day on the Somme*
Martin Middlebrook £3.95

1 July 1916 was the blackest day of slaughter in the history of the British Army. 'The soldiers receive the best service a historian can provide: their story told in their own words' – *Guardian*

☐ *A Better Class of Person* **John Osborne** £2.50

The playwright's autobiography, 1929–56. 'Splendidly enjoyable' – John Mortimer. 'One of the best, richest and most bitterly truthful autobiographies that I have ever read' – Melvyn Bragg

☐ *The Winning Streak* **Goldsmith and Clutterbuck** £2.95

Marks & Spencer, Saatchi & Saatchi, United Biscuits, G E C . . . The UK's top companies reveal their formulas for success, in an important and stimulating book that no British manager can afford to ignore.

☐ *The First World War* **A. J. P. Taylor** £4.95

'He manages in some 200 illustrated pages to say almost everything that is important . . . A special text . . . a remarkable collection of photographs' – *Observer*

A CHOICE OF PENGUINS

☐ *Man and the Natural World* **Keith Thomas** £4.95

Changing attitudes in England, 1500–1800. 'An encyclopedic study of man's relationship to animals and plants . . . a book to read again and again' – Paul Theroux, *Sunday Times* Books of the Year

☐ *Jean Rhys: Letters 1931–66*
Edited by Francis Wyndham and Diana Melly £4.95

'Eloquent and invaluable . . . her life emerges, and with it a portrait of an unexpectedly indomitable figure' – Marina Warner in the *Sunday Times*

☐ *The French Revolution* **Christopher Hibbert** £4.95

'One of the best accounts of the Revolution that I know . . . Mr Hibbert is outstanding' – J. H. Plumb in the *Sunday Telegraph*

☐ *Isak Dinesen* **Judith Thurman** £4.95

The acclaimed life of Karen Blixen, 'beautiful bride, disappointed wife, radiant lover, bereft and widowed woman, writer, sibyl, Scheherazade, child of Lucifer, Baroness; always a unique human being . . . an assiduously researched and finely narrated biography' – *Books & Bookmen*

☐ *The Amateur Naturalist*
Gerald Durrell with Lee Durrell £4.95

'Delight . . . on every page . . . packed with authoritative writing, learning without pomposity . . . it represents a real bargain' – *The Times Educational Supplement*. 'What treats are in store for the average British household' – *Daily Express*

☐ *When the Wind Blows* **Raymond Briggs** £2.95

'A visual parable against nuclear war: all the more chilling for being in the form of a strip cartoon' – *Sunday Times*. 'The most eloquent anti-Bomb statement you are likely to read' – *Daily Mail*

A CHOICE OF PENGUINS

☐ ***The Diary of Virginia Woolf***
Edited by Quentin Bell and Anne Olivier Bell

'As an account of the intellectual and cultural life of our century, Virginia Woolf's diaries are invaluable; as the record of one bruised and unquiet mind, they are unique' – Peter Ackroyd in the *Sunday Times*

☐ Volume One	£4.50
☐ Volume Two	£4.95
☐ Volume Three	£4.95
☐ Volume Four	£5.50
☐ Volume Five	£5.95

These books should be available at all good bookshops or news-agents, but if you live in the UK or the Republic of Ireland and have difficulty in getting to a bookshop, they can be ordered by post. Please indicate the titles required and fill in the form below.

NAME _____ BLOCK CAPITALS

ADDRESS _____

_____

_____

Enclose a cheque or postal order payable to The Penguin Bookshop to cover the total price of books ordered, plus 50p for postage. Readers in the Republic of Ireland should send £IR equivalent to the sterling prices, plus 67p for postage. Send to: The Penguin Bookshop, 54/56 Bridlesmith Gate, Nottingham, NG1 2GP.

You can also order by phoning (0602) 599295, and quoting your Barclaycard or Access number.

Every effort is made to ensure the accuracy of the price and availability of books at the time of going to press, but it is sometimes necessary to increase prices and in these circumstances retail prices may be shown on the covers of books which may differ from the prices shown in this list or elsewhere. This list is not an offer to supply any book.

This order service is only available to residents in the UK and the Republic of Ireland.

● ● ●